HIGH PRAISE FOR GEORGE JONES
AND HIS
"NO-HOLDS-BARRED ACCOUNT"*

I Lived to Tell It All

"AN ULTRA-CANDID VIEW OF A MAN WIDELY
REGARDED AS HIS FIELD'S GREATEST VOCALIST
. . . This is about as far as you can get from a
sanitized show business autobiography; rather, it is a
man purging the depths of his soul . . . [Jones] has
become positively loquacious about his past."
—*Chicago Tribune*

"[AN] ANECDOTE-RICH MEMOIR." *People*

"POIGNANT, MOVING . . . It's a book as
unforgettable as the man and his music . . . George
Jones opens up and writes candidly and intimately
. . . *I Lived to Tell It All* is George Jones—the good
news, the bad news, and the just plain fun."
—*Oxford Review* (Atlanta, Ga.)*

"HE'S THE GREATEST VOICE IN COUNTRY MUSIC
. . . HE'LL ALWAYS BE MY FAVORITE SINGER."
—Tammy Wynette

Please turn the page for more extraordinary acclaim . . .

I Lived
to
Tell It All

QUANTITY SALES

Most Dell books are available at special quantity discounts when purchased in bulk by corporations, organizations, or groups. Special imprints, messages, and excerpts can be produced to meet your needs. For more information, write to: Dell Publishing, 1540 Broadway, New York, NY 10036. Attention: Special Markets.

INDIVIDUAL SALES

Are there any Dell books you want but cannot find in your local stores? If so, you can order them directly from us. You can get any Dell book currently in print. For a complete up-to-date listing of our books and information on how to order, write to: Dell Readers Service, Box DR, 1540 Broadway, New York, NY 10036.

GEORGE JONES

I Lived to Tell It All

with

Tom Carter

A DELL BOOK

Published by
Dell Publishing
a division of
Bantam Doubleday Dell Publishing Group, Inc.
1540 Broadway
New York, New York 10036

Grateful acknowledgment is made to the following for permission to reprint previously published material:

ACUFF-ROSE MUSIC AND WARNER BROS. PUBLICATIONS, INC.: Excerpt from "I Can't Help It (If I'm Still in Love with You)" written by Hank Williams, Sr. Copyright © 1951 and renewed 1979 by Hiriam Music (BMI) and Acuff-Rose Music, Inc. (BMI). International rights secured. All rights reserved. Used by permission of Acuff-Rose Music, Nashville, TN, and Warner Bros. Publications U.S. Inc., Miami, FL 33014.

MCA MUSIC PUBLISHING: Excerpt from "These Days I Barely Get By," words and music by George Jones and Tammy Wynette. Copyright © 1975 by MCA Music Publishing, a division of MCA, Inc. All rights reserved. International copyright secured. Used by permission.

POLYGRAM MUSIC PUBLISHING: Excerpt from "I Was Country When Country Wasn't Cool" written by Rhonda Kye Fleming and Dennis W. Morgan. Copyright © 1980 by Songs of PolyGram International, Inc. All rights reserved. Used by permission.

SONY MUSIC PUBLISHING: Excerpts from "He Stopped Loving Her Today" by Claude Putnam, Jr., and Bobby Braddock. Copyright © 1978 Sony/ATV Songs, LLC d/b/a Tree Publishing Co. All rights administered by Sony/ATV Music Publishing, 8 Music Square West, Nashville, TN 37203. All rights reserved. Used by permission.

STARRITE PUBLISHING: Excerpt from "Life to Go" by George Jones. Copyright © 1959 and renewed 1987 by Starrite Publishing Co., a subsidiary of Glad Music Co., 14340 Torrey Chase, Suite 380, Houston, Texas 77014. All rights reserved including international rights and the rights to public performance for profit. Used by permission.

WARNER BROS. PUBLICATIONS: Excerpt from "A Picture of Me (Without You)" by Cole Porter. Copyright © 1935 (renewed) by Warner Bros. Inc. All rights reserved. Used by permission of Warner Bros. Publications U.S. Inc., Miami, FL 33014.

ISBN: 0-440-22373-3

Reprinted by arrangement with Random House, Inc.

Printed in the United States of America
Published simultaneously in Canada

July 1997

10 9 8 7 6 5 4 3 2 1

OPM

Preface

The shoppers stirred impatiently on the Florida grass, looking closely for bargains at the yard sale. I imagine they picked up and laid down used dishes, glasses, pictures, linens, and the other stuff, one man's trash intended to become another's treasure.

One guy lifted up two trophies that looked like they belonged on someone's mantel.

"George Jones: Country Music Association's Male Vocalist of the Year," read one inscription.

"Is this really a trophy given by the Country Music Association to George Jones?" asked the buyer. "Is this an official Country Music Association award? How in the world did it get in a garage sale?"

No one seemed to know.

Had the seller or buyer been able to find me, and had they asked, I couldn't have answered either.

I had likely been drunk and given the prestigious awards to someone who gave them to someone else who somehow directed them to the discount table at someone's suburban sale. Or maybe I just got high and left them someplace after an awards show. The priceless awards were bought for coins that day. The buyer returned them to me later in Nashville. They were the real thing and today sit inside a trophy case in my house.

The awards had left me during the troubled journey that was my life, a journey across a sea of whiskey and a mountain of cocaine in a vehicle of self-destruction. I was once dying of terminal restlessness. My secondary poisons were drugs and alcohol.

Friends, family, doctors, therapists, and ministers had tried to save me. All of that concern from all of those people was to no avail. Finally, the power of one love from one woman made the difference.

It may sound corny. But it's definitely true. I'm proof—*living* proof.

I don't know why anyone would want to hear about my sordid past, but I'm told a lot of folks do. People have been telling me I should write my life story for decades.

"It was all I could do to live through the life," I told them. "Why would I want to write about it?"

And so I never began the task, not until 1992, when someone satisfactorily answered my question.

"You hold a lot of influence over a lot of people," he told me. "Your story could prevent people from sinking into drug or alcohol abuse."

I decided to write. My story, to my way of thinking, will be an overwhelming success if it prevents just one person from taking the crooked path I took. I took a lot of whiskey when I was young.

Then the whiskey took me for thirty-five years.

And it took me straight to the bottom. I surfaced time and time again, but always sank once more until I abandoned the millstone of alcohol and, similarly, cocaine.

I have enjoyed a decorated musical career. But I'll swear that as many, if not more, folks are interested in my highly publicized personal life as are interested in my music.

Someone said that headlines dealing with my criminal behavior and civil negligence have represented forty years' worth of advance publicity for my story. I guess that's true. My cowriter, Tom Carter, came to my house to pick up the legal files that have dotted my life. He loaded the entire trunk of a luxury car and piled papers on the back floor and seat to the ceiling. He couldn't see out of his rearview mirror.

Then he hauled two more similar loads.

I suspect that was about one fourth of my legal papers. Moving around so much, I've lost a lot of files and records.

I've retained many lawyers, and one told me that I had been sued more than a thousand times in my career, mostly for failing to honor personal-appearance contracts because I was too drunk, or too full of drugs, or both, to do the shows.

If it appeals to the most lowdown kind of human behavior, you name it and I've done it. You'll read how I've paid an expensive price for my cheap thrills.

Through it all I kept reading articles that said I was the greatest country singer alive. And singers I respect were constantly saying that too. I was always appreciative, but I never understood how such a supposedly good singer could be such a troubled person.

My talent, though it brought me fame and fortune, never brought me peace of mind.

I called on a lot of friends, family, and former acquaintances in writing this book. My memory, from time and personal abuse, isn't the best. Some of their memories jogged mine, but were different from my exact recall. In those cases I used my version because I wanted this book to tell my story. I don't think there are any inaccuracies. I know there is no insincerity. So much misinformation has been printed about me, and I never understood why. The truth was always outrageous enough. Why did writers feel they had to add anything to it?

I know a lot of folks aren't going to like my story because I wasn't always a likable person. And while my life has changed, it hasn't changed for some of the reasons some folks would like to hear.

I haven't been saved by Alcoholics Anonymous, for example, and I didn't have a religious experience and join the church. I think that AA has been wonderful for a lot of folks, and I respect the life-changing improvements others have had through spirituality.

I quit drinking and using drugs because I got sick and tired of being sick and tired. My body and my mind gave out, and I gave in to anybody or anything that would help me get sober. I got so far down that I would have been willing to move to a reservation and eat herbs and roots if that would have guaranteed sobriety.

But I didn't have to do that. I had only to yield to a

good woman's love—simply to let someone love me when I didn't love myself. They say love can change the world. I'm here to testify that it changed one man. I had to stop abusing myself. I became my loved one's favorite loved one. How dare I mistreat someone she loved so much?

I know that a lot of readers are going to be disappointed because I don't analyze my life and experiences more than I do in the following pages. I didn't supply a lot of the answers they want because I don't have them. I still don't know why I did many things. I have theories, but I don't have concrete answers.

Neither do a lot of professional people with smarter minds than mine. Near the end of my drinking days, I was actually refused admittance to one rehabilitation hospital where a doctor flatly said I was incurable.

Mrs. George (Nancy) Jones proved that educated fool wrong.

I also know that a lot of my show-business peers are going to be angry after reading this book. So many have worked so hard for so long to maintain their careers. I never took my career seriously, and yet it's flourishing.

I never wanted to be a star and only occasionally wanted to be a performer. I always wanted to be a singer. I was happiest singing for one person who was listening as opposed to a thousand who weren't.

Sometimes the one person who listened closest was me. So I have blown off paying engagements for giant audiences only to get lost with my guitar, my thoughts, and my voice. By myself.

I've been behind bars, but none more binding than my own psychologically self-imposed prison. I've been beaten by mean and furious men, but never more savagely than I've battered my own body and mind. I've been financially broke, but not as impoverished as when I was spiritually bankrupt.

I've lived more in a month than most men do in a lifetime. When one lives hard he lives fast. At times the living was so fast that I literally didn't know the day, the time, the town, and, occasionally, not even the year. That kind of living is no life.

Yet, miraculously, I lived to tell it all.

And in the following pages, to the best of my ability, I'll tell it all to you.

GEORGE JONES

Acknowledgments

The manuscript of Dolly Parton's 1994 autobiography contained a list of acknowledgments intended to bear more than three thousand names. Her publisher wouldn't allow that, so Dolly cut the catalog in half. The remaining roster looked like a small-town telephone directory.

I also was going to try to name everybody who played a pivotal role in my life and in the writing of this book. But I think readers get weary of reading names they don't know, just as they get weary of acceptance speeches at awards shows where performers thank everybody from their kindergarten teacher to their foot doctor.

Besides, the people who were truly important to me, and who truly believed in and helped with this book, know who they are. And they know how I feel about them. They don't need reassurance by being a part of anybody's impersonal list.

But I'd be remiss without thanking my wife, Nancy Jones, whose name appears about as often as my own in the following pages. God should give all of the angels a name, and each should be called Nancy.

Tom Carter, my cowriter, got me to tell things I've never told anybody, and I was never uncomfortable. Anyone wanting to write his life story should work with Tom.

Jane Hailey, Tom's part-time assistant, worked all night several nights to bring this book in on time, and she came up with the title.

Mel Berger, my literary agent, went back to the publisher's bargaining table many times after I got cold feet and called off the project.

David Rosenthal, my editor at Villard, came to Nashville at his own expense to outline the book's promotion, and then put his money where his mouth was. I've known what it's like to record an album for a label that doesn't promote it. Now I know what it's like to write a book for a publisher that does.

Evelyn Shriver is my personal publicist, and is the best in the nation.

If I try to name others, I'll inadvertently leave someone out. There have been too many Jones Boys (members of my band who have come and gone), bus drivers, jailers, lawyers, arresting officers, bartenders, preachers, drug and alcohol counselors, friends, songwriters, bookies, managers, booking agents, United States presidents, hoodlums, and the random rest in a roll call of likable losers.

They have something in common in that I owe them, every one. Yet I owe each in a way special to him or her. And the closest I can come to repayment is to come clean about my life. And so I have about how I lived— and "I lived to tell it all."

Thanks.

Chapter 1

The grasshoppers were so thick that summer their swarming blocked the sunlight. Like the Old Testament locusts that fell on Egypt, they covered the parched East Texas ground like a rug. I had a brother-in-law, W. T. "Dub" Scroggins, who was much older than me, and I called him my uncle. His cash crop, cotton, had survived hail and high winds that year. But it would never stand up to the bugs.

Dub was never one to get hysterical, and he kept his composure when others lost theirs. His head was always as level as his spirit was sweet. He had a wisdom that sprang from the soil. He gave the ground his toil, and it gave him a savvy that made him smarter than his years.

I stayed with him and his wife, my sister Helen, on their farm twenty miles southeast of Waco during summers when I was a boy. I lived the rest of the year with my parents, brother, and sisters in one of three humble houses in East Texas.

Dub woke me one day that summer before daylight.

"George," he said, "the grasshoppers are going to take the cotton. I don't give it much more than a week. They're devouring every farm in this county. I've been thinking about it, and today we're going to take back what's ours."

We ate breakfast before sunrise, but that was not early enough to beat the insects to the field. By the time we had walked to Dub's seventy acres, the grasshoppers had already flown from the weeds into the cotton, where they'd eat all day. At sundown they'd fly back into the weeds, where they would roost, filled with the cotton that Dub had planted by hand. There was probably a drop of his sweat in every boll.

My sister Helen is ten years older than me, and she was married at sixteen, before I started the first grade. I looked up to Dub, literally and figuratively, and thought he looked the way God would if God wore denim. This time, I was looking to Dub to see what he would do. Even as a child, I understood the tragedy that was happening before me—tons of ruin from insects weighing less than an ounce each.

From inside Dub's barn, I heard the swing of his hammer. He was driving nails into scrap lumber, fashioning it into a sled. It was no more than a four-foot-square platform surrounded by two-by-fours that were waist-high to me. It had a rail, and I was supposed to hang on while I drove Dub's mule through the cotton.

He opened a burlap sack filled with bran. Dust boiled inside the barn's stale air when Dub thrust a scoop into the grain. The barn was like a furnace even though the sun was just barely in the sky. I've never been anywhere hotter than Texas in the summertime.

Dub poured the grain into a five-gallon bucket and added syrup. He stirred the mixture into a thick cereal.

"We're going to feed the grasshoppers today, George," he said. I thought I saw a smile.

Then he poured out a white-gray powder. A tiny cloud of dust again fumed upward as Dub poured arsenic into the mixture.

"Whatever you do, don't get any of this in your mouth," Dub said.

I drove the mule and sled that held the pail of poison through the cotton rows. Dub walked a few feet behind and slung his homemade brew from the bucket onto the cotton. In seconds, the bushes became the final resting place for the hungry grasshoppers.

As the sun eased over the horizon, its light glistened on the sticky bolls and the goo dripped onto the ground. Dub soon had globs of poisonous molasses clinging to his brogans.

The grasshoppers died the instant they ate, their fat bodies stuck in the mixture that had been their last meal. The cotton was dotted with dead bugs.

At least part of the crop was saved for another year. I could feel Dub's excitement about his home remedy's success. I stopped that mule only long enough for Dub to dip more poison into his bucket from the tub on the sled. We stood there, sweating and laughing at the wake of dead grasshoppers behind us.

"Get up there," I yelled at the mule, and the sled and the killing went forward. Even Dub's dog became excited and soon was barking wildly at something it had pinned down in nearby Johnson grass. Dub and I approached the dog curiously.

"Watch your step, George," Dub said. "It might be a snake."

Dub saw it first, a skunk with its tail raised and pointed toward our hound. It could spray its stinky mist in a heartbeat, and the stench wouldn't evaporate from its target for weeks. Dub told me about a man whose English saddle was sprayed. The man scrubbed it with lye soap and a brush, but never got rid of the smell. He had to bury the saddle.

"Get away from here, boy!" Dub shouted, and I got excited and ran like I was on fire toward the waiting mule. I was yelling, and that's probably what spooked the old mule. It bolted with the sled and sloshing poison in tow. Trouble is, the mule didn't run down the cotton rows. It ran across them. Cotton bushes were uprooted and flying like bowling pins. I was hollering at the mule and wanted to dive for the sled, but I feared the flying poison.

Soon the tub was empty, and it began rattling loudly on the sled. The noise frightened the mule even more, and he cleared the cotton patch and started up the lane for the barn. By now nothing was left of the sled except one or two boards, and they were fast becoming splinters. I kept hollering and waving for the mule to stop. That also scared the mule, and Dub was right behind me, hollering and waving for me to stop hollering and waving.

There was a gate between the lane and the barn, and the mule ran toward it full-tilt. I don't think it even slowed down before it went through. Dub said he could hear the barbed wire ping before it snapped on both sides of the gate.

The gate and sled were little more than splinters. The tub that had contained the poison was reduced to dented sheet metal. The mule was bleeding from cuts from cotton bolls and the shattered gate.

I started crying because of what I'd done and because Dub was screaming. I just knew he was going to be furious, and I ducked when he raised his arms. When they came down, they didn't strike me. They wrapped around me. I could feel his heavy breathing inside his embrace. My tears ran into his sweat.

"Ain't no reason to cry, George," Dub said. "We're a lot better off than the grasshoppers."

We waited for the mule to cool off before Dub smeared something like lard on its scratches. We spent the rest of the day building another sled and hammering out the battered metal into another tub. At daylight the next morning we were out there again, Dub sloshing his killing paste and me driving the mule.

I refused to turn loose of the mule the second day. Helen brought food at noon, and I ate with one hand. I wouldn't take the other from the mule's reins.

I lived with Dub and Helen again the following summer and was joined by my sisters Ruth and Doris. We had no electricity, and no money for ice, so Doris did what a lot of folks did—she put milk and other perishables in the well to keep them cool.

She tied a glass jug of cow's milk to the water bucket and let both sink gently beneath the dark water ten feet below ground level. The next day Doris drew a bucket of water, forgetting about the milk jug. It banged against the side of the well, shattered, and the water filled with glass and unprocessed cow's milk.

Doris was always blaming me for what she did, so when I saw Dub walk his mules up to the gate after a day of plowing, I ran to him.

"Doris is going to tell you I broke the milk in the well, but she did it."

She told him her story just as I had predicted. He didn't believe her for an instant. Doris cried, but not as much as she did when Dub told her she'd have to drain the well—by hand.

The nearest water was seven miles away in Mount Calm. Dub couldn't afford to give up the use of his wagon and team for the day required to haul it. Besides, the small amount of water he could carry would not have lasted long. And we could never drink the new rainwater that would fall into the well until it was drained of the spoiled milk.

"There is just no way around it, girls," Dub told my sisters. "That well is going to have to be drained, bucket by bucket."

I think he would have made me help Doris if she hadn't lied.

When Dub arrived in the middle of the next morning, the girls were arguing about who had drawn the last bucket of water and crying and fighting. He had cut his plowing short because he knew those two could never finish such a big job.

"Why are you drawing your well dry in the summertime?" an old man shouted from the dirt road in front of

Dub's place. He'd been watching the goings-on for some time before he spoke. He couldn't understand why farm folks were pouring drinking water onto the ground in the sweltering summer heat.

"Smell the well!" Dub answered. "These here silly girls broke a jug of cow's milk in the water, and it's not fit to drink."

The old man spit out tobacco, laughed, and approached the well.

"You got a Mason jar?" he asked.

"Why sure," Dub said.

"Go get 'er for me with some pounds of salt."

With the precision of an Indian medicine man, the old fella measured the salt into the jar and poured it into the bucket. He lowered the bucket into the well and told Doris to pull the rope up and down to churn the water.

"That salt will dissolve, and what don't dissolve will settle," he said. "And when it does, your water won't stink no more, and it will be fit for drinking after you boil out the salt."

Before the old man left, Dub paid him with all of his remaining salt. The old man argued about taking it. The next day, his prophecy came true.

These stories about cotton-eating grasshoppers, a runaway mule, and spilled milk are among many warm memories of growing up during the Depression in the East Texas wilderness. Times were hard, and pleasures were few.

In childhood I didn't know I was poor. Years later I knew, but by then I had the riches of memories.

My boyhood had another side. A dark side. My sister

Ethel died at age seven, five years before I was born. That was the first time, my people say, that George Washington Jones, my daddy, ever took a drink.

He died on September 7, 1967, at seventy-two, from a clogged artery in his neck. Doctors said the obstruction had been neglected for too long. It was difficult for them to operate because Daddy's arteries had been affected by the miles of liquor that had run through them.

Daddy moonlighted as a moonshiner. He made beer and whiskey and sold it to the rough loggers around the Big Thicket, the nickname for East Texas, where the green thickets are unlike the rest of the barren state. My daddy even sold, and sometimes gave, beer and whiskey to the lawmen who were supposed to arrest bootleggers like him. He used the money to provide for my five surviving sisters, my brother, and me, his youngest. He cared for, and he cared about, his family. Until he got drunk.

By the time I was twelve my daddy was working at the shipyard in Beaumont for a steady wage. Nobody in the family was supposed to talk to Daddy when he came in drunk. That set him off.

Sometimes my mother, Clara, couldn't hold her tongue, and nagged him about drinking. He'd beat on the table for her to fix him some supper, no matter how late, and she'd cook and complain. Then the fight was on.

"Be quiet, Mama," Helen would whisper. "Don't upset him, and he'll just go to bed."

But if Mama had a mind to, she'd keep up her nagging, and finally Daddy would snap. He'd slap her around and maybe turn over the table she had set. Helen had to get between them more than once to keep him from beating Mama. Then he'd start on Helen. He'd go into a rampage and upset every piece of furniture in the house. Some of the kids would get under the bed until someone could get him into his own. Then my sisters would tiptoe around the house putting things back together until well into the night.

He'd get up the next morning, sick, and everything would be in its place. He never knew that hours earlier it had all been a shambles.

Sometimes he'd roar into the house in the middle of the night, stumbling from kerosene lamp to kerosene lamp, lighting them and cursing for everybody to get up and sing. My sleepy sisters and I would have to sing him to sleep. I'd strum my guitar, and they'd try to harmonize, singing gospel songs. Helen said that when he dozed off, I'd hear his snoring and shoot out the window, just as some of my sisters had done earlier. I was always the last one to go. I had to stay and strum because if I stopped, the absence of the guitar might awaken him and he'd go into another tirade.

We were our daddy's loved ones when he was sober, his prisoners when he was drunk.

One of my daddy's beatings of Helen made Dub furious. "And to save her life," Dub said, "I married her three days later."

The marriage lasted fifty-four years, until Dub's death in 1993. Death has also taken another sister, my brother, and both of my parents.

I trusted Dub more than any other man on earth. In 1992 he recalled that in the early 1980s I was coming back from one of my many financially broke spells. I played various dance halls then for admissions money, paid at the door, or for a flat fee, paid in cash. I gave the money to Dub for safekeeping and to prevent me from blowing it. He said he once had $162,000 of my money in a brown paper bag hidden behind the seat of his pickup. The truck wasn't worth much, and Dub said he never locked its doors. He eventually took the money into his house. But imagine if someone had stolen that junk truck. They never would have thought to look behind the seat where the only other cargo was lint and debris.

Helen has long since had children of her own and grandchildren who will soon be leaving home. They don't fight the land anymore. The hardest thing they do today, thank God, is turn down the thermostat. Dub was still the softest-hearted but leather-tough man I ever knew when he died. He fell as I began to write this book, and Helen said she thought he suffered lingering pain but he wouldn't talk about it. She forced him to go to the doctor, who told Dub he'd been carrying a broken shoulder for two weeks. When I called him, he never mentioned his injury. All he could talk about were the good times we had had when I was a boy.

Dub began to deteriorate in 1979 after working for a cement company where he sprayed poisonous chemicals to maintain the grounds. His nerves began to die to the extent that he dropped things and didn't know it. He frequently didn't know where he was going. So he was forced to quit and lived mostly in retirement until his death.

My wife, Nancy, and I flew to Woodville, Texas, in June of 1993 for Dub's funeral. The service was held at the Raleigh Funeral Home, where the crowd of mourners spilled into the yard. One of Dub's granddaughters read a poem about him, and a woman I'd never met sang "A Picture of Me (Without You)," one of my hit records from more than twenty years earlier:

> *Imagine a world where no music is playing*
> *Or think of a church with nobody praying*
> *If you've ever looked up at a sky with no blue*
> *Then you've seen a picture of me without you.*

That's how I felt for the longest time knowing Dub was gone. I hadn't seen him regularly in years. But I had always known I could see him whenever I wanted to. His passing left me with a deep sense of personal loss.

Some said the loss could be heard for days afterward in my music—music that has taken me a long way from my dusty Texas boyhood. I've traveled a roundabout way to the top. Sometimes my path has taken me back to the bottom. I've lived in mansions and been a prisoner in hotels where I couldn't remember the name of the town.

I've stood tall in the spotlight, I've lain drunk on the floor. I've lived more lives in mine than ten men do in theirs.

Sometimes my problems have seemed unconquerable. Yet they were no greater than Dub's when the grasshoppers were eating his summer cotton.

He got through, and, somehow, so have I. Sometimes I've wished that I could have been content with less, like just laughing at life, grasshoppers and all, and settling for a cooling drink from Doris's milk-water well.

Chapter 2

The Model-A Ford puttered along the darkened dirt road of the Big Thicket, an East Texas wilderness that was a logging haven during the Great Depression. The nine passengers couldn't see the poor lumbermen's shotgun houses sitting just inside the towering timber's shadow.

The car's headlights reflected on the gravel ahead, flickered, and went out. The car was cast into total darkness inside the nighttime forest.

My dad was driving. He struggled to keep our jalopy on what he guessed was the road. He turned the wheel hard into a curve, and that forced my mother, a short and large woman, firmly against the passenger door. Children screamed as it sprang open.

Mama flew out of the car and into the cinders at perhaps thirty miles per hour. She tumbled through discarded railroad ties and spikes until a ditch stopped her momentum. She had turned over and over, and the next day she turned black-and-blue.

But she never turned loose of her baby.

I was three years old when that happened, and I'll remember forever the kind of love it represents. Mama always put her children and their welfare first. She and Daddy raised a family that was as rich in love as it was poor in possessions.

And we were rich in another way. The Jones children had a wonderful sense of values. They knew right from wrong thanks to the watchful teaching of their parents. This was driven home to me when I was seven and got the only real whipping Mama ever gave me. One was all it took.

I had stopped by the house of Mr. and Mrs. Walton, our neighbors, and walked into their bedroom. There, I saw a pocketknife on the dresser. It shined and was the prettiest thing I thought I had ever seen. My young mind ran away imagining how sharp that knife was and all the things I could do with it.

To this day I can say that I didn't think I was stealing when I put that knife in my pocket. It just seemed to my innocent mind that something I liked so much ought to belong to me.

Mama was sitting on the front porch shelling beans or peeling potatoes when I walked into our house. She stepped inside and said, "What's Old Man Walton doing coming this way? He don't never come this way."

Instantly, I knew I had done wrong. I shoved the knife under the mattress, jumped onto the bed, and pretended to be asleep.

"Mrs. Jones," I heard Mr. Walton say, "I don't know

how to tell you this, but your son Glenn [my middle name] came by the house a bit ago and I know my stuff was on the dresser. Nobody else has been in that house and I hate to say that he took my knife, but I wish you would ask him."

I could feel my heart pounding against the mattress as I tried to shrink under the covers.

"I'll do more than *ask* him if he's got that knife," Mama said.

Mama seemed taller that day than she ever had as she hovered above me and asked if I had Mr. Walton's knife. I was so scared that I would have sooner walked over hot coals than try to trick her.

"Yes, Mama," I said. "I do." And I pulled the knife from under the mattress.

Mr. Walton was given his knife, then Mama took me outside. She cut a switch and walked me to the garden, where she whipped me up one row and down another. I thought the corn would tassel and bear ears before she would ever quit.

It would be a few years before I was old enough to appreciate that whipping and realize that it really did hurt my poor mama more than it hurt me and that it truly was given as an act of love.

Mama and Daddy had real wisdom that went with their concern for their kids. We were forbidden from cussing. If my Pentecostal mother had ever heard us use profanity, a whipping would have been in store.

Yet once my mama heard me say "son of a bitch." I was a desperate little boy at his wit's end who would achieve a part of his manhood in a matter of seconds, and perhaps she thought a child with a man's job ahead of him might need to cuss in the situation.

As a kid, I never liked to fight. But I was living in Beaumont, where another seventh-grader followed me home and taunted me with a gang of his friends. I was small and naturally afraid of all of those tough ole boys who came into town from farms where they had built up their bodies from hard work. This went on for days, maybe weeks.

The meanest boy's name was Dick, and one day he and his cronies followed me up to my back door. I guess Mama heard the commotion because she stepped onto the porch. Through the screen door, she saw me lose my temper and call Dick's bluff. I might have figured she was going to whip me, but it would be after the fight.

I called him a son of a bitch and lit into him with both fists. Once I got on him, I was obsessed with bringing him down. We lived in the Maritime housing project, and folks came pouring out of those houses from everywhere. They pulled me off of Dick, and he never bothered me again.

I knew Mama had heard me swear, and I knew she knew what I had been going through with Dick. I looked her in the eye, ready for her wrath. She just looked away. She never mentioned Dick, cussing, or fighting again.

Love and wisdom were about all Mama and Daddy sometimes had to give. We were heading somewhere on one Christmas Day when Daddy's old truck broke down with yet another flat tire. The Texas heat made the old tires soft, and they were easily punctured by the gravel of the back roads. Each flat meant Daddy had to jack up the truck, remove the tire, pull out the inner tube, hot-patch it, put it back inside the tire, inflate it, put the tire on the truck, and lower the jack.

All that was very time-consuming to a bunch of kids eager to celebrate Christmas. So Mama made our Christmas right there at the side of the road. She broke out apples, oranges, nuts, and other fruit that we never saw the rest of the year. Some of the girls got tiny dolls that were really no more than trinkets. Helen said she was almost grown before she got a doll big enough to resemble a baby.

On one Christmas I got a guitar that was about six inches long. It wasn't really a guitar at all, just an imitation. But we kids were as happy as larks. We didn't know that there were children in the city getting bicycles and clothes and whatever else. No one we knew was that prosperous. We'd never had anything significant, and we never missed what we never had. And soon after the roadside Christmas, we were back inside Daddy's rickety truck, puttering and singing along a path that was as rocky as our lives.

The spirit of Christmas lived throughout the year among the Big Thicket poor who loved each other. Seven of us carved our names into a giant oak tree at our Kountze house. We wanted to see the names endure, and we wanted to see them together. We probably spent an entire day taking turns with the carving knife. Helen says she thinks someone carved my name for me because she thought I was too small to handle a knife.

We loved mischief and played friendly tricks on each other. My late brother, Herman, had a wife who was afraid of the hobos who came to folks' back doors during the Depression. She used to latch the screen door, but it still had play in it and would rattle if shaken. I sneaked up to that door many times pretending to be a bum, yelling and rattling the door of a scared woman who was home alone. She yelled, sometimes ran through the house, and once ran out the front door and down the road to get away. I loved that.

During the changing of another of Daddy's many flat tires we kids got to playing in the woods by the truck and I found a trash pile that contained an iron wagon. It had an iron tongue and wheels. It was covered with rust, but I thought it was the neatest thing I'd ever seen. When I asked Daddy if I could take it he said no because there was no room for both the wagon and his kids in his truck.

Brokenhearted, I bawled for hours.

A man lived in a cabin about a mile behind ours. He found out about my wanting a wagon and made one entirely out of wood. He might have carved the wagon out of a log, I don't know. But it had a wooden tongue and even wooden wheels. There is no telling how long it took him to cut and carve that wagon. He wouldn't take a dime for it, and it gave me a million dollars' worth of pleasure.

I came into this world on September 12, 1931, inside a homemade house of logs in Saratoga, Texas, near Kountze and Beaumont, as the last of eight children. I was delivered by Dr. Roark, who dropped me because my twelve pounds and some odd ounces were too heavy for him. He came to our house to deliver a baby and also got to treat its broken arm, although I was too small for him to set the arm. He had been with our family for years and delivered the first of the eight kids, Ethel, who died. Then there was Herman, Helen, Joyce and Loyce (twins), Doris and Ruth (also twins), and me.

Folks said Ethel was killed by congestive chills, and there is no telling what that means in terms of modern medicine. She might have had simple pneumonia that could have been cured for the price of penicillin. If he had known, Daddy would have found a way to raise the money.

But Ethel was never taken to a hospital. The nearest one was in Beaumont, where Ethel would have been a charity case. That wouldn't have set well with Daddy, so he and Dr. Roark treated Ethel at home. Mama and Daddy gave medicine from the doctor's bag, but most of the treatment was not much more than wrapping Ethel's shivering body in sheets and holding her close to them, Helen has told me. Ethel stopped shaking one day just as she closed her eyes. They never reopened.

That's the kind of primitive medical treatment there was for Texas's rural poor during the Depression. My daddy taught himself to set bones out of necessity. He set Herman's broken arm when he fell off a horse and got so good at setting the bones of injured lumbermen that Dr. Roark used to send for Daddy when he had more patients than he could handle. A man came to our house on a horse once during the night because there had been a bad car wreck and Daddy was needed at the scene and later at the hospital to help set the bones. Helen almost tore her nose off her face once, and Daddy sewed it back with nothing to kill the pain. He used a sewing needle and household thread.

Daddy could swing an ax with the accuracy of John

Henry swinging a hammer. He could fix or build anything. I guess he had to learn because there was no money for workmen. He made each piece of furniture we owned and kept every clock in the house running on time. I can still remember his taking apart a complicated clock and putting it back together perfectly.

Not everyone had Daddy's touch.

A family who often had no food lived behind us. Because of bad diets and outright malnutrition, their bodies were often covered with giant swellings. Their mama would coat her children with sulfur and tell them to lie on the front porch in the sun. The risings would get to be as large as potatoes before their mama would take an old house knife or razor and cut her children's skin. As the blood and other fluids drained, we could sometimes hear cries of pain. But their mama didn't know what else to do, so she just did her best.

We raised or made almost everything we used, even our soap. Mama used to take fat off a hog and boil it in a pot over an open flame until it became hard and dry. The result was called cracklings. She then poured lye into the cracklings and cut the cracklings into bars. That was our soap, and we used it to wash ourselves and our clothes.

Our clothes would get so dirty in the hot Texas dust that Mama would have to wash them through two or three hand cycles in a number-three washtub. She never owned a washing machine.

My folks knew how to make do for their own about everything. We heated water for baths by drawing it from a well in the morning and setting it in a washtub all day in the sun. The water was outright hot in the summertime by sundown. Then three or four filthy kids would use the same water and lye soap.

I never saw an electric iron until I was a teenager. So Mama or Helen would take a solid steel iron and set it on the woodstove. It would get hot enough to press our clothes, which were stiff as boards after Mama soaked them in homemade starch.

One of the most effective tools Mama and Daddy had was their children. Each of us had a job, and we knew to do it right. Herman and Helen had to cut and stack wood, the hardest job, because they were the oldest. There were so many kids in our family that not one blade of grass grew in our yard. We kept it worn down. So the kids had to rake it and sweep it. It was never mowed.

I was still pretty small when Mama and Daddy decided I needed to help with the family load and develop a sense of responsibility. It was decided that I would get up in the morning before everyone else and start the woodstove.

The first time I built a fire I stacked the stove to the top with kindling. It was a thick, black iron stove with a black sheet-metal pipe to the chimney.

I saw that black steel turn bright red. I had overloaded the stove so much that it began to glow and crackle from the heat. The noise actually woke up Mama, who leaped from the bed waving her arms and screaming that I was going to burn the house down. Daddy and some of the kids jumped up and began to throw water. It hissed and made steam, and smoke rolled through the house. We had to open the windows and doors to let it out as everyone ran around in nightshirts and underwear fanning their hands to push the smoke outside. Daddy showed me how to build a fire after that.

Since there was no money for fun, we were a family who knew how to entertain ourselves the way modern young people can't. The simplest things were big deals. I can remember us sitting next to the half light of coal oil or kerosene lamps and listening to "Gangbusters" and "I Love a Mystery" on the radio. We kids would cling to each other on the floor around the old Zenith. We'd be totally silent one minute and screaming the next as the broadcast sound effect of a squeaking door or heavy footsteps came over the air. We took it totally seriously. One or two of us probably thought that what we heard was true. Then we'd go to bed, afraid to close our eyes because a villain we had heard on the radio might find his way to our house in the woods.

Age and prosperity can sure damage a poor child's imagination. And our imaginations were a rich source of entertainment.

Even Ethel's funeral, the best Mama and Daddy could afford, was simple. She was buried in a plain sundress that she sometimes wore to sing and dance and parade in for the family. From what Helen remembers, and from what I've been told, I think Ethel might have grown up to be a movie star.

But her dreams, and much of Daddy's spirit, were covered by the East Texas clay. Daddy lived another forty-one years after Ethel died. But he never got over the death of his seven-year-old daughter.

Family was the most important thing to most people during the Depression. Folks today can't imagine the kind of closeness that came from kinfolk wrestling those hard times together. Nothing was closer than blood. And nothing brought blood closer than going through hard times with each other.

You sure can't replace blood with alcohol, but folks said Daddy seemed to try. He took his first drink at thirty-one, a few days after Ethel's death.

He drank with heartbroken vengeance. He drank more in a month than several men together did in a year. Alcohol became the liquid balm for his splintered spirit. Eventually, Helen and Dub committed Daddy to a rehabilitation center for alcoholics. He never drank during the last four years of his life.

The Jones family makeup just doesn't set well with liquor. Daddy never got crazy except when he was drunk. Years later neither did I.

Daddy was an unusual drinker. He drank to excess but never while he was working, and he probably was the hardest-working man I've ever known. He wouldn't take a swallow during the week, even though he sold homemade beer and bootleg whiskey when the logging slowed down. Folks came at all times of the day or night to walk with Daddy back into the woods to his still. He'd take their money, but he wouldn't take a drink with them if they came when he had to work the next day.

I'd see him meet Mama on Friday evening in front of the H&H grocery store. He'd go inside, pay his bill, and charge groceries for the next week. He made sure his family would be fed and that his responsibilities were met. Then he took the tidbit that was left and bought a bottle.

He'd stay drunk all weekend, but at three-thirty Monday morning he was sober and heading back into the woods to haul logs.

As a boy I rode many miles inside the long, wide toolbox on the old truck that Daddy used for logging and making wood staves. The truck had no suspension, and I bounced all over those solid steel chains inside the box. I actually believe that's why I have hemorrhoids today. Daddy would sail down a dirt road and spit chewing tobacco juice from his open window. It often hit me squarely in the face.

He came home from work at a decent hour during the week and the family sang together. Our old walls, virtually hidden inside the Texas woods, almost shook to our singing of Pentecostal hymns. Daddy played the harmonica, what we called the French harp, I played the guitar, and the sun went down as our voices raised. We were usually in bed by seven-thirty. By that time it was dark inside the woods, and we had no electricity.

But our schedule wasn't so predictable when Daddy was drunk. That's when he came home late and woke up the whole house, demanding that everybody get up and sing, especially my sister Doris and me.

As a boy, I was a dreamer. I sat for hours and stared silently into space. Even amid my big family I sometimes felt alone. Years later I still felt alone, especially during my drinking and drugging days.

My family might be in the middle of a big sing, and maybe neighbors would come by. I'd be having a great time, then somehow I'd seem to drift away. I wondered how I could feel so much by myself around so many people. Years later I felt the same way in front of thousands.

I went to the seventh grade twice before my folks finally let me quit school for two reasons. First, I had no interest in anything that school had to offer. Second, Mama and Daddy got tired of me playing hooky. Helen never told on me, but she knew I missed school in spells, some as long as a month. I'd sneak away and go into Beaumont, where I walked the streets barefooted with my little guitar, singing and dreaming with a mind that no school could hold. Without telephones no one could call my folks to ask why I wasn't in class.

I was interested in music as far back as I can remember. Helen said I used to try to play an old guitar with a missing string when I was three by laying it horizontally across my lap. And I remember the battery-operated radio we had that Mama and Daddy played on Saturday nights during the Grand Ole Opry from faraway Nashville, Tennessee.

In our small house my sisters had to sleep three or four to the bed. But when I was small I slept between Mama and Daddy. The purr of the radio static and the lateness of the hour were too much for a sleepy little boy. I often fell asleep to the music that I strained to hear across the miles.

"But you wake me up if Bill Monroe or Roy Acuff come on," I told Mama.

My dad saw my enthusiasm for music and one day surprised me by saying I could go with Mama and him on their weekly trip from Kountze to Beaumont. I lived my young life in houses near Saratoga and Kountze and then inside the Maritime project house in Beaumont.

We rode the Doodle Bug, the train that ran directly to Beaumont and made nothing but milk stops. We got off and went straight to the Jefferson Music Company. I suspected nothing.

I must have thought I was in musicians' heaven. Guitars hung from the ceiling, and my mouth was wide as I gaped at more instruments than I knew existed. I'm sure I was spellbound.

My mood was interrupted when Daddy talked to the salesman. Over the counter the man handed Daddy a shiny Gene Autry guitar with a horse and lariat on the front. I can see its glow to this day. Then Daddy handed it to me. I can't count the number of Martin D-45s and other expensive guitars I've owned in my life. But none ever meant any more to me than that little ole Gene Autry.

I took it home, and it hardly ever left my hands. I slept with it a time or two. I began to play note by note and could play melodies long before I learned how to make a chord. It soon paid off for me.

I was eleven when I first sang for pay, and it happened by accident. I rode a bus from Kountze to Beaumont on a Sunday morning. I could always ride for free if I had my guitar and sang the driver and passengers a tune. Barefooted and wearing my usual bib overalls with one leg rolled up to the knee, I carried that Gene Autry guitar to a penny arcade on Pearl Street. A shoeshine stand sat in front of the arcade. I got on it and began to play and sing.

People were beginning to get out of church, and soon a half dozen gathered in front of me. Then ten, twelve, fifteen, and maybe as many as twenty came and went. I just kept singing and playing.

Somebody threw a nickel, and I was astonished. I

didn't know whether to pick it up or keep playing and try to keep the coins coming. So I played on. The change continued to fly, and someone placed a cup near my feet. I would have brought one from home if I'd had any idea people were going to pay me. I continued singing and continued to hear coins hitting the side of the cup. That was the true music to my ears.

Two hours later, after I had sung every song I knew two or three times, I counted my funds. I had more than twenty-four dollars! That was more money than I had ever seen, and my young mind actually thought it was all of the money in the world. My family could have eaten for a week or more on that much money in 1942. But they never saw it. I was walking on air when I stepped inside the arcade. I'm not sure I left with a cent.

That was my first time to earn money for singing and my first time to blow it afterward. It started what almost became a lifetime trend.

Helen worked all day cleaning a woman's house, raking her yard, doing her laundry and more for twenty-five cents. She did that fifty-two weeks before her salary was raised to fifty cents. She was ten years older than me, and I had made as much money in two hours as she would in a year.

I guess I could have returned to that same arcade and done the same thing again. Maybe I could have made it a weekly event and even advertised myself. But I never went back, and I never knew why. At eleven years old I was already doing, and failing to do, things for no apparent reason.

*   *   *

Singing that day in Beaumont wasn't my first time to sing for strangers. I first sang outside the family in church when I was about nine years old. That didn't pay anything, but I wasn't doing it for money.

I had met a Pentecostal preacher and his wife, Brother Burl and Sister Annie, and they preached and sang the Gospel. They let me sing with them in church and in revival gatherings around Kountze. I stood next to a wooden pulpit and looked across the congregation at farmers with red faces and white foreheads from where their caps had shielded them from sunshine. Those poor Pentecostals would raise their hands, close their eyes, and open their hearts before the Lord.

I did all the great old Pentecostal songs, such as "Jesus, Hold My Hand," "Farther Along," and "Canaan's Land."

I remember one time we went somewhere to preach and sing and it was raining. They had a loudspeaker on top of their car. We sat inside, where Sister Annie and I sang through the speaker before Brother Burl took the microphone to preach. The water pounding on the car roof did nothing to dampen our spirits. The joy of Jesus went forward.

I became a part of their lives and grew to love them.

I don't remember how old I was when Brother Burl bought a used car made in 1942. But I remember that I taught him how to drive. He didn't know that the only car I'd ever driven was his.

We went onto the dirt road, where I can still remember that kindly preacher grinding the gears, unable to shift from first to second. I sat in the passenger's seat and rolled with laughter. Fun came easily back then.

Before I met Brother Burl and Sister Annie, I was just a shy country kid who had trouble looking anyone, much less a crowd, in the eye. Working with Brother Burl and Sister Annie in those fiery Pentecostal meetings, I developed a little self-confidence as I sang the time-proven hymns.

The training I received in church was shown about two years later when I was singing in Beaumont in front of the Excello Café. I had a shoeshine box and shined shoes awhile, then played and sang awhile. By that time I had my own cup.

I was singing "Precious Jewel," a Pentecostal standard that I had sung many times in services with Brother Burl and Sister Annie.

Then, like something out of a movie, a long and bright yellow Cadillac convertible pulled up to the curb on a street otherwise lined with old cars. A man and woman sat inside. From that moment on I pretty much ignored the other folks standing around me. I couldn't take my eyes off the rich strangers. And each time I looked at them, they were looking at me.

Between songs, the woman asked me to join them in the car. I'm sure I hesitated. As I slowly walked to the car, I noticed it had California license plates. That made the experience even more mysterious.

I sat down beside the couple and seemed to sink to my waist in the leather on the softest seat I'd ever imagined. Back in those days, a little boy could get into a car with total strangers and not be afraid.

Then the man asked me if I'd like to go to California and be in the movies!

At that point in my life, I hadn't even seen many movies, much less thought about being in one. He asked if I thought my mama would let me go, and I told him he'd have to ask her.

I think you could have heard her yell all over the Big Thicket when those town folks asked if they could take her boy out west.

"No way is my boy leaving here!" she yelled. "No, sir!"

The strangers didn't stay around long.

Mickey Rooney had already been a big childhood star, and maybe I could have been just like him. I'll never know. The strangers drove away, and I saw the dust of East Texas rise behind their bumper.

Not much remains of the places where we lived when I was growing up. The old houses have fallen down, and their remains were sold for the price of used lumber. Someone walking through the thick woods of East Texas today who happened on the spot of one of my homes would have no idea that nine people once made a living and had a life there. A visitor might rest against a certain oak and wonder out loud about seven names, faded by time, that were carved in its trunk long ago.

Chapter 3

His name was Jake Marino, he's dead, and he's just one of the dozens of musicians I played with when I was hustling jobs in the bars around Beaumont. I had gone to Beaumont as a teenager with my dad as he followed the logging and other common labor trails.

On this particular night, Jake and I were playing Lola's and Shorty's, a roadside rough house on Beaumont's Pine Street where customers routinely danced as couples, drank in groups, and clobbered each other one blow at a time. Some folks occasionally looked twice at someone lying on the floor to see if he was passed out— or knocked out.

At Lola's and Shorty's, if you didn't have a gun, you were given one as you walked through the door. Not really, but that statement comes close to describing the atmosphere inside the rural Texas honky-tonks of the late 1940s and early 1950s.

Jake and I were on break between sets. There was no backstage area, so there was no getting away from the crowd. We stood eye level to the people when playing or when on break. We therefore became part of the group as drunks rushed to us to slur their words and breathe their booze while accidentally spitting into our faces. By the end of the night, the cigarette smoke was often so thick that, from the front, I couldn't always see people in the back. Even during cool weather the room was warm from so many dancing bodies pressed so closely together.

On this particular night I kept seeing one man. And I hadn't seen him before.

From working Lola's and Shorty's and other lawless joints, I learned to look over my shoulder at the people behind me while somehow looking at the people in front of me. I had mastered the art of silent self-protection.

The guy in question was walking among everybody but still somehow seemed to be alone. Curious, I approached him, and found out what I had suspected was true. He was there to repossess my car because I was two payments behind on the note, held by a credit company in Beaumont. The firm had sent him, a stranger, because I would have recognized one of the regular collectors.

"Are you here to take my car?" I asked him point-blank.

"Yep," he said. "I am. You're behind on your payments."

"What's it to you?" I asked. "You don't even work for the company that holds the note."

He tried to explain, and one thing led to another. In seconds I was on top of him. I was hitting him hard, and that accelerated the flow of blood.

Mine.

Consumed with beating him, I hadn't felt him stab me. Perhaps he used a straight razor because the blade was sharp enough to penetrate my heavy leather coat, even though it was the type of thick Western wear you don't often see today.

My buddy Willie saw him cut me, and my buddy Newt pulled the guy off me after busting his jaw. I lay on the ground, waiting for an ambulance to rock me over patchy two-lane highways to the hospital. The bottles and tubes above my head inside the swaying vehicle moved with every seam in the concrete. From my cot I stared at the ceiling, not knowing how much blood I had lost and perhaps just drunk enough not to care. I didn't realize how close I had come to leaving my life on the parking lot at Lola's and Shorty's.

Being cut that severely left a strange sensation. On one hand, I could feel the warmth of my blood seeping into the thick bandages. Outside my body, though, the blood quickly became room temperature and felt cold pressed by the bandage against my skin. The ambulance attendant kept telling me I was going to be fine, but I knew he said that to every patient, no matter how badly injured.

That incident was a long time ago. But one never forgets the feeling when he truly wonders if he is going to die. And on that cot I had fleeting thoughts that the inside of that battered ambulance would be the last thing I'd ever see.

Ninety stitches were required to stop the bleeding from a slash whose scar wraps around my waist to this day. For that night, I had all I ever wanted of fistfights, ambulances, booze, and bleeding. Little did I know I had not nearly gotten it all behind me.

I was about twenty years old when I was stabbed. But I began singing in those hell-bent-for-leather dives when I was about fourteen. One of my first playing partners was Dalton Henderson, and we performed days at KTXJ in Jasper, Texas, fifty-eight miles north of Beaumont. We worked nights in joints for a couple of bucks, then he and I stayed with his parents.

Dalton was a big part of my personal history in another way. The first time I ever got drunk I did so with Dalton and some other boys whose names I can't remember. I don't remember a whole lot about the ordeal because it was so long ago and because I got so loaded. We were riding in an old car and someone opened a bottle of whiskey. I remember being about two or three miles outside of Jasper in a pasture and throwing up. I was so drunk that I didn't notice I was standing in cow shit. I fell in it.

I remember trying to stand up and falling back down several times—literally "falling down drunk." The other boys and I were covered with cow shit when the highway patrol got us. That deal earned me four days as the guest of Jasper County. I don't remember what kind of county clothes I wore in jail, but I'll bet I was glad to get them. They weren't spotted with cow shit.

Shortly before I worked with Dalton I played with the Reily Trio, made up of a brother, his wife, and his sister. That was at KFDM in Beaumont, where we did a live show at 5:30 A.M. That job didn't last very long because I couldn't stand getting up that early and because the Reilys left Beaumont to play in the band of Lefty Frizzell, the country music legend who had big hits on Starday Records before I later joined the label.

Those morning radio shows were totally unlike anything you'd hear today. The entertainers performed live and acknowledged letters and the people who wrote them. Many listeners mailed song requests because they couldn't call the station. There weren't any telephones in rural East Texas in 1945. An announcer read the news along with farm-to-market reports about the price of grain or livestock. He also read obituaries of those who had died the previous day and told what funeral homes were handling their services. Predawn radio that reached the Texas countryside was not just a source of entertainment. Back then it was the listeners' link to the world.

And it made local celebrities out of the musicians who played over its airwaves. When I was fourteen, there were no bigger stars to me than the husband-and-wife radio duo Eddie and Pearl.

Along with their broadcast they also performed live at drive-in restaurants where people ate in their cars while listening to Eddie strum a guitar and blow a harmonica as Pearl played upright bass. I had recently bought a new flattop guitar and mounted an electric pickup inside. A buddy and I were sitting in his car listening to the music and watching people eat when he decided he would ask Eddie if I could play with him and Pearl.

Eddie said it was okay, and I tuned my guitar to his during one of his breaks. He told me what he was going to play, and I must have impressed him because I knew everything he did, which was mostly Hank Williams and Ernest Tubb songs. I had listened to him regularly over KRIC in Beaumont.

I had also gone to hear them a few times earlier at the Playground Park, an amusement park for children. The price of admission was ten cents. I remember because the price of a movie was nine cents plus two cents for tax.

The first time I played with Eddie and Pearl I didn't sing a note. I only played lead guitar. Later, when Eddie found out I could sing, he let me take the vocal part every now and then. Playing with people who played on the radio was a big deal to me. A real big deal. Soon I was working with them four nights a week in dance halls, plus one hour a day, five days a week on the radio, and playing the amusement park with them on weekends. That schedule paid me $17.50 a week plus room and board. I lived with other folks a lot as a teenage musician. And with Eddie and Pearl I probably worked more and earned less than at any other time in my life. I even remember our schedule being extended to playing six nights a week. I don't remember my pay going up.

We'd do three or four long sets each night, fighting to be heard above the drunks who were often fighting each other.

Doing that night after night took its toll on me. I can imagine how tiring it was to Eddie, who was older and had a fondness for whiskey. A lot of booze and little sleep will wear a man down quickly.

Eddie must have been real tired one night after we played the Bayou Club, about ten miles outside of Beaumont in the oil development country. He drove around a horseshoe curve that was low in the middle and had a bridge on it. It had rained a lot that night, and the road was under water. Eddie couldn't see the road, and I guess that's why he didn't follow it. It turned, but Eddie went straight—right into the bayou.

"Eddie, you're going into the river!" Pearl hollered. "You're going into the river!"

Eddie was drunk and kept driving until the water forced the car to stop. Water was over my feet inside the car and over my knees when I stepped out. Eddie went to sleep inside the car with water in his lap while Pearl walked back to the Bayou Club to get someone with a chain.

Once on higher ground the car started and Pearl drove us home. Eddie continued his nap. By the time we got home Eddie was awake and Pearl was mad. She went straight to the bedroom and wouldn't fix anything to eat as she usually did after a show.

So Eddie decided to feed himself. It wasn't long before Pearl charged back into the kitchen.

"What are you eating?" she wanted to know.

"I'm eating this here potted meat!" he shouted. "I'm hungrier than hell!"

And he kept chomping.

"That ain't potted meat!" Pearl yelled. "It's dog food!"

He'd been too drunk to notice that he'd eaten half of the dog food in the house.

I learned a lot from Eddie and Pearl and still have a soft spot in my heart for them. It wasn't easy for a married couple without straight jobs to make it as musicians on the radio when they didn't have hit records. Eddie had his faults, but he scuffled enough work to keep them alive.

I probably can't say enough about how rough-and-tumble those old beer joints and taverns really were. I remember after I left Eddie and Pearl I played with a guy who sang Ernest Tubbs songs. We ventured over to the Port of Houston on old Highway 90 from Beaumont.

Ships came into that port, and they were filled with non-English-speaking people. It was hard to communicate with them while they were sober and impossible when they were drunk.

The club owner literally strung up chicken wire to keep my buddy and me from getting killed from flying beer bottles. A customer might bump another while he was dancing and a fight would explode. Somebody would hit someone who had hit someone else, and soon there would be an outright brawl.

My buddy and I just kept playing because that's what the owner told us to do. Meanwhile, the all-out fight continued.

Bottles sometimes hit the chicken wire and shattered on the concrete floor. People danced on broken glass. At the end of a slow night the janitor swept up the pieces. At the end of a good night he shoveled them.

I went back to work with Eddie and Pearl and was playing the Playland Park when I noticed a young woman with her parents. She was Dorothy Bonvillion, and she became the first Mrs. George Jones. I talked to Dorothy and her folks after the show, and they invited me to their house for supper.

My mama had to sign legal papers for me to get married because I was only seventeen. I had no money and no job, and Dorothy's parents had no patience about that situation. They insisted that we move in with them and that I go to work with Dorothy's daddy. He made me a house painter.

I didn't want to paint houses. In fact, I didn't want to do anything for a living that didn't involve music. But that didn't pay enough to support Dorothy, me, and the baby that was soon on the way. I took a job at a bottling company driving a truck, but that didn't satisfy me either. Dorothy's folks treated me like I was a little kid, and the constant pressure of being under their watchful eyes was too much. I wanted to get away.

So Dorothy and I lived in an apartment for a spell but had to move back in with her parents because we couldn't afford the rent.

Due to the pressure from her parents, little money, and our youth, our marriage was probably doomed from the start. Dorothy and I were divorced even before Susan, my first child, was born.

The judge wanted to know how much I earned, and I estimated about seventy dollars a month. He ordered half of that for child support. I missed my first month's payment, and by the time I was two months behind I was put in jail. On the fifth night my sister Loyce and her husband bailed me out.

I still had no money, and that meant I'd be going back to jail, where there isn't too much financial opportunity. I had no reason to believe I could ever make the child support payment and no reason to think I wouldn't land right back in jail, where I could do no one any good.

So I joined the marines.

It was steady work. I could make a financial allotment

for my dependents, and, best of all, I could get out of Texas and the troubles that seemed to follow me there. I was eighteen years old.

I was stationed in San Jose, California, where I met Cottonseed Clark, a nightclub musician and radio personality who let me sit in with his show one night. I did a Webb Pierce song, and Cotton ate it up. He offered me a job for twenty-five dollars every Saturday night. That's the most I had ever been guaranteed to earn for one night's singing.

I had duty every other weekend, and I had to finagle my way out of it so I could earn my twenty-five dollars. If I could have worked every Saturday night I would have earned one hundred dollars a month, far more than my military pay.

People have asked what I remember most about the service, and I don't answer with talk about guns or six-mile hikes and the like. The most vivid memory I have is coming in at four o'clock in the morning on New Year's Day, 1953, after playing a show. I lay down in the darkness, and the entire barracks was silent except for one voice. It belonged to the guy in the bunk next to mine.

"Hey," he said. "Your buddy is dead."

I didn't know who he was talking to or what he was talking about.

"Hank Williams," he said. "Hank Williams is dead."

He showed me the front page of the newspaper with a headline that screamed that country music's greatest singer-songwriter had been found dead in the back of a car on the way to a show in Canton, Ohio. That sounded as far away to me as Europe, and I couldn't believe that someone who was so close to my heart had died in such a distant land. Music was the biggest part of my life, and Hank Williams had been my biggest musical influence. By that thinking you could say he was the biggest part of my life at that time. That's how personally I took him and his songs. And the composer of the tunes that would live for ages was dead at twenty-nine.

I lay there and bawled.

To this day I'm always complaining about the lack of good songs available to recording artists. Nashville has more songwriters writing weaker songs than at any other time. I've heard Merle Haggard, Faron Young, and veteran writers such as Jerry Chestnut and Hank Cochran say the same thing. The songs that reach number one today sell one or two million copies but are forgotten in less than a year. Nobody, including me, gets to record songs that are so good their popularity will stand the test of time.

> *Today I passed you on the street*
> *And my heart fell at your feet.*
> *I can't help it if I'm still in love with you.*
> *Somebody else stood by your side.*
> *And he looked so satisfied.*
> *I can't help it if I'm still in love with you.*

"I Can't Help It" was a hit for Hank Williams forty-four years ago. Its lyrics couldn't be more simple—or more profound. There's no telling how many hundreds of artists have cut that song. Today a song goes number one for the artist who records it, and no one else ever cuts the tune. No one else wants to. They'd rather write their own rush job, publish it, make a fortune from the popularity of today's country music, then write more musical mush to repeat the cycle.

But the songs of Hank, Lefty, Johnny Cash, Willie Nelson, Merle Haggard, and a few others will live forever. Not a year goes by when one of those songwriters doesn't get a new recording or two of one of his timeless compositions.

When Hank died, I had no idea that his tragic passing would be the first of several among country stars I'd eventually get close to.

I met Johnny Horton, who died in a car wreck, and became good friends with Patsy Cline and Jim Reeves, who died in plane crashes in 1963 and 1964. Jack Anglin, of Johnny and Jack fame, was killed while driving to Patsy's funeral. He was also a friend of mine. I had a hard time with the death of Marty Robbins in 1982 when he was taken as a relatively young man by a heart attack.

Country music today is an international industry. But when I came to Nashville in the late 1950s it was a struggling business where everybody in it knew everybody in it. We were a family. And most of us were trying for that first "real big" record. Back then, our music was so unpopular in the wake of rock 'n' roll that you could record a song that sold only twenty thousand copies and see it go to number one on the country charts. Most of the record-buying public regarded us as hillbillies. Our music was still called hillbilly music in a lot of circles.

Even in Nashville there were folks who looked down on those of us on Sixteenth Avenue South, where we recorded three-chord songs that were played on tiny AM stations scattered mostly in the rural South. And because we were not a part of polite society, and because we were struggling to take our backwoods music to town, we bonded. People get close to each other when they're working for the same cause.

I think that's another reason I felt so close to Hank Williams, even though I hadn't even seen Nashville when he died. Hank had done more to make our music popular than anyone before him, including the legendary Jimmie Rodgers, who made the first country music record in the 1920s, and even Ernest Tubb, who was a household name in the 1940s and 1950s when he became the first country star to have a legitimate film career. As a kid in East Texas, I never would have dreamed that someday I'd work for Ernest on long tours of one-night shows.

As for Hank, I suppose my grief for him was no greater than that of millions of other Americans, but it might have been. Most folks had only known Hank through his music. But I had also known him personally long before I ever moved to Nashville. There aren't too many people who can even say they saw Hank Williams perform. But I did, and I even got the chance to perform *with* him.

He came to KRIC when I was doing the afternoon radio show with Eddie and Pearl. He was booked to play the Blue Jean Club that night and wanted to promote his show. He talked a little bit on the air to Eddie, and then Eddie asked Hank to sing "Wedding Bells," Hank's latest single record.

Hank accompanied himself on rhythm guitar, and I was supposed to play electric lead guitar behind the most popular country singer in the world.

But I didn't play a note.

I was so intimidated at the sight of Hank Williams and the thought that I was in his presence that I was paralyzed with fear. I simply stood there and watched him arch his back and let that hurting voice coming from his skinny frame fill the room.

The only thing I did with my guitar was hold it.

Hank wore Western clothes on stage or off. That day was no exception. He didn't change when he left the studio.

After the one-hour show he visited with Pearl for a long time. I was still in shock and didn't say a whole lot. I just stared. Pearl told him how much I admired him and his music, and that pleased an adoring fan who was fourteen. Time, alcohol, and drugs have not been kind to my memory. But my recollections of my afternoon with Hank Williams are as vivid as yesterday. And they will be forever.

I came out of the service in November 1953 and went back to Beaumont. That's where most of my people were, and that's where I had done most of my singing before the military came into my life. I didn't do much for about a year except play music in dives where I sang and drank the nights away. What I didn't know about drinking before I went into the service I had learned by the time I got out. I was twenty-two years old, and for me liquor went with country music real naturally, especially inside those Texas honky-tonks. I'm not making excuses for drinking, I'm just saying I was always around drunks, and that's when I began to drink regularly. A lot of folks say they have to be drunk to put up with drunks, and I was no different. I also think that all of us are the result of our surroundings, especially when we're young.

Booze was easy to come by. Folks were always wanting to buy a drink for me, and a lot of them got mad if I turned them down.

They didn't get mad very often.

I took a day job as a disc jockey on KTRM in Beaumont about a year after my military discharge. I soon had a night show at the station and enjoyed the work more than any job I'd ever had outside of a nightclub. I used to talk over the air about the bars where I was scheduled to sing. That made for a lot of free plugs for my own shows, and that translated into money that club owners didn't have to spend on advertising. They liked that, and I always had a lot of people at my shows.

There has always been pretty strong word-of-mouth communication in the music business. I'll give you an example. If a singer needs a lead guitar player, every guitar player around town seems to get word of it. That's still true today, even in Nashville, where an estimated thirty thousand people work in the music industry.

So I had no trouble finding out that Jack Starnes and H. W. "Pappy" Daily were looking for me in Beaumont. They owned Starday Records. (The "Star" was for Starnes and the "day" was for Daily.) They had heard about my singing, and they had heard a couple of acetates that had been played on the radio. (An acetate was a recording that was used to make duplicate recordings back in the days of pressed wax records.)

I was told they wanted to sign me to a record deal, and I was overjoyed. They were the first people with ties to what to me was a major label to show any interest in my voice. Their distribution, at that time, didn't go much beyond Texas, but I don't guess I thought about that.

But my first records for the label didn't exactly shake the nation in February 1954.

The first Starday "studio" was actually Jack's living room, where he had tacked cardboard egg cartons on the walls to absorb sound. There was one microphone for the singer and all of the musicians. We cut our music live. That means we played it and it was recorded exactly as it was played. There was no such thing as overdubbing, where the vocal and instrumental tracks are electronically stacked on the recording, the way records are made today. In my early recording days, if one person on the session made a mistake, everyone had to play the song again or leave the mistake on the record.

There was a single lightbulb in the center of the room and one "engineer," a guy who turned the recording machine on and off. Today the engineer sits in a sound booth and is visible to the singer and musicians.

When I did my first session for Starday, the engineer sat in another room. I couldn't see him, and he couldn't see me. I knew he wanted me to start singing when he flipped a switch that turned off the overhead light. I stood there waiting in the dark. When he turned the light back on, the musicians and I kicked off our song.

Can you believe we were trying to make a product for radio airplay under such primitive circumstances? That's how a lot of records were made back then. We just did the best we knew how. (My second session for Starday was inside a real studio.)

The first session produced "No Money in This Deal" and "Here in My Heart," two songs I wrote.

I can't imagine being as nervous today as I was when I cut my first two songs for Starday at age twenty-two. When anybody gets nervous they rely on their reflexes, and I was no exception. I simply did what I had been doing all along, singing like my musical influences— Hank Williams, Roy Acuff, and Lefty Frizzell.

"Well," Pappy said after hearing those interpretations of my songs, "you've sung like every successful male singer in the business. But the world has already got a Hank, Roy, and Lefty, and it's satisfied with what it's got. Do you think you could sing like George Jones? I'd like to hear how *he* sounds."

"I don't understand," I said. "Those guys are who I like."

I was so naive that I actually didn't realize that Pappy and Jack were trying to find someone with a different sound, his own sound. And so, inside that makeshift studio, I searched for the voice of George Jones.

That was probably the birthplace of my own style. I still used Hank's, Roy's, and Lefty's phrasing, but I used my own voice, which was considerably higher forty years ago than it is today.

I remember hearing "No Money in This Deal" on the radio for the first time in 1954 over station KTLW in Pasadena, Texas. It was played by Tater Pete Hunter, a famous area disc jockey. I was standing beside him the first time the song went on the air. The song ended, and Tater must have put on another record because I remember talking to him.

"Well," I said, "how do you like my record? I want the honest truth."

"I don't like it," he said. "I've heard a lot better."

I've been asked if his honesty hurt me. The answer is no. I've always tried to be honest, and maybe that's why I never resented honesty in others. Years later, when I missed hundreds of personal appearances because I was drunk, people around me tried to get me to lie.

"Tell the press you were sick, or that your sister was ill, or that your bus broke down," they said.

"Hell no," I said. "Tell them I was drunk."

Country music is the most honest music in the world, and I think the people who sing it should be honest. A country music fan is the most loyal creature on earth as long as you're honest with him. I'm not proud of some of the things I've done, and I haven't gone around talking about all of them. But if I was asked, and if I answered, I answered honestly.

That's one of the reasons I'm still working and playing some of the world's largest concert halls today. I can't tell you how thankful I am for those shows, their wonderful crowds, and the fact that they're all a long way from Lola's and Shorty's.

Chapter 4

In 1954 I was playing Almadee's, a Houston drive-in restaurant, and on a night off I went to the Princess Drive-In, another of the scores of drive-in restaurants that were so popular in Houston and other American cities in the 1950s.

There was a spirited carhop there, and I had trouble taking my eyes off her. I began to flirt and asked her to come see me at Almadee's. Not long after that I had a recording contract, but not before I married the carhop. The former Shirley Corley became the second Mrs. George Jones.

I don't remember much about the ceremony, including the date. I've never been good at remembering dates. But Shirley was my wife for fourteen years, during which time she gave me two sons, Jeffrey and Brian. And I gave her a lot of grief.

Shirley and I might have been miscast from the start. Uncle Dub often said that she didn't like having a husband who was an entertainer and that she was embarrassed because I sang in public. I don't know. But I know she didn't want to go with me years later when I moved to Nashville. She stayed in Nashville for three months, then returned to Texas, where she had friends. I'm sure it was hard for her, a young woman living in a strange city while her husband was on the road singing country songs. So she was less than supportive.

Little did I know in 1955 that Shirley's lack of support for my career would eventually break my heart. I remember coming in off the road several times, tired and lonely, only to find her gone. I interpreted that as a lack of concern for me and what I did for a living, and that made for problems.

Shirley was a good woman and a good mother, but obviously we had our difficulties. She's no longer alive, and I don't intend to say anything unkind about her. I'll tell you a few more things about her later.

My 1955 recording of "Why Baby Why" was my biggest hit on Starday Records. It was a bigger hit for Webb Pierce and Red Sovine, who heard my version and recorded the song as a duet for Decca, a major label with national distribution. I've heard folks talk about all of my glory years on Starday Records. The fact is I was only on that label for two years. On March 9, 1957, "Don't Stop the Music" started its climb to the number-ten slot on the *Juke Box* operators' survey. That was my first tune recorded on Mercury, my record label until 1962.

After "Why Baby Why" my single records were "What Am I Worth," "You Gotta Be My Baby," "Just One More," and "Yearning," a duet with Jeanette Hicks that was my last record for Starday. By the middle 1950s, I was starting to get established as a recording artist in Nashville. It would be a few more years before I'd move to Nashville and have my own band.

My 1950s recordings were getting the majority of their airplay in Texas, so that's mostly where I worked.

I had a 1950 Packard and hired a painter to put my name on the side in big letters. He painted the titles to my hit songs on the fenders. I pulled up to my shows in those roadhouses driving that mobile advertisement.

Pappy Daily became serious about promoting me and hired Gabe Tucker, program director at KIKK, Houston's largest country music station, as promotions director for Starday. Gabe had been Ernest Tubb's manager and a standup comedian on "The Eddy Arnold Show" on TV, so he had a lot of contacts in the recording industry. He became a big help to my early career, and we are friends to this day.

Because of his position, Gabe had no trouble listing "Why Baby Why" as number one in the country market. He sent copies of the surveys listing my song as number one to every major radio station in the country. Program directors and disc jockeys from around the nation called him.

"Houston is a pretty big market," they would say. "If this George Jones guy is number one down there, he must be pretty good. So we're going to chart his song in this market and see how it does."

Gabe taught me a lot of little things about promoting a record, and most of them didn't interest me. For example, he often arranged for photographers to be present whenever I played a package show (a show with other artists).

"Now after the show," he would always remind me, "I'll get the photographer to photograph you with these stars, and you be sure you stand to the photographer's left. That way, when the picture is published, yours will be the first name mentioned in the caption."

I was content just to be in the pictures and never thought about where I should stand. I don't think the other country acts were aware of the standing strategy. None ever said anything about where he or she stood except for Buck Owens.

Gabe remembered one night backstage at the Houston Jamboree when Buck insisted on standing to the photographer's immediate left and told Gabe he wouldn't let anyone else hold that position.

That left-side rule was a big thing with Gabe until one day when I was part of a group picture with Pappy Daily. I didn't realize I had taken the place at the left of the line.

"Move away from there!" Gabe shouted. "We can't do this to poor old Pappy. He's our bread and butter. You can't have your name in the magazine before his."

Gabe began to run around the line, moving people all around, and the other acts must have been wondering what was happening.

All of that seems ridiculous to me today.

I've seen lots of acts fight over who gets top billing on a show and who gets to close the show. There was a time when closing the show was important to me because back in the days of big package shows, the closing act was commonly regarded as the most popular. Today I'm just as happy to open the show so that I can do my part and get on my touring bus to watch television and maybe, if I'm lucky, a good football game. I've even had arguments with a few promoters because I wanted to be offstage in time for a television show and they wanted me to stay because they thought I'd hold their crowd. It's funny how some of the things that once meant so much to me in this business, and in life itself, don't worry me now that I've got a few years behind me.

A documentary was made about my life in 1990, and one of the people interviewed was Loretta Lynn. She told a story about an extended tour I did with Buck Owens in the 1960s. Buck and I argued each night about who would go on last and therefore get top billing.

"Now, Buck," I used to tell him, "you closed the show last night. Let me close tonight in this town, and you can close tomorrow night. We'll take turns, and that will be fair."

He wouldn't hear of it. Buck's career was smoking hot, and I guess he wanted to milk it for all it was worth.

"I'm the star," he would say, "and I'm going to close the show."

So I fixed him. We were somewhere in Canada. I was introduced, was of course supposed to sing *my* songs, take an intermission, then let Buck come out as the final performer of the evening.

It went exactly that way, except that when I was on-stage I didn't sing my songs. I sang only Buck's. I did "Under Your Spell Again," "Excuse Me (I Think I've Got a Heartache)," "Foolin' Around," "Under the Influence of Love," and the rest of the few hits he had recorded. I didn't leave one song for him to sing. I walked offstage and passed him in the wings.

"You're on," I said.

He wasn't amused.

Buck went out and did essentially the same show I had just done. The people didn't know what to think, and Buck didn't know what else to sing.

In 1994 Faron Young said that Buck had never been overly fond of me. About a month later, Buck said that our friction began because Faron paid him a hundred and twenty-five dollars nightly, which was twenty-five dollars more than he paid me, when we were featured acts on Faron's touring show in the late 1950s.

That extra twenty-five dollars was a lot of money back then, especially to a struggling country singer who was paying all of his own expenses. Faron and Buck argued that Buck was entitled to the additional money because he had to drive to Nashville from his home in Bakersfield, California, while I had to drive from mine in East Texas. They said his higher overhead justified additional pay.

I thought the matter would be simplified if Buck would simply move east.

Another night we played Charleston, South Carolina, with several other acts. Buck again insisted on closing the show.

I put on some baggy Bermuda shorts and walked quietly to the back of the stage. Buck was lost in a tender ballad when I walked behind his band in those shorts. Only the audience could see me as I danced a jig. I looked like a banty rooster in bloomers, and no one onstage could figure out why the crowd was howling as Buck tried to sing his tune. Before Buck could look around, I was gone. The audience settled down, and I pulled the same stunt again.

When Buck caught me he was angry once again.

In December 1994 Buck contributed information for this book and laughed about our early disputes. He had many kind things to say about my music and career, and I appreciated that very much. Age has brought wisdom to both of us.

Faron said I was resentful because Buck's home in Bakersfield did not make him a part of the Nashville family. Faron said Buck became most angry with me, however, because I kept telling Faron that Buck was ugly and regularly called him "gizzard lip."

What can I say? I used to drink a lot, say a lot of things I shouldn't have.

Faron and I also mixed like oil and water for years and for no reason. If we were together, we were drinking. If we were drinking, we were fighting.

He was doing a radio interview one time in a city where the mayor and his wife were present. Knowing that the honored guests and the radio audience could hear, I walked into the room and began using foul language. Faron, who happened to be sober, politely asked me to stop, but I persisted. He then confronted me, and we had a fistfight in front of his honor and the city's first lady. That did wonders for our careers. You should have heard the radio announcer adlibbing in an effort to cover up the free-for-all from his listeners. He talked real fast, like an auctioneer with high blood pressure.

Another time, Faron and I got into a fistfight and I fell on top of a floor furnace. Its grate was hot steel, which branded itself into my back and butt. I carried the marks from that one for a long time.

Then there was the time that Faron, Little Jimmy Dickens, and I were doing a show up north and Faron and Jimmy began to argue. Jimmy is even smaller than Faron. Jimmy is smaller than everyone. Faron pushed him, and I took up for Jimmy.

Faron and I began to shove each other, and it was only a few minutes until show time. Because we were drunk, we didn't realize how loud we were shouting. We were standing backstage and the sound of three men yelling leaked into the auditorium, where the crowd had paid to see singers, not a tag team.

"I'd give you two cents to whip his ass!" shouted a member of Faron's band to me.

"Where's your money?" I yelled.

"Now just a damn minute!" Faron said to his musician, who by then had placed two pennies into my hand.

That was all I needed. I lowered my head and charged Faron, hitting him squarely in the chest with my skull. He went down like a sack of wet cement.

We were wearing our stage clothes as we wrestled on the concrete backstage. Meanwhile, the show's emcee was talking louder and louder to conceal the sounds of profanity and crashing. No telling what the audience thought.

The fight was broken up, and Faron and I went on-stage wearing clothes that had been torn full of holes during the wrestling match.

Faron might have saved my life during our early careers. We were in a hotel room, where I was so drunk that I passed out in the shower. The water inside the stall began to rise. Faron soon noticed that it was leaking under the door and into the bedroom where he was sitting. He came into the bathroom and found me asleep sitting over the drain. My weight had stopped up the release of the water.

The holes in the drain left imprints on my hip. It was covered with dots.

A drunken Faron stared at those marks. Someone said he called the front desk and asked for a doctor right away.

"Jones has the worst case of measles I've ever seen," he reportedly said, "and they're spreading from his ass."

Back to Gabe, who was responsible for getting me on the Louisiana Hayride in Shreveport, the Deep South's answer to the Grand Ole Opry. A lot of acts who became big Opry stars cut their teeth on the Hayride.

The first night I played the Hayride I worked with Tibby Edwards, David Houston, Floyd Cramer, and a kid who had only a few records out. It represented a new music called rock 'n' roll. He was shy and didn't want to come out of his dressing room. He was surrounded by his people, who I guess were protecting him. So I spent very little time with Elvis Presley.

I remember he was friendly, but, again, we didn't really get to visit. I watched his show from the side. That was the first time I had ever seen anybody sing while shaking. I wondered what country music was coming to. But, of course, it wasn't country at all and probably had no place on the Hayride in 1955. Within a year, rock 'n' roll would be the most popular music in the nation, knocking country right out of the commercial spotlight.

Pappy and Gabe quickly realized that the only way they could draw people to country concerts was to present large package shows with a half-dozen name acts. Putting only one or two country acts on a bill was an invitation to financial failure for country promoters.

By 1956 rock 'n' roll's popularity was so far ahead of country's that Pappy insisted I try recording rock. I didn't want to do it, but I was young and wanted to please the powers that be in the music business. I would have done virtually anything to make it.

Pappy wanted a rock star, but he didn't want to jeopardize the little success I'd had as a country artist. I didn't want anybody to even know I was going to try rock. So he and I agreed we would record me under a different name.

In 1956, at Gold Star Studios in Houston, George Jones recorded under the name of Thumper Jones. The name came from Thumper the Rabbit, the character in Walt Disney's *Bambi*.

I was asked to write two rock songs and penned "Rock It" and "(Dadgummit) How Come It." You won't find those tunes today on any Dick Clark offering for the best of rock 'n' roll, and I don't think there is any danger of them being resurrected by the Rolling Stones.

They say people will do anything for love, and I loved the music business enough in 1956 to record songs I wouldn't sing today in my bathroom. It's hard to find copies of those two songs. During the years, as I have encountered those records, I've used them for Frisbees.

In the middle 1950s Gabe masterminded another promotional scheme that helped my Texas career tremendously. Veteran concert promoter A. V. Bamford came to

town to discuss promoting a giant package show in
Houston. Bamford was probably the most successful
country concert promoter of the day and had earned a
lot of credibility by promoting shows with Hank Williams. Bamford was the promoter of that January 1,
1953, date with Hank in Canton, Ohio, that Hank died
on the way to.

Nashville music publisher Buddy Killen was Hank's
bass player that day and remembers that Bamford came
backstage minutes before the show to tell everyone in
Hank's band that their boss was dead.

Killen said he told Bamford not to kid about something so serious. He said he looked into Bamford's eyes
and knew he was seeing the awful truth.

When Bamford wanted Gabe to help promote that
Houston show four years later, Gabe said he and the
station would get behind it, but only if the station took
10 percent of the gate.

"And," Gabe insisted, "we'll sponsor the Houston
show if there is another show in San Antonio and if
George Jones is the headline act."

Bamford accepted the proposition, and the San Antonio date in 1957 was one of the first times I was the
headline act on a big package. It was advertised as "The
George Jones Show" and featured Buck Owens, Webb
Pierce, Ferlin Husky, Cowboy Copas, Skeeter Davis, and
me.

Tickets were $1.50.

Gabe asked each star to pose with me, then published
a picture book. Everyone knew Gabe was a big shot at
Houston's KIKK radio, and they all wanted to stay on his

good side, so Gabe had no trouble getting them to do what he wanted.

The show was a sellout, a second was scheduled, and that was a sellout also.

Pappy Daily saw very quickly how beneficial the big live shows were to advancing my recording career. He wasn't overly crazy about sending me to the fans on shows around the country, so he decided to bring the fans to me. He got the idea to start the Houston Jamboree, which would be similar to Nashville's Grand Ole Opry. He wanted the show to be held each Saturday night and wanted it broadcast over Houston radio. He figured that putting it on the air would attract country stars who wanted to get their music on the radio.

Pappy Daily had gotten me to sign with Mercury Records by the time I first appeared on the Houston Jamboree. Another act on that label was Sonny Burns. Sonny and I had recorded some duets earlier, but none of them ever did much in terms of sales. Sonny, Gabe recently remembered, was Mercury's priority artist.

He insisted that Pappy give him some good songs, and Pappy obliged.

Sonny refused to record the songs, claiming they were no more than shit, Gabe said in 1994. So I became Pappy's second choice, and the songs were given to me.

"White Lightning" was released on March 9, 1959, and spent twenty-two weeks on *Billboard*'s Top 40 country chart. It held the number-one slot for five. (The song was written by J. P. Richardson, whose stage name was "The Big Bopper." He died in the plane crash with Buddy Holly and Ritchie Valens on February 3, 1959, and I have been sorry ever since that he didn't live to see his song go number one.)

I recorded "White Lightning" in Nashville in Owen Bradley's "Quonset Hut" studio. Pappy was the session's executive producer, but he turned the session over to Buddy Killen, who later became the president of Tree Publishing, the world's largest country music publishing house. Killen played upright bass on the record and even came up with the tune's kickoff. (It was a bass solo for a few bars.) I don't think I've ever heard another country song begin that way.

Other players were legendary blind studio pianist Pig Robbins, with whom I record to this day, and guitarist Floyd Jenkins.

I was drinking heavily throughout the session, and Killen later said we did eighty-three takes before we got one we could use. Killen said he wore the skin off his fingers playing that same opening and had to wear Band-Aids to cover raw blisters. Years later he said he could still remember the pain from playing that kickoff over and over on the stiff, woven-wire strings of an upright bass.

The word "slug" is slurred in that record. That's because I was drunk. But Killen said everyone was so tired of the song and all of the takes that he called the session to an end. If you listen to the original recording of "White Lightning," you can hear me stumble over the word "slug."

Killen also directed the recording of "Who Shot Sam," which I helped write. It came out in July of that same year and was on the survey for thirteen weeks.

This means I spent a total of thirty-five weeks on the

Billboard charts in 1959 after recording two songs that no one else wanted.

"That was when Pappy Daily really began to concentrate on George Jones," Gabe said. "And we determined that George Jones could smell a hit, and we decided to play our new songs for him first."

I wish they had decided to give me bigger advances against royalties.

I made a lot of money for Pappy Daily, Starday, and Mercury. Basically I was a naive guy who was overly trusting of some people who proved to be untrustworthy. I was never paid royalties on a regular basis. It became very frustrating to me to hear my songs on the radio, see them listed high in the charts, and yet not have enough money to hire a band. I played with house bands throughout the 1950s. I sometimes had to perform with bands with which I'd never even rehearsed! I even played with some who played a song in one key while I struggled to sing in another! Then I would throw my guitar in the car and drive all night to some dumpy motel where I would try to get a few hours' sleep before repeating the routine.

I was drinking the whole time to soften the grind, and the booze kept me run-down. I drank to have a good time, but not always. Sometimes I did it simply to ease the boredom of life on the road alone.

I came in drunk one Saturday morning after driving all night from a show somewhere. I went directly to the office of one of Pappy Daily's assistants. I demanded that I be paid everything I was owed, but he couldn't say exactly how much that was. And the only number he seemed to know was eleven.

"Well, just how many records have we sold?" I demanded.

"I'd say about eleven thousand," the assistant said.

"Well, how many advance orders do we have for our next release?" I asked.

"Oh, I don't know," he said. "About eleven hundred."

I got real sick of that real quickly.

Someone said I was given nine hundred dollars, but I figured I had a lot more than that coming and I got rowdy. I wouldn't leave his side. If he moved behind his desk, so did I. If he went to the men's room, so did I. I threatened to whip him, and he took off out the back door.

But not before calling the police.

I was taken to jail, which had its temporary quarters in the fire station. I was let out after I sobered up, and I apologized to the assistant for acting up. But I never apologized about the money.

One of the reasons I was suspicious about not getting my money is that I had seen how swindle had helped kill Lefty Frizzell. I first met Jack Starnes right after Lefty had left his management, claiming he was not paid all the royalties that were due him. He had recorded giant hits on Columbia Records, such as "If You've Got the Money, I've Got the Time," "I Love You a Thousand Ways," "Always Late," and "Mom and Dad's Waltz." I've said many times that my three greatest musical influences were Roy Acuff, Hank Williams, and Lefty Frizzell.

At one time Lefty had beautiful stage clothes, a new guitar, a new car, and a twin-engine airplane. Who ever heard of such prosperity for a country star in the early 1950s? All of that was mysteriously taken from him, and almost overnight. The man was the Elvis of his time on one day—and broke the next. There was no solid explanation about where his money went. He was basically a good old country boy who felt betrayed. He couldn't handle the pain.

His spirit broke after he realized he was financially broke. So he hid inside a shell of self-pity. He didn't want to work or go out.

Alice, his wife, became very religious, and he felt further from her than ever. She made him go to church, and he wound up dating some of the women there. He got caught, and he and Alice separated inside their own house. She made him live in the basement and locked the door that led to the upstairs.

He needed a woman who would say, "Hold your head up, better days are coming." He needed a woman like I found in Nancy, my current wife. Who knows? If Nancy hadn't done for me what some wives have failed to do for their husbands, I might have wound up like Lefty—destitute and alone.

Lefty lived in that basement with a bed and a stove and ate soup and other canned food. Can you imagine a man whose singing had touched millions having to live alone in such confinement? His drinking, which had been bad for years, grew worse.

In his darkened room below the ground, the idol of millions became ill on July 19, 1975. An ambulance was called. En route to the hospital, he suffered a massive stroke according to medical records. He was admitted to Nashville Memorial Hospital, where doctors struggled to keep him alive.

Lefty Frizzell, forty-seven, was dead by nightfall.

The last time I saw Lefty alive was in his basement. It was about 9 A.M. He was hopelessly drunk, and so was I. He drank that vodka like it was Kool-Aid. Seeing him there in that awful state suddenly made me sober.

My heart became as broken as his attitude. I wanted to reach out to him but didn't know how. Other folks who claimed to be his friends had come by. Some brought him vodka, and I wondered what kind of friends they really were.

I wanted to say so much to him, but ultimately I didn't say much at all. We both knew he was on the bottom, and there was no point in talking about it out loud. That wouldn't have helped a thing.

I thought of all the mornings I had awakened at my sister Loyce's house to the sounds of Lefty's hits. She never played anyone's records but his. I might be so hungover that I couldn't hold anything down except fried potatoes and ketchup. Loyce made them for me whenever I wanted them. The food satisfied my hunger, the music satisfied my soul. Funny what we remember in this life.

And when I remember Lefty I remember that voice, those hits, and a gentle spirit who also trusted folks who were untrustworthy.

I honestly believe that helped to kill him.

Gabe, Pappy, and I realized that my success as a country singer, no matter how big it became, would always be limited unless I appeared on the Grand Ole Opry. But it was hard for a Nashville-based singer to get a recording contract in the middle 1950s if he couldn't assure a record-label executive that he could perform on the Opry,

which had been the sounding board for country entertainers since its beginning in 1925. And long before I
came along, the show was broadcast over the NBC radio
network. An entertainer could get a hit record simply by
singing the song once on the Opry.

It isn't hard to understand then that most artists
wanted desperately to be on the Opry, and so did their
record labels. Pappy Daily went to Nashville many times
to court the decision-makers at the National Life and
Accident Insurance Company, owner of the Opry, and at
WSM, the fifty-thousand-watt station over which the
Opry was broadcast.

But nothing seemed to work. I wasn't wanted at the
Grand Ole Opry.

Pappy sent Gabe to Nashville, and that didn't work
either, even though Gabe pulled every string he had. Not
getting me immediately on the Opry was frustrating for
Gabe. He was turned down by some of the same men
who had asked him for favors on his Houston radio
station.

"I was practically at my wit's end," Gabe said. "That
was one of the hardest shells I ever tried to crack."

Opry officials knew how much money an artist could
make on the road if he was successful on the Opry.
Therefore, the way I heard it, some of the Opry big shots
wanted bribes before admitting a new singer. A lot of
Nashville's veteran music executives swear today that
was the case in the middle 1950s, but I can't say for sure.
I never really tried to find out because it wouldn't have
made any difference. I wanted to make it on my talent,
not on somebody's pocketbook. If my singing wasn't
good enough to get me on the Opry, I didn't want to go.

I had too much respect for the artists who had gone ahead of me. The very thought of singing where Roy Acuff, Bill Monroe, or Hank Williams had sung was overwhelming to me. I attached a respect to the Opry that bordered on reverence. The Opry was later called the Mother Church of Country Music. I agree with that description. I wasn't going to pay my way into that church, and neither were Gabe or Pappy.

Then, in 1956, for reasons I've never known, I got the call. I was asked to be a guest for one night on the Opry. Pappy and I drove on two-lane highways all the way from Houston to Nashville, a distance of 780 miles.

I'd like to tell you a lot about that first night on the Opry, but I can't remember. I think that's because I was in a nervous fog. A country singer making it to the Opry in 1956 was like an athlete making it to the Olympics. I was simply too overjoyed to realize what I was doing. Thank God I had done it long enough elsewhere to do it without thinking.

Jimmy Dickens loaned me a guitar because for some reason the Opry officials wouldn't let me play my own. I don't know why. I went onstage, sang my song, and could hear my heart pounding above the applause. I would have sung for those folks all night, except that I had been told I could only do one song. I thought about going back for an encore, but then I decided against it. I sure didn't want to break any rules.

I must have done something right. On August 25, 1956, I appeared on the Opry again, this time as its newest member. As a kid I had never thought I would even *see* the Opry, much less sing on it, much less be a member. And in time, the legends I've mentioned became not only my coperformers but my friends.

My life and career were unfolding too fast, but I loved it.

In the summer of 1956, nobody could have convinced me that country music wasn't the world's greatest business.

Chapter 5

All I heard was the whistle.

Stonewall Jackson and I had worked a little club around Albuquerque, New Mexico, and had drunk some beer after the show. Someone hurled a bottle at him so hard that it whistled past his head.

I had been drinking, and everyone always said I was a different man when I drank. Drinking made me aggressive, especially on behalf of my friends.

I asked Stonewall what had happened, and he said someone tried to alter his head with thrown glass.

"Who did that?" I yelled at no one. "Who's the dumb son of a bitch that tried to hurt my buddy?"

"I did!" said someone from the darkness.

The voice took a human shape that got bigger as it approached. I soon was staring into the eyes of a cowboy towering above me. I must have weighed all of a hundred and forty pounds.

"You ain't got no right to be throwin' bottles at my friend," I said.

I threw a punch that missed before I was clobbered with a roundhouse that knocked me out. I was later told I flipped over backward in midair.

I landed facedown in a puddle that was about eight inches deep. Stonewall said he could see only the back of my head protruding from the water. He ran to me, but the cowboy and his buddies got there first. They began to kick me as I lay unconscious. The air was filled with fists and feet, and Stonewall said he feared I would drown as I lay there unaware of what was happening to me.

Seeing that I was out of commission, and probably because they were tired of kicking, the cowboys turned on Stonewall. They beat him so severely that his eyes swelled shut. He couldn't open them the next day.

We both took a terrible whipping, and then the drunken good ole boys were gone. They probably thought they had left me for dead.

Stonewall was able to shake me awake about the time the police arrived. I went into the men's room to blot the blood and to take off the stage suit I was still wearing from our show. It was the only one I owned, and the following day I had to buy some street clothes to wear on our next show.

That fight never made any headlines. Yet it could have been fatal if Stonewall hadn't gotten my head out of the water. That wouldn't have been much of a way to die, but my life back then wasn't much of a way to live.

I liked Stonewall a lot. I don't get to see him much today because our schedules have taken different ways. But he was just an old country boy like me who came to town to try his luck. His luck unfolded faster than most's.

He was a sharecropper in Georgia when he drove to Nashville in a battered pickup truck. He parked outside Acuff-Rose Publications, the largest music publisher in town, and entered without an appointment.

That was on a Wednesday.

He played a tape for Wesley Rose, who immediately set up an audition for him for the Grand Ole Opry on Thursday. Stonewall sang live on the Opry on coast-to-coast radio on Friday.

Stonewall called the old man who had held his share-cropping job open in case he didn't make it in Nashville. "Go ahead and give my job to somebody," he said. "I think I'll stay up here and sing."

George Riddle, who became the first permanent member of my band in 1960, recently discussed the fight involving Stonewall and me and said that I seemed to get into at least one fight on every tour. He laughed and said that I came off the road with as many injuries as some folks who fought in the Vietnam War.

In 1959 I was traveling in a car in the Northwest with Mel Tillis and some other entertainers. I had just gotten my arm out of a cast when Mel and I began to argue.

"The next thing I knew here came a fist from over the backseat," Mel said in early 1995. "I held George's arm down as hard as I could over the top of the seat so he couldn't swing at me again."

" 'Goddamnit, you've broken my same arm,' George

hollered at me," Mel remembered. "And I had, I had broken his very same arm, and we had to take him back to the hospital to have it put in a cast all over again."

Mel said he thought I should have bought my own cast and put a zipper on it. He thought that would reduce my doctor bills.

Back then, I seemed to get drunkest on my days off— the time I waited in a town for the show date to come up. I was somewhere in the Midwest in 1962 during a waiting spell that earned me another trip to the hospital. I was staying at a hotel with Red Sovine and his band, who were also on the show I was waiting to give.

Pacing and restless, I got drunk inside the hotel. We had played as much cards as I could stand. So I cornered Red.

"Red, I'm fixin' to whip your ass," I told him.

Red always was the diplomat. He had been around drunk and rowdy behavior for years, and he knew exactly how to undo the situation.

"George," he said, "you don't want to whip my ass. Anybody can do that."

I pondered that statement for a long time, then told him he was right. Red smiled and sat down. I smiled and staggered.

Then I took out after Dale Potter, Red's fiddle player. Dale ran into the bathroom and stayed there most of the day. Each time it got quiet for any length of time, I went over and kicked the bathroom door.

"I ain't forgot you, Dale!" I said. "You've got an ass-whipping coming."

I became real unpopular—not just with Dale, but with everybody in the room who wanted to pee. A lot of people were drinking beer. Guys were walking down the hall to other rooms because Dale wouldn't let them in the bathroom, where he had barricaded himself.

I kept drinking and waiting on Dale all day. Somebody said he made himself a pallet in the bathtub and went to sleep. When I decided he wasn't coming out, I lost my head and broke my hand. In my drunkenness, I attacked a solid-steel steam radiator. I was madly beating the thing while beating my hand into something like hamburger meat. I shattered a lot of bones and wore another cast for a long time.

Not long afterward I was playing the Chestnut Inn in Kansas City, Missouri. The place featured country music and strippers.

The country singers performed for an hour, then the girls danced for an hour. I'd put my heart and soul into a ballad, but some drunk would eventually holler, "Bring on the girls!"

One of the girls took a shine to me, but I didn't pay her any attention. In fact, I pretty much ignored her for the entire week I was booked, except for the last night, when I got drunk.

Her manager drove her and me to her place.

He said he would wait in the living room and for us to go ahead and have our fun. He said she was a nice girl. He said she liked me a lot.

He didn't say she was his wife.

She and I had just gotten into bed when the door burst open. It was her manager-husband. Over his head, he held a solid-steel chair.

I was on my back, naked and defenseless. All I could do was throw up my arm, which he quickly broke with that chair. I barely got out of there with my clothes and my life. I went to a hospital and got my fix of molded plaster. Because of that ordeal, I held a microphone in one hand and my arm in a sling for the rest of that tour and several more that year.

So much of country music, in those days, was performed in rough roadhouses and taverns. There were package shows held in auditoriums, but the majority of shows were called "shows and dances." Working folks who had labored all week came to drink, dance, and get rowdy in an effort to blow off a little steam. I could rise above it, unless I was drinking myself. In the late 1950s and early 1960s I didn't drink every day, but on the days I drank, I drank a lot. Some of the environments where I played were so depressing I felt I had to have a drink to stand them.

Stonewall and I played a prison somewhere in Texas as featured acts on a tour with Ernest Tubb. We traveled on Ernest's bus, and that was a welcome change from the thousands of miles we had been logging in cars. It would be a few more years before I would get my first bus.

Stonewall and I sang with Ernest's Texas Troubadours as our backup musicians. That day we played that prison in Texas, we decided to walk around the grounds.

I have never liked confinement.

We talked to some of the men, and I noticed the desperation in their faces. I'd been in jail, but that was my first time behind penitentiary walls. Whoever I looked at was already looking at me. A prisoner approached Stonewall, who tried to make small talk.

"How much time you got left?" Stonewall asked.

"I been here for eighteen years and still got life to go," the man said.

After we left the prison, I thought about that man and his words. His remark chilled me to the bone. I had hated the prison, but knew I'd be leaving. That man hated it more and knew he'd never leave. I wanted to get that prison out of my mind. But I couldn't. And so I began to write.

> I went one night where the lights were bright just
> To see what I could see.
> I met up with an old friend, who just thought the
> World of me.
> He bought me drinks and took me to every honky tonk
> In town.
> Then words were said and now he's dead, I just had to
> Bring him down.
>
> Oh I've been here for eighteen years and still
> Got life to go, I've still got life to go. I've still got
> Life to go.

I wrote "Life to Go" in late 1958, and it was released on June 8, 1959. It rose to number two on the *Billboard* chart and remained on the survey for twenty-three weeks as a hit for Stonewall Jackson. It became Stonewall's first number-one song on other country charts and was also recorded by Webb Pierce for an album.

My writing that tune was one of the few times that a good thing resulted from a dreary experience from life on the road. Usually, I simply got drunk and did nothing creative when I got tired, blue, or just plain sick of the monotony.

I wasn't the only country singer playing one-night shows, then racing to repeat the same show in a different town the next night. And the boredom seemed to be overtaking all of us from Nashville, as country music was being taken on the road more than ever. A lot of entertainers vented themselves, I'm ashamed to say, not only by heavy drinking but by the juvenile act of tearing up hotel rooms.

I was no exception.

Johnny Cash has made no secret of the fact that he mixed his whiskey with amphetamines, pills that give you artificial energy. He talked about that in his life story, *Man in Black*. Touring country singers first began taking the pills as substitutes for sleep. Eventually, we took them because they made us feel good, because they were available, and because we were in the habit.

Johnny has talked about getting high on those things and painting an entire hotel room black for want of something to do. Another time he released a bunch of live chickens inside a hotel. I'm glad that Johnny has been drug-free for many years and his reckless days are farther behind him than my own.

Jimmy Dean, in 1994, remembered that he was not allowed to check into a hotel in the late 1950s in Canada because Johnny had destroyed a room there. The hotel had boycotted all entertainers, Jimmy recalled.

We'd do anything back then to lift our spirits.

Stonewall and some other guys even put me inside a coffin once and carried me backstage. They pretended to be pallbearers while I folded my hands across my chest and never moved. The stupid promoter thought he was going to have to cancel the show and refund ticket money because his act was dead. He thought the hillbillies he had hired to entertain had actually brought their dead buddy into the auditorium.

Folks said the real show was watching him when I leaped from that coffin.

One road-weary release came from tearing up a motel in 1962 with Johnny and Merle Kilgore, who is Hank Williams Jr.'s executive manager today. That's a fitting job for Merle, who started in show business at age fourteen when he carried Hank Williams, Sr.'s guitar and ran errands for the legend. I first met Merle on the Louisiana Hayride.

Merle tried his hand at recording and had a few hit records. But his biggest songs were "Ring of Fire," which he and June Carter wrote for Johnny, and "Wolverton Mountain," which he wrote with Claude King and which King recorded in 1962. "Wolverton Mountain" was a blockbuster record when Merle and I were featured acts on the touring Johnny Cash Show.

We played Gary, Indiana, and I couldn't get the song out of my head. I was drunk and kept singing the song over and over at the Holiday Inn after the concert. Merle and Johnny got so tired of hearing me that they hid.

But I found their room. I begged Merle to help me get the song out of my head, and he urged me to record it. I don't know how that would have helped me that night, but it would have given him additional royalties.

The more I talked to Merle and Johnny the more I thought about the tour and how I didn't like it. Saul Holiff was Johnny's and my manager at the time. Because

Johnny was the tour's headline act, I took up my unhappiness with him. Johnny and I argued, and I accidentally broke a lamp. For some reason, I lifted the partially broken lamp and smashed it on the floor. Then it was really broken, and I somehow felt better. That's the goofy way I used to think on some of my drinking days.

"One broken lamp," Johnny said dryly, like an accountant. "That will be forty-five dollars."

We all laughed at the obvious humor. Johnny had paid for destroyed motel property so often that he could pretty much assess damage on the spot. He'd been billed by Holiday Inns in the past and knew the price tag on each piece of their disposable property.

"I'd never seen anybody trash a room before," Merle recalled recently. "Johnny was totally cool because this was old hat to him. I didn't know what was going to happen next."

I ran to the other side of the room and smashed another lamp.

"Two lamps," Johnny said coolly. "Ninety dollars."

I got caught up in the momentum of what I was doing. The next thing everybody knew I had pulled down the main curtain.

"One curtain, that'll be three hundred dollars," Johnny said.

I fumed at Johnny, telling him it shouldn't cost that much.

I ran into the bathroom and pulled the porcelain top off the commode. I hurled it into the bathtub, and the top shattered.

"One commode top, one hundred seventy-five dollars," Johnny said calmly. He was as laid-back as a sleepy auctioneer.

Johnny lay there and watched me destroy the room all around him. He never raised his voice, and I never lowered mine. Then I walked out.

On the final night of the tour, Merle, Johnny, and I were in Saul's room to get our pay. I was the last in line.

"Now, George," Saul said, "before I pay you I want you to know that there are a few deductions here."

"What deductions?" I asked.

"You remember that room in Gary, Indiana?" Saul asked. "One pair of drapes, three hundred dollars."

That's exactly how much Johnny had predicted they would cost!

"One commode top, one hundred seventy-five dollars," Saul said, and the price was exactly right again, according to Johnny's estimate!

I stood there and watched my pay shrink before my eyes.

Saul itemized every expense to the penny, and each time his figures agreed with Johnny's predictions. Until he got to the lamps.

"Two lamps," he said. "Forty-five dollars."

"You mean forty-five dollars each, don't you?" I asked.

"No," Saul said. "This paper from the Holiday Inn just says two lamps for forty-five dollars."

"Those lamps were beautiful," I said. "That's a good buy. That's a real good buy."

At that point I never complained again about the cost of my rampage.

*   *   *

By 1958 I was able to move Shirley and our two sons from Beaumont to Vidor, Texas. I bought a house on Lakeview Drive and then another on Hulet Drive. I left Shirley and the boys there when I went on the road and looked forward to each of my returns. Sometimes I came in drunk, and there was always hell to pay with Shirley. Another time I brought home George Riddle, and he wound up staying with us for a while.

He would fly or drive with me to our show dates and then help me get back to Texas. George worked for me for about four years, during which he played rhythm guitar and sang high harmony on some of my biggest early records, including "She Thinks I Still Care," "A Girl I Used to Know," and "Not Exactly What I Had in Mind."

Shirley was glad when George started traveling with me. She thought that a constant companion would settle me down and that I wouldn't get into mischief when I was out of her sight.

Boy, was she wrong.

I had met George while attending the Disc Jockey Convention, which eventually became the Country Music Association Convention, in 1960 inside Nashville's Hermitage Hotel. George had gotten out of the service the day before and come to Nashville to try to break into the country music industry. He was walking down a hallway and recognized my voice. Without an invitation he walked into my room. There he saw George Jones flat on his back, strumming a guitar in the middle of a bed.

Riddle hung around for a while, and I mentioned that I needed to hire a harmony singer. I had to have someone who knew my songs, who was willing to travel, and who could leave the next day.

"I can sing harmony, and I can go tomorrow," Riddle said.

I tested him on the spot by breaking into "White Lightning." He nailed his part, and the next day he rode with Jimmy Dickens, promoter Rex Reinhardt, and me from Nashville to Hobbs, New Mexico. I broke him in right—four men, instruments, clothes, and perhaps fifteen hundred miles—in one sitting!

Riddle and I played every dive that would have me for a year, working with house bands where they had them and working as a duo where they didn't. He paid me a high compliment recently when he credited me with getting him a recording contract with Mercury Records and said that I saw to it that he had billing on every show he ever worked with me. It's nice to be able to help somebody, and it's nice they remember in a business where too many people too often forget. I'll tell you later about my open-heart surgery in 1994. But I'll tell you now that George Riddle came to see me the day after the procedure, even though I hadn't seen him in years.

I suppose the biggest compliment that Riddle paid me was that he remembered in all the time he and I worked together that I only missed two shows due to drunkenness.

"There were plenty of times he went on when he was loaded, but I only saw him miss two shows, and one was on 'George Jones Day' in Beaumont," Riddle remembered. "We told the crowd he was sick, and Johnny Cash filled in for him."

Riddle also bragged that he remembered once when I

not only showed up but arrived a week early. We were booked at the Flame Club in Minneapolis. We drove all night and most of the next day from Nashville and were exhausted when we pulled into the parking lot.

There, rising above the lot, was a glowing sign that said, WILMA LEE AND STONEY COOPER HERE TONIGHT. I quickly fumbled through my briefcase to discover that I had the right club on the wrong date. I left Riddle with friends, and he waited for me to return in seven days.

I stayed at the Capitol Park Inn during most of my time in Nashville in those days. I came in after a Christmas trip home to Texas and told Riddle that I'd found a hit.

The song had been written by nineteen-year-old Dickey Lee. Twenty-two years later, Lee said he was still trying to write a song that would become that popular. It was pitched to me by Jack Clement, who had a little studio in Texas at the time and later moved to Nashville, where he wrote songs and produced records for some of the biggest names in country music, including Waylon Jennings during the 1970s and 1980s, Waylon's heyday.

On April 14, 1962, I saw the release of "She Thinks I Still Care." The song was on the *Billboard* survey for twenty-three weeks, six of them at number one. It has been recorded by scores of artists and in 1974 spent two weeks at number one after it was rerecorded by Anne Murray, who changed the hook line to "*He* Thinks I Still Care."

For years after I recorded it, the song was my most requested, and it became what people in my business call a "career record," the song that firmly establishes your identity with the public.

In the fall of 1963, I went to New York City and sang on Jimmy Dean's ABC network television show. I was nervous and had a hard time singing without a live audience. We wrestled through an afternoon of rehearsals, but even in Manhattan, where there wasn't one country radio station, the only thing Dean and his crew wanted to hear was "She Thinks I Still Care."

Just before the song's release, I told Riddle to hire a band that would be called the Jones Boys, the name of my band to this day. I suppose you could technically say that up until then it had been George Jones and the Jones Boy. But Riddle expanded the band by four, hiring Billy Wayne on steel guitar, Jerry Star (formerly with Wanda Jackson) as our lead guitarist, Gary Prawl (whose name I couldn't remember, so we changed it to Gary Parker), and Glen Davis, who is now a staff drummer at the Grand Ole Opry.

Billy was the first to leave the group. That meant I had no steel player and one spare uniform. The uniform was tailor-made of polyester and rhinestones. It was bright red with white trim. It wasn't the kind of suit you'd find at Robert Hall Clothes, and it would have been very hard to buy in a different size for a new player.

I wanted to replace Billy with a good player, but, more important, I didn't want to have to buy a new uniform. So I sent Riddle from somewhere on the road to Nashville to pick up a steel player who was like Billy in talent and size.

Shot Jackson was a master Dobro player who worked at a music store. He knew every good musician in town. Riddle went directly to him, and Shot raved about a new guy who had just come to town. George interviewed

Weldon Myrick, who went on to become one of the most sought-after steel guitar recording session players in Nashville history. Riddle was overwhelmed with his playing in 1961. But unless Weldon reads this book, he'll never know that the reason he wasn't hired was because Riddle figured he wouldn't fit into Billy's used uniform. So we hired Hal Rugg.

For a while, all six of us, plus our instruments, traveled in one car. Shortly afterward we pulled a trailer, but that still left six grown men inside a sedan. And we were working one-night shows with five hundred miles between each show. A lot of folks came to our shows and thought I had it easy. I often did—after I got to the show. In those days, the hardest part of a show was not performing it but getting to it.

In the early 1960s, before the popularity of interstate highways and radial tires, one of six men in a car almost always had to go to the rest room. Somebody was always hungry, tired, grouchy, lonely, or otherwise irritated. But truck stops and restaurants weren't as plentiful then as they are now.

Maybe you've driven across the country with your family. Have you ever done it with no room to stretch your legs, when you had to be at a certain place at a certain time, and try to sleep in the car so you could repeat the same routine the next day?

The driver gets so bored that he contracts highway hypnosis. I was actually riding once with a guy who came to a curve in the road and jumped out. The car went down an embankment with me bouncing around inside. (Seat belts weren't mandatory back then either.)

You guessed it—I broke my arm and had to have it placed inside a cast!

Another time I was drunk in the backseat when Riddle pulled into a restaurant. He left me sleeping, and when I awoke I could see a giant mound of dirt through the back window. I had been dreaming, and the miles had taken their toll. I didn't know where I was, but that didn't make any difference.

I bolted from the car and charged into the restaurant.

"Don't you ever do that to me again," I yelled at Riddle.

"Do what?" he asked.

"Don't you ever let me ride, then wake up when I can't see nothing but dirt," I said. "I thought I had died and was in my grave!"

People all over the room were staring.

Chapter 6

A young country singer today knows he's on track when his record label hires an image consultant, gets a national advertiser to sponsor a tour, and places him with a financial consulting firm.

But when I was coming up, you weren't a bona fide country star until you had a bus with your name written in big letters on the side. Getting that first bus was a rite of passage, and that's no exaggeration.

Customized buses are still as much a part of country music as ballads. Artists have traveled for years from show to show in buses like the one I currently own, which has a satellite television, a range, microwave oven, double bed, wall-to-wall carpeting, wood paneling, mirrored ceiling, central heat and air-conditioning, and more. Country music coaches are swanky houses on wheels.

In December 1994 Nashville's WSM radio reported that Dolly Parton had spent $750,000 on just the interior of her new bus.

My first bus, acquired in 1962, didn't cost that much, and it wasn't as elegant. It was a used, dented, and rusty contraption that I bought from a Western swing band. It wasn't customized, but was instead hollow on the inside, where there was little more than bare sheet-metal walls. Except for a few seats up front, all the "furnishings" were portable and weren't fastened down.

Some friends wanted me to get a bus because they thought that would prevent me from trading cars so often. I can't count the hundreds of cars I've owned. Even to this day, I sometimes buy a car and trade it before the new smell fades. But I used to be worse.

Before I formed my band I played Minneapolis with George Riddle and we drove to the show in my car. He sang a few songs before I went onstage. While he was performing, I traded cars with a guy I had met at the show. Riddle came offstage, I gave him my car keys, and he went to the car he thought was mine. He was fumbling with the lock when the new owner asked him what he was trying to do. A mild argument resulted before Riddle got his wheels straightened out.

The Jones Boys nicknamed my first bus "The Brown Bomber." Later they changed that to "Gas Chamber."

Diesel fumes seeped through the floor into the cabin if the bus was stationary. Not many cars had air-conditioning in those days, and there certainly wasn't any on that bus. Have you ever traveled in solid steel across a steaming highway above a hot engine in the summertime? Heat beats down from the sun at the same time it rises from the floor. When the two meet where passengers sit, the effect is unbearable. The guys and I sweated away many pounds inside that old thing.

Gary Prawl decided that whoever manufactured the bus should have put vents in the floor that would force air into the interior at highway speed. There was no ventilation until I got drunk outside Joe's Lounge in Chicago Heights, Illinois, and emptied a pistol into the floor. Our air-conditioning was bullet holes. When we moved, the air leaked in slowly. When we sat, the fumes still came in quickly.

I couldn't afford to customize the jalopy, so I put used bunks inside and didn't anchor them. They shifted if the driver took a curve too quickly. We sat on folding chairs, and occasionally a chair and the guy sitting on it fell over as the bus rounded a corner.

People have always been fascinated with modern minstrels who travel from town to town on a bus to earn a living. To this day, someone at almost every place I play wants to get on my bus. They want to ask how many people it sleeps and if I take a shower on there and things like that.

We played New Braunfels, Texas, shortly after we got the Brown Bomber, and a young woman got on the bus. She had had a few drinks. The guys went to the back and were changing clothes when the bus began to move. That wasn't unusual.

In about ten minutes we were in open country, sailing down a Texas two-lane with the windows open, bound for San Antonio. The bus kept going faster and faster. Pretty soon the guys in the back began to yell at me to slow down.

"I've never seen him drive this fast," one said. "How much did he have to drink?"

They kept worrying, and the speed kept accelerating. Glen Davis and George Riddle braced themselves by pressing their hands against the ceiling and wobbled up the moving aisle to ask me to take it easy. By then the fence posts looked like a picket fence rolling by the window.

Glen or Riddle grabbed the driver's shoulder and discovered it belonged to the visiting girl.

You never saw so many grown men stumbling over each other as they rushed to get her to stop. The boys had thought I was driving, and I had thought one of them was.

We finally wrecked that bus.

Instead of hiring an experienced driver from Nashville, as I would today, I hired someone I knew in Vidor. The band and I simply called him Tubbs. As I look back, I wonder if he had ever been out of Vidor. He said he had, but he was always getting lost. A band member or I would drive to the highway that we were going to take to our next destination, then we'd put a map in front of him.

"Now, Tubbs," one of us would patiently say, "just stay on this road and you'll be fine. Don't get off this road."

"Okay," he always insisted. "I've got it this time."

We'd go to the back of the bus for some serious drinking or to go to sleep. Within thirty minutes Tubbs would be stopped at the side of the road.

"I'm lost," he always said. And he always was.

We had finished a show in Anderson, California, and

were on the way to Salem, Oregon, when we took an unwanted detour off the side of a steep mountain in Grants Pass.

Riddle said he remembers a crash, bolting upright on his bunk, and seeing things flying around him. His mattress flew off his bunk, and Glen estimated that Riddle passed him on that bedding at fifty miles per hour.

The bus turned over, and everything inside went in every direction. The bus's interior was totally black on that dark slope as we skidded on the side windows toward the bottom of the mountain. All you could hear was the sound of rocks scraping against glass and metal and grown men screaming. I don't remember what finally stopped us.

The same thing happened to the band and me in 1964 in another bus on a two-lane highway in the Smoky Mountains. No one was injured that time.

After the first accident, I was taken to a hospital in Grants Pass, where I was treated for broken ribs. My stomach and chest were wrapped in bandages, and it hurt just to breathe, let alone walk. The boys were bruised and broken from head to foot. One wore an arm cast, and all wore heavy bandages when they worked the next show without me. I had taken an airplane back to Vidor.

My reputation for missing personal appearances due to drunkenness had begun to spread as early as the early 1960s. Some of the boys thought the crowd would think we had pitched a bender and gotten into a brawl and that I was too hungover to make the show. But newspaper reporters, who eventually wrote many mean things about me, did me a favor after that bus wreck.

By the time the boys got to the show, the news wires had carried the story about George Jones and the Jones Boys barely escaping death on a steep mountain pass. The band members said lots of fans were concerned and thanked the band for coming despite the accident.

Eventually, my reputation became so bad that people said I was drunk no matter why I missed a date. Of course, the truth of the matter is that I *was* drunk when I missed most of my dates. There came a time a few years later when some underhanded promoters took advantage of my reputation by advertising that I was going to appear without ever booking me. I honestly had no idea I was expected. On the night of the show, the promoters would sell lots of booze to the crowd and tell them that George Jones would be there shortly. A few hours later they would announce that I wasn't coming after all, implying that I was drunk and somewhere else. They usually told the crowd they could have their money back, but by then most of the people were too loaded to care if I showed up or not. The promoters therefore sold tickets and whiskey around my appearance without my ever appearing.

But whatever has or has not happened in my life since I bought my first coach, it has always been back to the bus and back to the road.

During the early 1960s I was a binge drinker. I'd go as long as three weeks without a drink, then stay drunk for three or four days. That's when my hostility surfaced.

I've been drunk and picked fights with men twice my size just because liquor made me feel aggressive. I've been a gentleman with nightclub owners who insisted I have a drink with them, then another, then another, and so on. That was often a disaster.

I played a club in Baltimore in 1962 for a week and never took a drink the entire time. The nightclub owner kept hounding me to get drunk with him.

"I want to be able to say I got drunk with George Jones," he told me every night.

I never knew why people wanted to say they drank with me. Was it because I had a few songs on the radio or because I was getting the reputation of being a two-fisted drinker? But I met that kind of temptation every place I went, and years later when I tried hard to get sober, the constant pressure from fans and promoters to drink was a terrible handicap. Some people like to give drinks to a drunk, and I don't think much of those folks.

Riddle met secretly with that particular Baltimore nightclub owner and told him I was on a sober roll.

"Leave George alone," Riddle told him. "Don't try to get him to drink. You don't want what you think you do. Seeing George drunk is not always a pretty sight."

But nothing else would do for this guy.

"I'm paying the bills around here, and I've given George Jones a week's worth of work," he said. "Does he think he's too good to drink with me?"

I've never felt too good for anybody. To this day I don't like snobs. But today I wouldn't let that man's remarks get to me. I'd consider the source and go on my sober way.

"Okay, my friend," I told him on the last night after my last show. "Break out the bottle."

We killed a fifth of whiskey and got into another. And then I got out of my mind.

I threw an ashtray at a mirror behind the bar, and glass flew in all directions. The club owner came out of his chair.

"What are you going to do, tear the place to pieces?" he shouted.

"Only before I whip your ass!" I said. And I meant it.

He pleaded some more, then ran from the room, scared to death by the man going crazy in his nightclub. I broke glasses, smashed mirrors, bent metal chairs, broke the legs off tables, tore down curtains, shattered whiskey bottles behind the bar, and more. I was out of my drunken mind.

The club owner, hysterical, ran back into the room and jumped on me. I knocked the shit out of him several times. I'm glad I had already gotten paid for my week's work. He ran out of the room once more, and I never saw him again. I was never invited back to play his club.

The next day I felt terrible about what I'd done, and I was mercilessly hungover. (The combination of a hangover and motion sickness from riding a bus is terrible.) There were plenty of times I did awful things and paid money for my misbehavior the next day. Riddle said he doesn't think I paid that guy. He said he had warned the guy about my drinking and that he thought the man had it coming. So we just got on the bus and left town.

Riddle and I left our bus at the Mexican border once to do some drinking in the cantinas between show dates. We caught a taxi and were having a good time until I got drunk, and then my mean side surfaced. It almost cost us our lives.

I began to feel my alcoholic oats when I noticed five

mean-looking Mexicans looking at us in a bar. I don't think they liked gringos, and I didn't like the way they were staring. They had scarred and greasy faces, like the bad guys you might see in a Clint Eastwood movie.

I decided I'd make conversation. I asked if their mothers had any children who had lived.

They didn't understand a word I said, and one or two might have thought I was trying to be friendly. Then I called them five smelly sons of bitches. They still didn't get it. I said the same thing again, and that time they got my tone.

"I don't think they ever did know what George was saying," Riddle said recently. "But when he began to scream and cuss so loudly, and when they could see the look on his face, they got the idea."

That's when they pulled out the knives.

Riddle and I fled without paying our bill. I weighed so little that I could run like a deer. Riddle kept looking over his shoulder, and each time he did, he saw the summer sunlight glistening off the flashing blades they were waving at us. By then the Mexicans were shouting, and I couldn't understand what they had to say. But I also got the tone.

Riddle saw a taxi, and we ran into its side. We hit with the thud of stray deer running into a car on a dark highway. Dust boiled from the tires as the driver locked all four wheels.

We dove into the backseat, and Riddle began to roll up the windows. The Mexicans and their knives were only a few feet away. Riddle by then was hanging over the front seat, cranking the passenger's window up while hollering "Drive, drive, damnit, drive!"

The taxi driver didn't understand English.

Riddle had just cranked the fourth window to the top when he had an idea about how to communicate. The Mexicans, meanwhile, were pounding on the taxi and kicking its side. One had jumped onto the trunk. Maybe he thought he'd come through the rear window and slice us to pieces in the backseat.

"Border, border, border!" Riddle began to yell.

The driver got it.

He was still looking at us in the backseat when he put the accelerator to the floor. The guy on the trunk rolled off, and the jolt forward broke the other men's holds on the door handles.

"I worked for George Jones for four years and had some pretty hair-raising experiences," Riddle said later. "I have to say that was the most scary, and probably the most scared, I've ever been in my entire life. I can't remember the name of the town, but I thought that was going to be the place where I would die."

We were taken to the border and the bus.

Today the public realizes how important a bus is to a country singer's livelihood. Swiping his bus can be like swiping a carpenter's hammer and saw. I guess that's why people have attacked my bus when they've been angry at me.

I was booked to play Pikeville, Kentucky, in 1975 when the band made the show but I didn't. I had found out that one of my previous managers was going to seize the gate receipts, so I knew I'd wind up playing the show for no compensation. But the promoter had spent money advertising the concert as one where no alcohol was served. He therefore didn't have the luxury of lubricating the crowd with liquor. With nothing to settle their nerves, their anger mounted. A lot of irate fans demanded their money back, and apparently the promoter quickly saw that he was going to take a loss.

His first thought was to call the sheriff, who happened to be his uncle. The uncle's first thought was to seize my bus and let the promoter sell it.

Justice moves quickly in small towns, where everybody knows everybody, but nobody knew my whereabouts.

With no bus, my band had no way back to Nashville. The only transportation for a six-member band and my friend Billy Wilhite, who used to accompany me in those days, was a six-passenger car. The promoter seized that too and wouldn't even let anybody in my organization sit in it. He didn't know the car was rented until he received a call from Hertz, whose lawyers must have sounded more ferocious than his sheriff uncle. The car was returned to Billy, who returned it to the rental agency.

Meanwhile, my bus and the band it was supposed to haul were still stranded.

Clarence Reynolds at the Commerce Union Bank in Nashville held the papers on the bus, and he called the sheriff. The bus had seen a lot of miles and madness, and when Clarence told the sheriff how little the bus was worth and how much money I owed on it, the sheriff asked how he could find me to give it back. Finally, the band, bus and all, got home.

There's a secure feeling in being inside thousands of pounds of steel moving at sixty-five miles an hour with the curtains drawn. You can shut out the world. But you always have to stop, and the world is always waiting when you do.

Living the majority of your waking life on a bus also breeds claustrophobia. The sheer confinement of a few square feet holding eight to ten adults can make everyone on the bus extremely restless. The obvious outlet is humor.

Darrell McCall used to play bass and sing high harmony for Faron Young, Ray Price, and occasionally for me and a few others. Faron frequently did long tours with Hank Snow in the early 1960s, and Darrell used to get off Faron's bus eager to play pranks on Hank, who was generally a serious type. (Darrell once said that after you ride a bus for so many miles your mouth feels like the bottom of a birdcage.)

Hank used to love to shoot home movies. He shot film of almost every place he played all over North America. That was back when Hank and Faron would go out on forty-day tours, be home for one night, then go back out again for forty more.

During Hank's one night at home, he often wanted to show his home movies to the band that had just accompanied him on the tour. In other words, he wanted to show them on film what they had just seen in real life. They were sick of the view.

But Hank was their boss, so they felt they had to watch his movies. Darrell thought he'd break Hank of the habit.

He secretly got hold of Hank's movie camera and filmed things he shouldn't have. He photographed hubcaps, piles of dog shit, and other things that weren't a part of the lovely landscape. Faron said recently that

Darrell used to turn on the camera and toss it in the air, filming the world in a spin. Hank would send his exposed film to his wife and ask her to have it processed so that it would be waiting for viewing when he and the band returned to Nashville. He'd have his unwilling guests in place, turn off the lights, hit the projector switch, and see Darrell's handiwork.

Then he'd call Faron.

"That goddamn Darrell has ruined my film," Hank would fuss. "I shot beautiful film, and he has replaced it with film of dog shit! Now, what are you going to do?"

Faron never did anything except to laugh.

A lot of people feel they should be able to do anything they want when they're at home, and that bus is home to a touring singer. I've carried barbecue grills on my bus and stopped by the side of the road, away from people, to eat and relax before climbing back on and going to the next town. To this day I sometimes arrive in a town where I've already paid for a nice hotel room. But there are plenty of times I never see the hotel's interior. I'd rather dress on my bus.

I think the willingness to do what we want to do at home is why some country singers have behaved so recklessly inside their mobile houses.

Billy Wilhite was one of the best friends I've ever had. I met him in Texas in 1957, and he started coming around my shows and traveling with me now and again before I got my first bus. After I did, he did various jobs for me, and eventually he and I lived together in an apartment in Nashville.

But first we lived on a bus, where I lived any way I wanted.

It was 1975, and I hadn't been divorced from Tammy Wynette for very long. I was booked on a package show with the Statler Brothers and Tammy in Tampa, Florida, and was supposed to go deep-sea fishing with Billy the next day. But Tammy and I got into an argument that reminded me of the way we fought when we were married. I got drunk and decided I wanted to go to Nashville.

The band wanted to stay in Tampa, so I took off on the bus without them—just Billy, Gordon Wooden (my driver), and me. We went by way of Florence, Alabama, where I was living at the time, and were headed down Georgia 278 near Atlanta. I was loaded on vodka.

Billy remembers my coming up the aisle to where he was sitting near the front, talking to Gordon. I was carrying an open bottle of Smirnoff's.

"How about a drink?" I asked him.

"No thanks, George," he said. "You know I had heart trouble here a while back and I don't want to drink."

I asked him another question, and he said that his heart problem was the result of angina he had suffered six months ago.

That seemed like enough recovery time to me.

"You're going to take a drink," I said.

"No I'm not," Billy insisted.

Right there on my bus, I pulled out a .38 caliber pistol. Once again I'm recalling the behavior of a man who used to live inside my body. I'm not proud of it today. But I made a deal with myself when I started writing this book. If I honestly did something, even if I'm honestly ashamed, I'm honestly going to tell it.

I sat down at a small table across from Billy. By then my bus (not the Brown Bomber) was as nice as that of most country entertainers. This one had a place to eat and play cards.

I was perhaps four feet from Billy when I waved that pistol in his face.

"Take a drink," I said.

"I ain't gonna do it, George," he affirmed.

So I fired a round.

I intentionally missed him. Billy remembers that the bullet sailed about a foot from his head and went out the roof above the front windshield. Gordon jerked, and the bus swerved. You can imagine how loud a gunshot sounded inside the close surroundings of a bus.

"Take a drink!" I demanded, pushing that bottle closer to his face.

"I said no. I'm not taking a drink!" Billy shouted.

I fired again, with no intention of hitting him, and that bullet went on the other side of Gordon. A scrap of metal hit him as the bullet penetrated the bus wall. Gordon stiffened, frozen with fear. He still hadn't turned around to see what was prompting the gunplay. He just stared into space and drove.

I picked up my argument with Billy and fired a third and then a fourth shot at the window across the room from him. Glass shattered, and at our speed some of the fragments sprayed into the air and around the room. I had never intended to hit Billy, only to scare him, and it had worked.

I finally fired my last bullet, and Billy knew it.

I held a five-shot gun, and he knew that I never kept a round under the hammer. So he decided to take the situation in hand by taking the gun away from me.

"Stop the bus, Gordon!" he said, and Gordon locked the brakes. We lunged forward.

As soon as the bus was stopped, Gordon leaped out of the driver's seat. He and Billy pounced on me and wrestled me to the floor, where they took away my gun.

They put me in a lower bunk, and one of them sat on me while the other searched for all my bullets. Convinced that they had found them, they kept my gun and dared me to get out of the bunk.

They had the gun and the bullets, and I had my orders.

Folks have told me that I have telepathy, and lots of things have happened in my life that would support that. On that day, even though I had passed out, I woke up about the time we were approaching Florence. I just somehow knew I was getting close to my destination. Billy had already decided to take me home and not let me ride on to Nashville.

Folks have also said I was a different man when I wasn't drinking, and there are plenty of examples of that too. I can't count the times I've given money to the less fortunate, although I'm not bragging. I just want to make the point that even during my drinking days I did things I thank God I could afford to do—when I was sober.

Billy remembers that on the day of the bus shooting I poked my head out from the bunk's curtains as the bus was coming to a stop. He could tell I had sobered up some.

We pulled to a halt, and I was the first one off the bus.

I walked past Billy, who was still sitting down. I had four one-hundred-dollar bills on me, and I stuffed them into his shirt pocket.

"Buy you some nerve pills," I said.

And, for a few days, I was off that bus.

Chapter 7

A touring entertainer meets more people in a month than most folks do in a lifetime. I never ceased to be amazed at the unusual circumstances surrounding some of the meetings, especially among people who later became some of my best friends.

I bought a house in Lakeland, Florida, in the late 1960s, and the seller told me that my next-door neighbor was a real son of a bitch.

"Stay away from him," he said. "He's a raving idiot!"

The neighbor, Cliff Hyder, became one of my best friends. He remains so to this day.

I opened a gift shop on Nashville's Music Row in the late 1980s and decided to give a free show for the first customers. I sang one of my hit records, "Bartender's Blues," a James Taylor tune. A girl who I'd never met was invited to sing harmony. I thought she was magnificent, and that was my introduction to Trisha Yearwood. In February 1994 I recorded "Bartender's Blues" again and selected her as my duet partner. By that time she had recorded many of her own hits and held platinum albums.

In 1964 I had recorded "The Race Is On," one of my biggest records and one that is a part of my road show to this day. It's an up-tempo song that some folks considered rock 'n' roll when it was recorded. Consequently, I was the only country act booked on an otherwise all-rock show in Austin, Texas, about a year later.

One of the bands on that program was real scraggly. I didn't like them because I thought they needed baths and told them so. To make matters worse, the young rockers had no equipment, so they asked to borrow mine. I said yes, and the group played so loudly through my amplifiers that one of them exploded.

Gary Adams, who was in my group at the time, said something to the band's lead singer, and the guy said something back. A scuffle was soon under way. Gary put the guy in a hammerlock, then forced him up a stairway where I was sitting with Sonny Curtis, my steel guitar player.

"This guy and his buddies blew up our amp, and he ought to pay for it!" Gary said. The guy cussed and reluctantly pulled a hundred-dollar bill from his pocket. Gary said he handed it to Curtis, who handed it to me.

That unruly singer was Mick Jagger of the Rolling Stones.

Today I consider the Stones the world's best rock 'n' roll band, and I even recorded a duet with its lead guitarist, Keith Richards, in 1994. We did "Say It's Not

You," a song I had originally recorded three years after the shoving match with Jagger. Keith remembered my first version and wanted to sing it for an album, *The Bradley Barn Session,* released during the writing of this book.

Early on in my career, I recorded "You Gotta Be My Baby" for Starday, which was released on July 14, 1956. One time I performed the song on a show in Odessa, Texas. I met a girl that night and tried to take her out, but she was getting attention from a disc jockey on KOYL. I didn't want to offend the disc jockey because I wanted him to keep playing my record. But I also wanted the girl. I couldn't figure out how to get on her good side without getting on his bad. That was my first encounter with Waylon Jennings.

In the early 1960s, I was sitting in Tootsie's Orchid Lounge, an old Nashville tavern across the alley from the Grand Ole Opry that was home to many singers and songwriters. I met Gary Adams that night when he came walking into the joint, his first stop after graduating from high school. He had come to town looking for a job in the music business. I was the first guy he met, and I hired him to be my guitar player.

"Man, this music business is going to be easy," he remembered thinking when he told the story years later.

I hired him because he had come to Nashville at the recommendation of Johnny Paycheck, a musician and singer who was then one of the Jones Boys. I knew that Paycheck had sent Gary to Tootsie's, and I knew that Johnny knew we had a show a couple of days later in Roswell, New Mexico.

So I left one hundred dollars with Gary for Paycheck

and him to meet me in Roswell. They were to take a train.

"The tickets for the two of us cost eighty-five dollars," Gary remembered years later. "We had fifteen dollars left to live on for two days. The first night on the train, Johnny got drunk. He was into karate at the time, and the next thing I knew I heard a scream and the crashing of glass. He had put his hand through a window in the men's room.

"We had to get off the train and let a doctor sew up his hand, and that took the rest of our money," Gary went on. "In all, it took three days getting out there, and we nearly starved to death because we had no money. Johnny sobered up and told George that he had fallen down."

Johnny played steel guitar for me for a while after that, and we have been friends ever since. It's been a friendship that has remained through our successes and failures. Johnny was riding high on the popularity surveys with "Take This Job and Shove It" while I was laying low, missing shows due to drunkenness. And our friendship, through the years, has stood even when we couldn't stand each other.

We were drunk and got into an argument one night somewhere in Virginia. We were riding in a car while most of the other Jones Boys were on the bus. I ordered Johnny to pull to the side of the road and get out. I told him I was going to whip his ass.

Johnny jumped out of the car, and I locked its doors. In seconds Johnny saw nothing but taillights. I left him stranded on dark asphalt somewhere in the rural South.

Gary hounded me for an hour to go back and pick him up, and I finally tried to do that.

But he was gone.

We found him walking down a street in a tiny town shortly before daylight. That's when a policeman pulled me over for reckless driving. I told him I was looking for that guy over there, pointing to Johnny. The cop approached Johnny, who said he'd never seen me in his life and wouldn't think about accepting a ride from a stranger. He later told the cop the truth. Johnny and I had our laugh and pressed on down the highway as the sun was coming up.

The Jones Boys and I played Milwaukee one time, and I bought a moped, a motorized bicycle that weighed about eighty pounds. It was intended to haul one passenger on short trips at slow speeds around town.

I insisted that Johnny and the other band members take turns driving it on our way from Milwaukee to Vidor, a distance of perhaps fifteen hundred miles. The moped's top speed might have been forty miles per hour. Because it was so light, it bounced each time it hit a tar crack in the two-lane highway.

The rest of us followed in a car, and most everyone got plenty of sleep. At that pace, there was little else to do.

Obviously, I bought the moped because I was drunk. Why else would I buy such an impractical machine so far from home? I could have bought one just like it in Vidor and not have worn it out getting it home. By the time we reached Vidor, the moped's engine was smoking from burning oil. I think the journey took about three days and nights, which I didn't mind too much, as I kept stopping for more whiskey.

But Johnny hated the entire trip, which he finished with many bruises and cuts. He had hit some railroad tracks the wrong way in another small town late at night. The machine jolted, and he flew over the handlebars. Somebody woke me to see Johnny sprawled on the pavement. Gary was laughing so hard you could hear his voice echo through his open window across the countryside.

That made Johnny furious, so he tried to pull Gary from behind the wheel for another fistfight. I was laughing so hard I almost got sick.

Glen Davis and other members of the band took shifts riding the moped. But after the crash, they had to point the bent handlebars at an angle to make the bike go straight.

I was in a poker game in the late 1960s somewhere in Texas with Willie Nelson, Wynn Stewart, and a new singer-songwriter who was working for $750 for his band and him. He had hauled his group all the way from Nashville in a leased bus, and he had to buy their food and lodging. He didn't make much profit, and Wynn and I won almost all of it. He had to go out after midnight to find his road manager to get the cash to pay us. After the game I wondered if he'd be mad about his financial bath and if I'd ever see him again. But I wound up recording several tunes written in the 1970s and 1980s by Tom T. Hall, truly one of the greatest country songwriters of all time.

Hall has said many times that he got into the music

business to drink beer and chase women. Not me. I preferred whiskey.

Tom's motivation has been shared by a lot of country singers through the years, including today's stars. I hear a lot of talk about how modern country stars live cleaner lives than my friends and I used to live. I don't know if they live cleaner or just more secretly.

We did what we did and didn't care who knew it. It hurt our careers, but we weren't in the music business primarily for careers. We were in it for the music and because its pace and schedule allowed us to live the way we wanted. It's easy to get drunk and chase women when you're working on the road. It isn't that easy for men who have to come home at a certain time every night.

I had my share of one-night stands with women, and I'm not proud of the way I treated my second wife, the late Shirley Arnold, who married J. C. Arnold after our divorce. Occasionally, however, I met a woman who I thought meant something to me.

In 1963 I thought I was in love and realized later that it was boyish infatuation. I was old enough at the time to know better. But I was still too young to resist.

On May 4, 1963, Melba Montgomery and I saw the release of "We Must Have Been Out of Our Minds," a song that rose to number three and was charted for twenty-eight weeks. Melba and I eventually saw the release of six other songs, but that first duet was our biggest record by far. She had written the song while traveling with comedians Lonzo and Oscar in a used van on the way to California.

"I wrote the whole song on the back of a postcard in less than one hundred miles," she said recently.

She was a down-home girl who was as country as me. She had come to Nashville in 1959 as part of a trio with her brother and a friend. Roy Acuff heard her sing and hired her away from the group to be his featured girl singer, which she was from 1958 to 1962.

She recorded a song on Nugget Records, a small label owned by Lonzo and Oscar, and I heard her on the radio. I determined that I wanted to meet her.

I told Pappy Daily to call her and ask her to meet us at Nashville's old Quality Inn. I thought it was our first meeting, but she later told me she had met me a short time earlier at another bar.

She said I had been too drunk to remember.

The day she walked into the Quality Inn I immediately asked her if she had a song she thought she and I could record. I really wanted her as my duet partner.

With no accompaniment, inside a little motel restaurant, she began to sing "We Must Have Been Out of Our Minds." I fell in love with the song instantly. In fact, I began to sing harmony and actually finished the song with her the first time I heard it.

"We can record that one," I said.

"You've got yourself a recording contract, kid," Pappy said.

Melba couldn't say a thing.

I had giant records years later with Tammy Wynette, and there were many other successful duet partners, such as Porter Wagoner and Dolly Parton and Conway Twitty and Loretta Lynn. I'm not saying Melba and I were the first to sing male-female duets in country music because we weren't. And I'm not saying we were the best. But Melba said recently that she thinks we popularized the male-female format, and I agree.

My affections for Melba surfaced almost immediately after we began working. But my drunkenness and the fact that I had a wife did little to make her want to commit to me. She said not long ago that I was never mean to her but that sometimes I embarrassed her.

We played Roanoke, Virginia, with several other acts, including the Osborne Brothers, a bluegrass duo. Melba and the brothers were recalling one of my shenanigans at that show when I began writing this book. It all came back to me.

I had been drunk for about a week and didn't feel too well come curtain time. Melba said my guitar was in tune, but I insisted it wasn't and ordered one of the Jones Boys to tune it.

The band kicked off with "White Lightning," my opening number in those days, and I walked onstage with that guitar. I sang one verse and one chorus, then decided it was out of tune. When the band took an instrumental break, I broke the guitar.

In front of thousands of people, I furiously pulled the instrument off my shoulder and beat it on the floor. Wood and splinters flew in all directions.

Then I walked offstage past Melba, who was standing in the wings. She stood there patiently on each show we did. She took her place after doing her set and watched me do mine. Then I would call her out to sing our hit duet.

I had done one half of one song before storming off. I didn't even tell the crowd good-bye, and they were furious. They began to stomp and yell. Things began to get a little scary. My band left their instruments onstage and scampered to safety.

The audience was getting madder and madder by the minute.

Melba had never seen an entertainer act that way, and she'd never seen a crowd on the brink of becoming a mob. So she fled to her dressing room. The audience continued to yell and cuss.

Fifteen minutes later audience anger was at its height, and Sonny Curtis knocked on Melba's door.

"George has locked himself in the men's room and won't come out," he told her. "You've got to do something before these people tear the place down."

Melba came out of her dressing room to the boos of the crowd, loud even though she was well inside the building's interior. She walked timidly to the men's room and knocked.

I hadn't answered for anyone else, but as soon as I heard her honeysuckle voice, I let her inside.

"And there weren't no seats in there," Melba remembered, "so George just sat down on the commode and put his head in his hands. I just stood there and talked."

"George, this crowd is going to come backstage and get us," Melba said, "and they've got us outnumbered. These people are mad and raising Cain. You got to go back out there!"

People you care about can get you to do things other folks can't. I wouldn't have gone back for those thousands of people, but I agreed to go back for Melba.

"I'll go back out if you'll let me play your guitar," I told her. "Mine is broken."

"You can play mine," Melba said, "but if you break it, I'm going to take what's left of the neck and break it over your head."

She meant it, and that made her cute. So my new girl singer and I walked hand in hand out of the men's room. I went straight to the stage, did my show, called her out, and sang some more. The show was longer and better than it would have otherwise been. And the next time I left the stage, I left the crowd standing on its feet.

Melba didn't put on airs for anybody. And even though country music's popularity was only a fraction of what it would become, it had already attracted female artists who would play political games to further their careers.

Not Melba. She was real. I was drawn to the reality and thought I wanted to draw her to my side for the rest of my life.

I told her I loved her and asked her to marry me. She said no and began to date Jack Solomon, my lead guitar player for three years. They grew serious, and I could see I was losing what I was never going to have.

So I came up with a plan. If Melba wouldn't accept my private proposal, I'd see how she'd do with a public one.

"We were onstage, and George had been drinking," Melba remembered. "We only used one microphone in those days, and I had to stand real close to him. We'd be singing, and he'd start telling me not to marry Jack but to marry him. The crowd could hear it all, and I was embarrassed to death. I'd keep right on singing. Well, I had the high harmony part. George wouldn't be singing because he'd be asking me to marry him, and I'd be singing harmony all by myself. And Jack was just standing off to the side playing his guitar, not paying attention."

Melba Montgomery married Jack Solomon in 1968. They're married to this day. I'll always have a soft spot in my heart for her, and the last time I talked to her I told her that someday soon she and I were going to record again.

I meant it.

Tom T. Hall once said he thought the country singers of the 1960s and 1970s weren't the bad people that their reputations for fast living indicated.

"I think mostly we were just a bunch of good ole country boys trying to have a good time," he said, talking about alcohol and pill abuse.

I just think that most country singers, including many of the women, didn't take seriously the booze and chemicals they took for recreation. I didn't. Not a lot meant a lot to me if it was an interruption of what I thought was a good time. Older whiskey, louder music, and younger women were pretty much my thing.

But sometimes life hands a sobering experience to men who don't want to get sober. That happened to me.

On Friday, November 6, 1965, the band and I played Shelly's Nightclub at 4500 Spencer Highway near La Porte, Texas, a small town of about twelve thousand on the southeastern border of Houston. The place was packed, as I was riding high in the charts with "Love Bug," a record so hot that I rerecorded it twenty-nine years later with Vince Gill. The band and I finished the La Porte show, and I don't remember if we played on Saturday.

It was during a time when my last bus had broken down, and I was shopping for another new used one. So I had rented a large van that might be called a recreational vehicle today.

On Sunday afternoon, we were heading south toward McAllen near the Texas-Mexico border and listening to the radio, as we almost always did. The music was interrupted by a bulletin.

"Country music singer and Grand Ole Opry star George Jones," said the announcer, "if you're listening, call the Houston police department immediately!" The voice sounded urgent. I was filled with curiosity and numb with fear.

We stopped at the next pay telephone, and someone in the van got out to call. His face was bleached when he got back on board.

He asked if I remembered seeing Jacqueline Young Friday night. I called her Jackie and said of course I remembered. She was the secretary of my fan club and had come on my van to ask me to dictate words for a Christmas card she wanted to send to fan club members.

She had been drinking and taking pills when she got on the van. We were alone, and then she passed out. I decided not to awaken her and went from the van to the stage and did my show. When I returned she was gone.

"The police said they have determined you were the last person to see her alive," said my band member on that Sunday afternoon.

"Alive?" I said. "What do you mean?"

A few hours after I had left her, Jacqueline Stanford Young, age twenty-five, was found dead inside her car, parked in an open field on Highway 146, four miles from where she'd been seen with me. She'd been beaten with a tire iron, but a coroner later ruled that she had died from "manual strangulation."

Someone had taken his bare hands, after beating her senseless, and choked the life out of her gasping body. She probably died looking straight into the eyes of her killer.

I was the primary suspect.

The Jones Boy who talked to the police gave them our location, and it wasn't long until my camper was surrounded by deputies and highway patrolmen. They asked the boys and me a lot of questions, and what we said must have satisfied them, as they said we could go on to McAllen to do our Sunday-night show if we would drive back to Houston on Monday to take lie detector tests.

As I look back on it now, maybe they were trying to see if I would run. When I arrived in McAllen, other highway patrolmen were there to watch me. They came inside the nightclub and stood in the back the entire time we did our sets. In those days, we did two hours, took a fifteen-minute break, and did two more hours.

What I didn't know was that the *Houston Chronicle,* then the largest newspaper in the largest state in the nation, had run a copyrighted story that morning that quoted the victim's grandmother Mrs. Emily Stanford. The woman said that her granddaughter was "crazy about country music" and intended to hear George Jones. Further on in the story, a sheriff's lieutenant said that "investigators" had learned that Jackie had in fact attended my show and gotten on board my camper.

I was being indirectly tried by a newspaper that was a

part of the national news wire services. The story was offered for publication all over the country.

Updates on the story were published for days. On many occasions, when a story appeared about a development in the case, it mentioned again that the woman had been with me only hours before her death. One headline in another newspaper accused me of knowing more than I was telling investigators. The fact is the band and I knew nothing, and we cooperated fully.

After our La Porte show, we had gone to a party at a Holiday Inn with some other women. They vouched for us. But that didn't satisfy the investigators, who still demanded that we take lie detector tests. I was eager to do it, so I could quickly establish my innocence.

QUIZ SINGER IN SLAYING OF DIVORCÉE, said a *Chronicle* headline four days after the unsolved murder.

"Singer George Jones and members of his troupe returned to Houston today to 'do all we can' to clear up the mysterious murder of 25-year-old Mrs. Jacqueline Young," read the first paragraph. That story indicated how much I was cooperating with investigators, until the next paragraph implied that I had something to hide.

"Instead of visiting the sheriff's office, as newsmen had been told they would, the entertainers closeted themselves at an undisclosed motel for questioning by Capt. M. F. Patton and sheriff's investigators Arnold Loesch and Harold Carpenter."

The words "closeted" and "motel" stood out to anyone who had decided I was guilty. Given my reputation for reckless behavior, there were probably plenty of such folks. Lots of people always want to believe the worst, especially about people who live in the public eye and even more especially about entertainers.

On Friday, a few hours shy of a week after the murder, the Houston newspaper ran a two-column story whose headline read, 15 TAKE LIE TESTS IN SECRETARY SLAYING.

"Jones, members of his band, and others associated with the group, were cleared Thursday after 12 of them submitted to polygraph tests here and in Austin."

That paragraph was the third from the bottom of the story, and it was the first to indicate my innocence. But the damage had been done.

One member of my group had a hard time with the lie detector test. He had tried to put the make on the victim, and perhaps he felt guilty about that. He couldn't settle down during the test, and the first time it was given he was implicated. I think he failed it a second time too, and an investigator told me he was sure the guy was guilty.

I knew him to be a nervous person, and the other Jones Boys and I urged him to relax during testing. He did and was finally cleared.

The year ended without an arrest. On January 2, 1966, the *Houston Chronicle* published a story that was an overall look at the unsolved case.

SLAYER OF JACQUELINE YOUNG STILL HUNTED, read the first line of the headline. HE LIVES HIS LIFE WITH MURDER AS HIS PARTNER. The writer tried to imagine how the guilty fugitive might be living outside the law: "And for 57 days now, wherever he is, and those who hunt him feel he is here, he has lived with murder."

Once again, my name was mentioned in the story. Meanwhile, I was running around the nation doing one-night shows, sometimes noticing more policemen than usual at my performances. It was clear that I was being watched.

I was often drunk and didn't pay attention, but the next day the guys in the band would talk about the whispers they had heard and about some fans who had asked them if George Jones knew more about that slaying than he was telling. Occasionally, a drunk would actually ask one of the Jones Boys if I'd done it. Given my condition during those days, I'm glad he didn't ask me. The fight would have been on before he finished the question.

In the summer of 1966, a man working in Dallas told someone that he had killed a girl after my show. The man he told called the police. There was an arrest, and in September former Houston gas-station worker Victor Eugene Miller II was convicted of murder. Ironically, his nickname was Roger Miller, the name of another famous country singer. His trial was covered by a press that often continued to mention that Jackie had spent her last hours with me.

Miller was handed a life sentence.

Perhaps twenty stories about the killing appeared in the *Houston Chronicle,* some of which I still have. I have no idea how many stories appeared in other newspapers around the world. *Detective,* a popular crime magazine at the time, ran a multipage spread, complete with pictures of Jackie and me. The implication about her death and George Jones was obvious. The results of the bad publicity can't be measured, not even to this day. Members of my family, still living in Texas, had to put up with the whispers and stares, but said little to me about it.

The investigation, from the time of the murder to Miller's sentencing, had taken almost ten months. Some folks will remember it forever. Two days after the killing, Sheriff C. V. Kern was quoted in the *Chronicle:* He said the case would be cleared up in a week.

Chapter 8

Looking back, I think I was newsworthy in that murder not only because of my recording career but also because my performance venues had become more and more important. It's true that I was still out there on the "kindlin' circuit," working one-night stands in dives where my songs were just backgrounds for brawls. That syndrome would last for years to come.

But I had also been playing the nation's big auditoriums on package shows in Milwaukee, Philadelphia, Los Angeles, Chicago, Denver, Dallas, Miami, Boston, Atlanta, Phoenix, and other major cities. All of that was a pretty big step from Vidor.

And I had helped make history in 1964 when I was a part of what some folks think was the most important country music show ever performed up to that time—

the first country show at Madison Square Garden in New York City.

Press came from across the nation to see if hillbilly singers (that's what we affectionately called each other) could draw enough Yankees to fill the giant room. As it turned out, the show was held over for three additional performances. Each was sold out.

Imagine, that was twelve years before Waylon Jennings and Willie Nelson staged their famous Outlaw movement, one of the most successful marketing schemes in country music history. Dolly Parton was a senior in high school. It was the year Merle Haggard had "Sam Hill," his second single record, and five years before Johnny Cash got his network television show.

Garth Brooks was two years old.

Yet there we were, ten country singers with their bands, in the world's fashion and financial center to perform music that could be heard mostly on about two hundred and fifty small AM radio stations tucked into the nation's heartland. Those of us on the program wondered if anybody would come.

The New York Times gave us a generally favorable review. "The country music jamboree was as ambitious, colorful, star-laden, uneven, beautiful and banal as a circus," wrote Robert Shelton in the May 18, 1964, edition. "There was a bit of noise, a lot of nostalgia, but enough good music-making for this circus to be one that country music fans would long remember," *Life* and *Time* magazines later wrote about us.

I wish Shelton hadn't called our show a circus. He obviously liked it and saw that the fans liked it too. But he just couldn't stand to be too kind to music that was still thought to be the anthem of the ill-educated common class.

Garth, Vince Gill, Reba McEntire, Alan Jackson, George Strait, and Brooks & Dunn—any one of those acts could play alone at Madison Square Garden today and sell out the place.

Thirty-one years ago, it took the combined efforts of Ernest Tubb, Buck Owens, Webb Pierce, Bill Monroe, Bill Anderson, Stonewall Jackson, Skeeter Davis, Porter Wagoner, Leon McAuliffe, and me. The show's master of ceremonies was Ralph Emery, who was then the nation's leading overnight country disc jockey on Nashville's WSM, one of the few AM powerhouses that programmed our music.

Patsy Cline would have been on the show, but she had died in a plane crash the previous year. Some fans kept hollering for Jim Reeves, who wasn't there and who would die in a plane crash later that year.

I'm glad I got the opportunity to perform but regret the impression I made the first time I played New York City. I was back there with the Jones Boys in 1993 and found out that some fans still remembered my 1964 entrance. Or, more specifically, my exit.

I was accustomed to giving the fans my all. Remember, my usual set in rural roadhouses was two hours, followed by a break, before two more hours.

But Ralph Emery remembered that in New York I was told I could do two songs. Two songs! I had driven my band all the way from God knows where, paid for their lodging and meals, only to be told that I could sing for about six minutes. I don't like to be told what to do regarding many things. I refuse to be told what to do regarding my music.

Ralph remembered that the 1964 New York City show was also my introduction to performance unions. Working the South, I was accustomed to some good ole boy running a rickety soundboard while trying to mike the singer and sometimes all of the musicians through one microphone. He usually shone a single spotlight too, moving its beam to whatever musician was taking a break. The lead and bass guitars usually had amplifiers that they set on top of folding chairs. Not too much was too sophisticated.

In New York there were too many unnecessary jobs and too many people to do them. My God, we were trying to put on a country music show, not a Broadway play. Everybody working on the production belonged to a union. And all of those unions said the show had to end promptly at 11:30 P.M. If the show ran overtime, Ralph remembered, the promoter would have to pay a five-thousand-dollar fine, plus double the hourly rate to each union member in the house. That was a lot of money in those days.

Needless to say, the promoter put a lot of pressure on Ralph to keep the show running on schedule and to be *sure* it ended on time.

I walked onto the stage, and about eight spotlights hit me in the face. I was blinded. I could hear the crowd, but I couldn't see it. I opened with "White Lightning" and was thunderstruck when the crowd's applause exploded. I had feared those people wouldn't know my music, but I could faintly see a few in the first row singing along.

I felt accepted, and I felt good. I felt no urge to quit. I eased into "She Thinks I Still Care," and the people applauded all the way through the instrumental introduction and into the first verse. At that moment I would have forgiven the Yankees for winning the Civil War.

I guess the crowd expected me to leave the stage at the end of that second song, the way the previous acts had done after two tunes. I went into a third.

Ralph was down in something like a hole. Maybe it was an orchestra pit. With the blinding lighting, I couldn't see him too well either, but I could make out his silhouette. He seemed to be jumping and waving his arms a lot. He kept shouting into a microphone, and I could hear the echo of his distorted voice floating around the room.

"Thank you, George, for those great songs," he said. "And now let's bring out our next performer."

"Why's he saying that," I wondered, "when I'm still singing?" To hell with the unions. I was still wondering why Ralph kept trying to bring me off as I went into my fifth song.

What I didn't know was that the promoter had told Ralph to do whatever he had to do to get me off the stage. The clock was ticking toward eleven-thirty and the crowd still hadn't heard the show's closing act—guess who?—Buck Owens.

Bill Monroe, who had been one of my idols since the 1930s, could see Ralph's dilemma and walked quietly to the announcer's side.

"You can't get George to come off, can you?" I would later learn he said.

"No," Ralph replied, "and I think the promoter is going to have a heart attack right after he loses his shirt on this show."

I guess the union stewards were licking their lips, anticipating all the money they were going to make when the show ran overtime.

I just kept singing. I was standing in the middle of the biggest and most important stage I had ever been on when they grabbed me. In front of thousands of people, Monroe and a member of his band slipped out of the shadows, into the spotlight, and put an arm under each of my arms. They physically lifted me off the floor. My voice trailed to silence as I was pulled from the microphone's reach.

Still, I kept singing and even began to kick a little. But that didn't help. I was too high off the floor for my feet to touch it. That's how I left the stage—smiling, kicking, and singing.

My band didn't know what was going on. They had fought many promoters through the years because I hadn't *gone* on. They weren't used to fighting one because I had *stayed* on. So they just stopped playing, gradually and one at a time. The music came to an awkward halt. By then a lot of the crowd was mumbling.

I was embarrassed. But I couldn't get mad at Bill Monroe for two reasons. First, he was much bigger than me, and second, he was my hero. And he had only been trying to help Ralph, who had done as much as anybody there to spread the popularity of country music.

Buck's musicians were plugging into my band's amplifiers before some of my guys had even gotten off the stage. Buck had been told to get through his two songs in a hurry, and he did. Applause hadn't even died from his first when he was well into his second.

Buck sounded his last note, and Ralph screamed something into his microphone about "Country Music Comes to Madison Square Garden is now history!"

Somebody stopped an official time clock at 11:29:40. The program had ended twenty seconds before deadline! The promoter had saved thousands of dollars. The people had gotten more than their money's worth. Everybody was happy—even me.

Ten singers and sixty band members walked out of what was then one of the nation's largest indoor arenas. Thousands of people heard the show, scores of reporters saw it.

But only one person had sung five songs.

I might have been thinking about that show, but I doubt it, when I played a show later that year with Melba Montgomery. Once again, people made a fuss about how long I stayed onstage. Once again, I thought they should be happy I had made it to the stage.

At that point in my career, I was missing perhaps 10 percent of my shows because I was too drunk to get to them or too drunk to go on after I did.

Melba remembers that she and I were part of a package show promoted by Carlton Haney, a big country concert promoter during the 1960s and 1970s. Country stars used to work hard to please him so he would use them on additional shows. Carlton indirectly paid a lot of entertainers' bills in those days.

A lot of acts actually feared him. Not me, not anytime, and especially not when I was drinking.

Melba, the Jones Boys, and I were playing Charlotte, North Carolina. Carlton told Melba and some of the lesser-known acts that they could only do two songs. He told me I could do five.

What about the audience? What if they liked Melba and wanted her to do more? Why shouldn't she? She was working hard to establish her career. The people had seen me before, but most of them had never seen her in person. So once again I didn't like the time limit, but I might have cooperated—until some idiot yanked the microphone out of Melba's hand in front of the crowd.

She had politely done what she had been told—sung her two numbers—and was about to leave the stage when some geek from the wings grabbed her microphone from her. It was like he was saying, "We've had your two cents, now get out!"

Rage flew all over me. I went out and did my five songs, took my applause, then started for the side of the stage. From there I called Melba.

She came out, and we sang our hit duet, which we weren't supposed to do.

Carlton began to holler at me from the wings, and I pretended not to hear him. Melba thought we were through and started to leave. I grabbed her hand and pulled her back to the microphone. We began to sing songs for that crowd that we had never sung together in our lives. I would have sung "Chopsticks" just to stay onstage and get back at those staging people for the rude way they had treated Melba.

Carlton Haney is a fat man with big yellow teeth and a thick Southern accent. He never called me George. He called me "Geoawge." It took him forever to say anything, and he always seemed to get three syllables out of one.

Melba said he was patting his chest at the side of the stage when she and I went into our tenth song. He seemed to be sweating a lot. We eventually sang every song we had recorded on our album. Because we hadn't rehearsed the tunes, we made a lot of mistakes. I didn't care. I wouldn't let her leave the stage. The people were going crazy, and so was Carlton—in a different way.

I noticed I didn't hear him screaming anymore. I glanced to the side, and he was gone. I turned back to face the crowd and jumped at what I saw. There, kneeling in front of me with his back to thousands of fans, was Carlton Haney. He was a short and obese man when standing. On his knees, he looked like a forgotten frog on a lily pad.

"Geoawge," he pleaded, his voice leaking into my microphone, "you've got to git off this heere showah."

With that, Melba and I walked offstage and Carlton struggled to his feet. He was stiff and limping when the curtain was closed.

I don't know why I did what I'm about to tell you. But then, I frequently didn't know why I did things when I was drinking.

The Jones Boys, featuring Johnny Paycheck, and I were playing a show and dance for the fire department in Fairfax, Virginia, in 1964. Everyone in the show had gotten up early and had been drinking all day. By show time I was soused.

The Jones Boys went on and played an entire set with-

I LIVED TO TELL IT ALL

out me. I was too drunk to come out of the dressing room.

"We'll be right back after our break with George Jones," Johnny told the crowd. A few had grumbled, but not much more. There was plenty of time left in the evening, and most of the audience expected to hear me sing plenty.

Johnny said he came into the dressing room and we argued about whether I would go on. He yelled and kicked things and threatened to whip me if I didn't. I'd heard it all before.

Johnny and another Jones Boy helped me to my feet and ushered me up to the side of the stage. The crowd couldn't see me. He and the band walked onstage to mild applause and picked up their instruments.

"Ladies and gentlemen," Johnny yelled, "give a big hand to George Jones!".

The band kicked into "White Lightning" and fans ran to the front of the stage. I stood behind the curtain and wobbled. Then I began to shake my head no. The music stopped.

Johnny, the only one who could see me, walked over to me as the crowd began to mumble and stir.

"Wonder if he's even here or if he's somewhere drunk," someone yelled.

"I'll bet he's drunk again," another said.

The people, without realizing it, were working themselves into a simmering anger that I would eventually ignite.

"What in the hell are you doing?" Johnny said to me in the wings.

"I ain't going out," I slurred, "unless you introduce me as Hank Williams."

Hank had been dead for eleven years.

Johnny argued some more, but the promoter and the people were putting pressure on him. I was too drunk to feel it.

So Johnny walked back to the center of the stage, blushed, and said, "Ladies and gentlemen, I'm sorry about the delay, but the wait was worth it. Here to sing for you-all is Hank Williams!"

Now everybody knew I wasn't Hank Williams. But the people were so determined to have a good time that they went along with it. But I didn't. I refused again to go onstage.

The music stopped a third time, and it wasn't a charm. I could feel the floor shake as Johnny stomped toward me. I smiled and staggered but didn't budge from my spot. Our conversation was so loud the crowd could hear us out front.

"I ain't coming out," I told him, "unless you introduce me as Johnny Horton."

Horton had been dead for four years.

"All right, you son of a bitch!" Johnny yelled, "I'm whipping your ass right here. When you go out there it will be with a bloody nose."

He began to dance around and churn his fists. He was drunk too, so he occasionally bumped into the curtain. It bulged each time he did. From out front, it must have looked like someone backstage was beating it with a broom.

"I mean it, asshole," he said. "I'll call you Johnny Horton, but if you don't come out, I'm coming back for you.

You can sing as Hank Horton or Johnny Williams for all I care, but you're liable to sing laying down. I swear I'll whip your ass."

"Did he say whip my ass?" somebody out front said.

The crowd had waited through one entire set and false introductions. The people were getting mad. Real mad.

They began to boo loudly as Johnny lumbered back to the microphone. "Here's Johnny Horton," he said, adding nothing else.

The band once again broke into "White Lightning," and George Jones, alias Hank Williams, alias Johnny Horton, stumbled toward the microphone at center stage.

I slowed my walk enough to sing "Back in North Carolina," the first half of the first line of "White Lightning." I never stopped walking, and I never sang another word. I went right across the stage, into the wings, and out the back door.

And the audience rioted.

They were coming over the footlights as band members dropped their instruments and ran. Some of the people hurled steel folding chairs onto the stage while others threw bottles. A few instruments were broken.

In about one minute I could hear the sound of sirens as I saw the sight of neon. I was running for a bar I could see about a block from the hall. I went inside, found a stool, and didn't go any farther.

I don't know why it took the entire band and half of the Fairfax police department at least three hours to find me.

* * *

On March 13, 1965, I saw the release of "Things Have Gone to Pieces," a song that was listed for twenty-one weeks on the *Billboard* survey, peaking at number nine. That song was historic in that it was my first single record for Musicor Records, my fourth record label in eleven years. I had been on United Artists from 1961 to 1964.

During the next seven years, I recorded a whopping two hundred and eighty songs for Musicor. That kind of output, even in those days, was unheard of. Thirty-two of the songs were single records. That means I had an average of almost five single records each year.

Norro Wilson, who coproduces some of my albums today, was talking recently about the technical perfection of today's records. If a line, for example, will fit in one verse better than another, it is electronically moved. If a guitar player wants to redo his part, his part alone is rerecorded until he and the producer are happy.

Today's records have more mechanical perfection than any recorded at any other time in history.

Some also have less heart. Artists today might take two or three days to record one song. When I was at Musicor, I might record an entire album in three hours, a practice that violated the musician's union's rules. I'd go through one take, Pappy Daily would play back what I had done, and then he'd usually holler, "Ship it." It would be at the pressing plant the next day.

Yet I recorded some of my biggest songs in that casual fashion, including "Take Me," "Walk Through This World with Me," "When the Grass Grows over Me," "A Good Year for the Roses," and "Sometimes You Just Can't Win."

Yet only one of those thirty-two songs went to number one. "Walk Through This World with Me" topped the charts for two weeks during the spring of 1967.

At first I fought Pappy, telling him consistently that I thought the song was weak. He kept pitching it to me, and I kept telling him no. He regularly brought it to me at recording sessions, which meant that he brought it to me often.

"I'm only cutting this here song to get him off of my back," I told the musicians at the session when we finally recorded it.

Pappy gloated when he finally got his way, and I was thrilled to have my first number-one tune in five years. (The last one had been "She Thinks I Still Care.")

I couldn't believe that a song I had resisted so much had done so well. I was thirty-six years old, had been singing for money for more than half of my life, and was still learning.

I still am to this day.

Chapter 9

In 1966 I tried to do something I've been trying to do ever since—slow down. People who've never rushed from city to city doing show after show think it's glamorous. Those people usually have seen the entertainment business only from the audience. They don't know what it's like to finish at 10:30 P.M., leave the auditorium at midnight, ride a bus four or five hundred miles to a sound check at 4 P.M., and hurry to a chain hotel to grab a quick shower and gulp fast food. After all, you have to get to a venue in time to repeat the madness during the next twenty-four hours.

All the while, you travel with the same dozen or so people you've seen every day for weeks as prisoners of a bus's cramped quarters. When that many personalities are mixed with that many miles under that much pressure, tempers flare and moods change.

And somebody always wants to be awake when others want to sleep. When I got my fill of that life, I often disappeared with just a bottle. I didn't turn back up until I was ready, and by that time there were usually a few lawsuits waiting from promoters whose shows I had missed.

My traveling today is considerably different. I try to work only three or four days a week and fly to the week's first date on a private jet with my wife, Nancy. My band, whose members travel in their own bus, does the sound check for me before I arrive at each show. After the performance, I ride a new bus with no one but Nancy and my driver, Pee-Wee Johnson, who's been with me for years.

As early as 1966 I decided I'd try to lessen my marathon lifestyle by sometimes bringing the fans to me instead of my always going to the fans. My wife, Shirley, and I got the idea for a musical theme park. Musical theme parks are all over the country today, but thirty years ago the idea of asking country fans to drive to suburban Vidor, a medium-market city, was new.

Today's theme parks provide showers and electrical hookups for recreational vehicles. So did ours, and it was therefore ahead of its time because recreational vehicles weren't as plentiful in 1966 and other camping facilities weren't as nice. Until then I had never commercially developed a piece of property in my life, and neither had Shirley. We just had a good idea that was ahead of its time, and we relied on some people, who may have inflated the construction costs, to do the work for us.

And, looking back, I realize I was too busy with my career to have the time to build a major tourist attraction. Without taking enough time off of the road, I tried to build a place for me to work off of the road.

I bought several tracts of land that lay side by side on Lakeview Road, not far from my house in Vidor. The first thing I did was build a ranch house on the new land. I spent more than $100,000, which built a lot of house in those days.

By then I had several quarter horses, a few Appaloosas, and some cattle. I had always had a special fondness for quarter horses. One of the most prestigious quarter-horse tracks in the nation is Ruidoso Downs near Roswell, New Mexico. A race named after me was held there for years.

My new spread was named the George Jones Rhythm Ranch.

Many years later, Conway Twitty opened Twitty City in Hendersonville, Tennessee, a suburb of Nashville. He and his family lived on the property, which was also a tourist attraction. I had planned something similar in East Texas.

There is no telling how much money I spent building a performance stage, grandstands, and rodeo grounds. There was the cash I laid out, along with the money I missed because I passed up performance dates to oversee the construction of my theme park.

On July 4, 1966, three years before man walked on the moon, I stepped foot on an outdoor performance arena intended to offer the world's best country music on a regular basis.

I've never been too good with money. I've always been able to earn it better than manage it. And I've always had a hard time saying no to people who needed it. A doctor once said I had deep-seated guilt about prosperity—that I felt unworthy. I don't know if that's true. But there has to be an explanation for the casual approach to money I once had.

There are all kinds of stories around Nashville about me getting drunk and throwing cash out the car window or flushing it down the toilet. That's something I don't want to believe, but I suppose if there's that much smoke there has to be a little fire. I probably did that a time or two.

Merle Kilgore said he once saw me get drunk and flush money down the toilet, then decide I should flush the empty whiskey bottle too. He said I threw it into the toilet, and the bottle shattered the commode. Water, he said, ran everywhere.

As far as my George Jones Rhythm Ranch grand opening, well, you never realize how many relatives, relatives of relatives, friends, and friends of friends you have until you have tickets for sale. They all want a free one. And everybody in the world seems to have cousins who want them too.

Those folks just seemed to come out of the woodwork, and I couldn't say no. I gave away about as many tickets to my grand opening as I sold. But still I made money because the debut was a financial success.

The talent was Lefty Frizzell, Merle Haggard, and several local acts. I had to pay all of them, as well as my own band, because I performed too.

And to all of those folks who believe I don't show up for shows, let me say that I was on hand for the very first, very last, and all shows in between at the George Jones Rhythm Ranch. That's because there was only one.

Dust collected on the grandstands, which were never used again after Independence Day, 1966. A sign that said CLOSED FOR THE SEASON was hung in a ticket booth. The season is still under way.

Each performer was paid, then Merle and I and our bands took off. We went to a motel where Merle dragged out a reel-to-reel tape recorder and played a new song that he said would be his next release. It was called "I'm a Lonesome Fugitive," and it came out five months later. It became Merle's first number-one record.

Not too long ago some of the old Jones Boys were talking to Tom Carter, who helped me write this book, about watching Merle thread his old-fashioned portable recorder to get their opinion of his tune. My band and I were probably the first people outside of Merle's organization to hear the song, so we observed history in the making.

But I wasn't thinking that way on July 5, 1966. By then all of the fireworks had been exploded and the nation had gone back to work. I should have done the same thing.

Instead, I went drinking. Somebody said I left home and didn't return for four days, but that isn't true.

I was gone for about four weeks.

Shirley had people looking for me everywhere. Pappy Daily was having a fit because I missed a recording session and no telling how many show dates. My band members, who were paid by the day, were unhappy because they missed so much work. All these years later I don't remember specifically where I was for that month or so. I mostly just floated around Texas on my earnings from the big Fourth of July show.

I was too often gone, and too often drunk, to fully realize the first signs that led to my second divorce. Don't get me wrong. I knew Shirley was unhappy. We argued a lot, and when she moved to Nashville, she only lasted three months before returning to Texas and her friends and relatives. She suspected there were other women, and there were. One-night stands were a way of life for my friends and me in those days. Shirley once caught me in the backseat with a gal outside a Texas honky-tonk. On more than one occasion, a member of my band took me home after an extended tour because I was too drunk to get from the airport to my house. I was a bad husband and an absentee father to two boys. But no matter what I do now, I can never recover their boyhood years. It's too bad that while they were undergoing a young childhood I was undergoing an old one.

Shirley finally had enough.

I had been taking strong drink for about twenty years and had not realized that the drink was finally beginning to take me. A lot of doctors would tell me years later that I was an alcoholic—that I had a sickness. Such thinking wasn't popular in 1966. Heavy drinking wasn't thought of as a disease. It was thought to be a character flaw. People didn't say with compassion that someone had a drinking problem. They said with disgust that he was a drunk.

I know that's what folks were saying about me.

Two things happened while I was married to Shirley that I can laugh at now, years into my sobriety. But no one was amused at the time.

Once, when I had been drunk for several days, Shirley decided she would make it physically impossible for me to buy liquor. I lived about eight miles from Beaumont and the nearest liquor store. She knew I wouldn't walk that far to get booze, so she hid the keys to every car we owned and left.

But she forgot about the lawn mower.

I can vaguely remember my anger at not being able to find keys to anything that moved and looking longingly out a window at a light that shone over our property. There, gleaming in the glow, was that ten-horsepower rotary engine under a seat. A key glistened in the ignition.

I imagine the top speed for that old mower was five miles per hour. It might have taken an hour and a half or more for me to get to the liquor store, but get there I did. A lot of cars whipped around me on the two-lane highway leading from our house to the store. I wonder if the old-timers around East Texas still wonder about a guy who they swear they saw mowing the concrete.

Another of my stunts has to do with a beautiful wooden fence that surrounded our house. I had had it built myself. I came home once just before dark, stopped my new Cadillac in front of the fence, looked it up and down, and drove through it. Then I turned and drove through it again. And again. And again. In the space of a few minutes, while drunk, I intentionally destroyed thousands of dollars' worth of fence and a new Cadillac.

All of my valuable livestock got out. I was sound asleep on my living room couch the next day when my brother-in-law Dub woke me and demanded that I help round up the animals. I was too sick and too ashamed to help, but I did it anyhow because I don't think I ever told Dub no.

Those are just two of the many reasons I was divorced. Here is one thing that wasn't a reason.

I didn't shoot J. C. Arnold.

For years, numerous publications about me have talked about my shooting Arnold in the ass with a shotgun after catching him with my wife. The publications have also said that I later took Arnold to a doctor myself and paid the physician to dig buckshot out of his butt. Many said that I paid the doctor additional money to cover up the incident.

When Tom Carter interviewed many of my old cronies for this book, even they insisted that I had shot Arnold because I was jealous over Shirley.

Arnold, Shirley, and I were in a small business together. When I was gone, as I frequently was, Arnold and Shirley became "close." I spoke to them about their situation, and I spoke harshly, to put it mildly. But all of my wrath came as words, not as buckshot.

I wasn't served any divorce papers. Shirley and I called her lawyer to our house, and I told him to give her what she wanted. I didn't think she asked for enough, so I gave her more. Nancy recently found a copy of my old divorce papers. They show that Shirley got that new ranch house plus three other houses we owned in Vidor. I had fifteen thousand dollars in cash and savings bonds, and I forked that over. I had a quarter horse that I gave her, a couple of cars, our house in Florida, and my touring bus. I even gave her all of my band equipment. I was earning some songwriting royalties at the time, and I gave half of them to her, along with five hundred dollars a month in support for each boy.

The only reason I didn't give her more was because I

had no more to give. After all, to hear her tell it, she had given me the best years of her life. And that was true.

I moved to Nashville as an established recording artist and a failed man. I had made a ton of money by the standards of the day and was essentially starting all over again. I went from life at the George Jones Rhythm Ranch to living with Billy Wilhite at the Executive Inn. We had a two-bedroom apartment that was okay. But it was no more than a glorified closet compared to what I had owned in Texas. I started drinking virtually every day.

I began each day with Bloody Marys to get rid of the previous day's hangover. I ended each with Jim Beam to guarantee the next day's hangover. Night after night, when I wasn't on the road, Billy helped me up the stairs. We were two men in midlife living like roommates at school. Billy remembers that each time he put me to bed he struggled to remove my boots, which I made difficult by bending my toes. He then took his fist and clobbered my foot. I straightened my foot, and the boots came off.

That's a pretty simple recollection. It illustrates how I was searching for any little thing that, in those troubled days, might make for a smile.

There are certain days that will always stand out in people's minds. Most folks can remember where they were or what they were doing when they heard that President John F. Kennedy, Martin Luther King, Jr., or Elvis Presley had died.

I have a vivid recollection of where I was when I first heard that I had lost my blood. That's what they called it back then—losing your blood—when you lost a close relative.

I was playing a little town in Michigan on September 6, 1967, when my sisters Helen and Ruth called before the show, which was at an outdoor park. They said they had tracked me down through Pappy Daily, and that I should come home.

"It's Daddy," Helen said. "He's in a coma or something. We've had to put him in the hospital."

I drove to Detroit, where I caught the first plane for Houston. I drove from the airport to the hospital.

I told you earlier how my dad never drank until after the death of my sister Ethel. After that, he had as much of a problem with alcohol as I did later.

I was braced with booze when I went into the hospital room where Dad lay surrounded by Helen, Ruth, Herman, Dub, and a nurse. I stood there, drunk and dumbfounded, listening to the weakening breathing of the man who had sired me. Before long I noticed that he and I were the only people in the room.

Old friends and relatives I talked to while writing this book said that my grief was too much to bear and that I tore up Dad's hospital room as he lay dying. My memory isn't the greatest, but that simply isn't true either. Believe me, I knew what it was like to get angry and tear up a room. It required a lot of inner fury and hostility.

I was hurting too much to be hateful.

It's funny what will go through your mind when your flesh and blood, who once would have done anything to help you through this world, is leaving it—and you're powerless. During the long hours on the propeller plane from Detroit to Houston and the car ride to Dad's bedside, I might have remembered that fine physical specimen of a man who could once chop an entire forest one tree at a time. Over the years he no doubt had toppled thousands of pounds of lumber.

Yet the whiskey got him ounce by ounce.

In his final days there were several problems. But one doctor stressed the hardening of arteries from the years of drinking. He said they were just too destroyed to be replaced.

"If only I had seen him sooner," he said to me.

If only I had been told about my dad's decaying condition, the doctor would have seen him sooner. I would have seen to that. But nobody told me anything until it was too late. My own family kept a lot from me back then. Years later they told me they thought I was drinking too heavily to handle the truth about a lot of things.

And yet I'm sure I was proud of how my dad, when he'd get sober for weeks, would work with the same spirit he had when he brought up eight kids as a common laborer. He once took a job selling Standard Coffee door-to-door. How hard must it have been for a man who had lived through the Depression to knock on folks' doors and ask them to buy coffee when he knew some couldn't afford light bread? But he never complained, and he became one of the most successful route salesmen in Standard's history.

My dad couldn't have raised a big family in the wilderness unless he'd been savvy, and he never lost that quality. One of his last jobs was as a door-to-door sewing machine salesman. He earned a twenty-five-dollar commission for each machine he sold with a five-dollar down payment. So he made customers' down payments

Me at age four.
Author's Collection

I was six years old when this shot was taken of me with my neighbor, Mrs. Hodge, in Saratoga, Texas.
Author's Collection

My dad,
George Washington Jones,
in 1945. *Author's Collection*

My late mother, Clara,
in 1974. *Author's Collection*

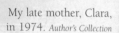

My parents, George Washington and Clara Jones, during a Christmas season celebrated after my brothers, sisters and I were all grown up.
Author's Collection

By age twelve I was a minstrel on the streets of Beaumont.

Author's Collection

As a teenager I sang in a beer joint with a guy whose last name was Smith. *Author's Collection*

Dalton Henderson joins me as I pose with the fiddle when I was seventeen. He worked on my first radio show on KTXJ in Jasper, Texas. *Author's Collection*

Here I am, age
seventeen, in
downtown
Nashville.
Author's Collection

Eddie, *left,* of Eddie
and Pearl, joins me
in singing for "the
Kitty." Fans were
asked to put money
in the wooden
kitty's mouth as our
pay for playing.
Author's Collection

I'm getting ready to visit my sister Loyce while on leave from the Marine Corps in February 1952. *Author's Collection*

In the service I managed to find time to entertain my fellow marines. *Author's Collection*

Here I'm in Galveston, Texas, during a military leave in the early 1950's. Note my style: swimming trunks and street shoes. *Author's Collection*

I'm standing beside a 1951 Packard. The car was about five years old when I began driving from show to show for Starday Records and, in order to obtain engagements, I had my name and phone number painted on the car. I owned the one shirt seen hanging in the window. *Author's Collection*

My first publicity photograph for Starday Records, 1955.

Starday Records

Here are some photos from my early publicity sessions for Starday. *Starday Records*

Here is a publicity shot taken in the mid-1960's. *Starday Records*

George Riddle, *left*, joins Patsy Cline and me to pose for one of the last photographs ever taken of Patsy. This was in Kansas City, Missouri, where we had gone to do a benefit show for disc jockey Cactus Jack McCall. Patsy died in a plane crash hours later en route to Nashville. *Charlie Dick*

Me with Pappy Daily and Mr. and Mrs. Gabe Tucker promoting my 1959 Mercury release "Money to Burn." Pappy is lighting comic money for photographers who caught us as we landed in Nashville from Texas. *Author's Collection*

In 1963, George Riddle stands to my immediate right as we play with a house band on one of our many one-night shows. *Judy Mock*

Arlie Duff, who wrote "Y'All Come," joins me backstage. *Author's Collection*

Here, a fan surprised me and got this shot when I was backstage. *Author's Collection*

George Riddle, *right*, sang harmony and helped me drive from show to show in the 1960's. *Judy Mock*

This is Jones Country at its best during a typical concert. *Nancy Jones*

Here, Uncle "Dub" Scroggins and I are standing in Jones Country in 1986. *Helen Scroggins*

A police officer has me in custody during an arrest for driving while intoxicated. I tried to knock away a news camera.

Hallway Productions

I'm at the point of exhaustion during an alcohol and cocaine binge in 1977.

Author's Collection

Here I am drunk onstage at a concert in the early 1980's. *Author's Collection*

After two failed attempts, I finally made it to New York City's Bottom Line club where I met up with Linda Ronstadt, *left,* and Bonnie Raitt, *right. Epic Records*

In 1980, Johnny Paycheck and I worked together on some recordings. *Slick Lawson*

Performing together live at Jones Country, Johnny Cash and I belt songs during a concert. *Beth Gwinn*

for them, took his commission from the company, and put a twenty-dollar profit into his pocket from selling sewing machines that were probably repossessed.

As he lay dying, I thought of those simple little Christmas gifts he had bought me years ago for pennies when pennies were a sacrifice. I would have given a fortune for those gifts when I was in the hospital.

Thirteen months earlier, my parents had celebrated their fiftieth wedding anniversary. I threw a party at my ranch and welcomed all of their old friends from around East Texas, along with their children, grandchildren, cousins, and anybody else who happened upon the place.

My parents were proud, and worried, about the success I was having. They were glad I was getting a name and earning a living, but they worried about my safety inside the rough honky-tonks. Mama had always wanted me to sing gospel songs.

So on my parents' special day I invited Sister Annie and Brother Burl. I couldn't remember the last time I had seen them, but Annie's voice was still a chime unto Jesus as she sang the timeless hymns.

Folks kept hollering for me to sing my jukebox or radio hits, but I never sang one. I celebrated their fiftieth year together by singing only hymns that had lived through the centuries. I remembered that as my dad lay dying.

I was glad I had thrown that party a year earlier, and I knew he was glad too, although he'd never say that to me again.

I remembered affectionately how my dad would

swear, as I had many times, that he would never drink again. Then my mother would find whiskey hidden where she least expected it.

I built a house for my parents down the road from mine in the 1960s. One day we were cleaning their lot and decided to burn a hedge, not knowing that my dad had hidden several bottles inside the bushes. They began to pop and explode like the Fourth of July.

It was funny at the time. But in the hospital, I smiled through my tears as I looked at the only dad I'd ever had, poked full of tubes that weren't doing enough to pump him full of life.

Everybody's dad dies. Everybody's dad wasn't mine. This had to be hurting my mother, brother, and sisters. Why did I feel so alone in the pain?

I'm glad I was able to pay all of Dad's funeral expenses. A simple service was held, and once again the blessed hymns of old were sung. I rode with my brother and sisters in a family car to the Restlawn Cemetery north of Vidor. A day later I was out of state and on-stage. I didn't know what to do, so I did what I knew best.

One of the former Jones Boys remembers that I seemed to be trying to force myself back into the routine that was my helter-skelter life. But forced fun rarely works.

We were coming away from a matinee somewhere in Texas, and I had had a few drinks. For some reason the air-conditioning on the bus wasn't working. We stopped at a light and a semitrailer pulled up next to us. My window was down, and so was the truck driver's. For no reason, I threw my drink into his face. He came out of his cab cussing and screaming while banging on my bus door. He wanted to get ahold of me.

The light turned green, and we left him jumping up and down amid the fumes of a belching diesel engine. Who knows why I did that? Was it just another one of my mindless drunken pranks? Or was it one more attempt to laugh to keep from crying, a way of life that I realize now I had adopted as permanent? Some of the guys in the band said for months after my dad's death I'd get drunk and talk on and on about him. Eventually, they paid no attention to what I said, and I never remembered.

But they did say I frequently talked about my dad's painful struggles to rehabilitate. Three years before he died, his children had him committed to an asylum, where he struggled inside a straitjacket. Can you imagine the humiliation of that strapping man inside that containment? He had whipped poverty, famine, drought, and various other blights with two bare hands. Yet those same hands could not free themselves from woven cotton.

That straitjacket only made him dry. It did little to make him sober. When his hospitalization was finished, his drinking resumed.

And as he lay dying, and as I looked at the dad who couldn't look back at me, I wondered if we had done the right thing. Should we have put him in a hospital for a drinking problem he couldn't control? Was it like putting him in prison for a crime he didn't commit?

Those are the random thoughts that ran uncontrollably through my hurting and confused mind during those awful days and nights. I don't ponder those questions today. I've changed a lot in thirty years.

There are questions I'm still not wise enough to answer, just wise enough to no longer ask.

Chapter 10

My move to Nashville once again raised my desire to have a performance place with my name on it. During the next twenty years I owned various nightclubs and theme parks where my friends and I played.

In 1967 I opened the first Possum Holler, a five-hundred-seat nightclub on Nashville's legendary lower Broadway Street. It was situated in the heart of the tourist district, across the street from the Ernest Tubb Record Shop, next door to the world-famous Tootsie's Orchid Lounge, across the alley from the Ryman Auditorium, then the home of the Grand Ole Opry.

A lot of country entertainers at that time were paying their bands by the day. The Jones Boys wanted to work as much as they could, so they played Possum Holler with and without me when we weren't working the road.

I worked Possum Holler as much as I wanted, but

probably not as much as I should have. But there was hardly ever a shortage of talent inside the old room, which had a high ceiling and was located on the top floor of an old building.

The club was open during the days when Nashville's country stars were an unofficial "family." We hung out together. Today's stars are so reclusive that they work entire tours together and never see each other. In an earlier day stars struggled together financially. Today they're rich by themselves.

Every songwriter in Nashville hung out at Possum Holler. A lot of songs that became hit records were written by, or pitched by their writers to, recording artists inside the smoky dance hall with its scuffed hardwood floor.

On Saturday nights at the Opry, stars did their sets, then walked over to Tootsie's for a beer or two before going back for another Opry show. When the Opry adjourned at midnight, many came to Possum Holler and stayed until closing time.

Billy Wilhite said he remembers seeing as many as twelve famous singers and musicians onstage at once inside my old nightclub. They came to see each other and to sing together. The audience got the benefits.

Those who casually played at various times inside my club included Merle Haggard, Jack Greene, Jeannie Seely, Mel Tillis, Charley Pride, Willie Nelson, Roger Miller, Kris Kristofferson, Carl Smith, Faron Young, Porter Wagoner, Dolly Parton, Webb Pierce, Ernest Tubb, Roy Acuff, Waylon Jennings, and Dottie West. Many brought their bands.

"I think it would be easier to try to think of the stars

who *didn't* come inside that place," Wilhite said, "and I can't think of one from that day and time, unless it was Johnny Cash. I don't think he was ever in there."

Possum Holler had a manager, bouncer, bartender, and four waitresses. The manager and bouncer are dead, nobody remembers who tended bar, and the waitresses, who are now married, won't own up to having worked there.

The Four Guys, a Grand Ole Opry quartet, owned a nightclub of their own at the time. Between sets at their place, they came to Possum Holler to relieve the Jones Boys. Except for the Jones Boys, the Four Guys was the only act who was ever paid. Everybody else just got up and did his or her thing free of charge. Many acts came to Possum Holler just to try out a new song on the crowd.

Merle Haggard released "Branded Man," "I Threw Away the Rose," and "Sing Me Back Home" the year I opened Possum Holler. He and his band, the Strangers, sang each tune inside the club.

Three years earlier, Dottie West became the first woman in country music to win a Grammy Award, with "Here Comes My Baby." She sang that song many times at Possum Holler.

For all of that talent and stargazing, no customer ever paid more than a five-dollar admission charge.

Possum Holler not only captured the stars of Nashville, it captured their spirits. The music business today is virtually run from 9 A.M. to 5 P.M. by businessmen, lawyers, and accountants. Its songwriters write on schedule, not necessarily on inspiration. The Nashville of the 1960s was a fun-loving, mischief-making paradise for a bunch of kids in adult bodies who didn't want to grow up. We made music for money. We had fun for a living.

Jimmy Dickens, one of country's biggest stars of the 1950s and 1960s, came into the club one night when he didn't know he was being followed by Roger Miller. Roger was a giant star. He had won five Grammy Awards just two years earlier. Miller was short, but Dickens was much shorter.

Without saying a word, Roger eased a hundred-dollar bill from his billfold and held it over Dickens's head.

"One hundred dollars to the man who can whip my little brother!" he yelled. Roger had pulled that stunt at many places, and it never failed to get a laugh. It brought the house down at Possum Holler.

Country stars used to have publicity pictures that were eight-by-ten-inch glossy prints of themselves with giant smiles. We never used the mood shots that are popular today.

One of the pinball machines had a girl in a bikini as part of its flashing sign. The likeness of a muscular man stood next to her. Someone cut out Ernest Tubb's smiling face from his publicity photograph and pasted it over the muscular guy's face. When a player's ball hit the button that made the bikini glow, Ernest's grinning face also lit up.

Ernest's biggest hit was "Walking the Floor over You." The refrain began, "I'm walking the floor over you, I can't sleep a wink, that is true." Someone changed the words and pasted them in a circle next to Ernest's face. The new words said, "I'm walking my winky to the floor with you."

Such mindless mischief told of an earlier, more fun, more innocent Nashville.

We never ran any drink tabs at Possum Holler. First of all, I didn't feel right in charging my friends. And I didn't want to run tabs on the tourists because I didn't know them. I would have had a hard time collecting because credit cards weren't so common thirty years ago. Our customers paid in cash, and they paid for their drinks by the round.

But not one guy. When the bartender turned away, this customer took off, leaving nothing but an empty glass. Well, almost nothing.

"I came in here to have a drink because my mouth was hurting, but the drink didn't help a bit," said a note he left. "I know now what the problem was."

He had left his false teeth on the bar.

Country stars used to come to Possum Holler for a few belts before getting on their bus or airplane for the long journey to their next show.

One night Billy Wilhite, Roger Miller, and I got pretty well oiled and barely got out of the club in time to catch a flight. We were seated in first class, where we were talking about how well someone had sung at Possum Holler. We had a few more drinks.

The next thing I knew Roger was talking to the flight attendant. The next thing I knew he was talking on the intercom.

"May I have your attention, may I have your attention, please?" Roger said. Each passenger grew quiet, thinking he was hearing the pilot's voice. "Engine number one has just gone out," Roger continued.

People gasped.

"Engine number two has just gone out," Roger said.
Folks were really scared.

"Engine number three has just gone out, engine number four has just gone out," Roger went on.

Someone yelled that the airplane only had two engines.

"This is a recording, recording, recording, recording . . ." Roger said.

He then stepped from the first-class section into the main cabin. Roger had had his own network television show, and everyone on board recognized him. They knew instantly that they had been taken, and they loved it. They actually applauded.

"And now, ladies and gentlemen," he said, "I'm going back to my microphone, where I'll be joined by the great George Jones."

The passengers clapped, and at thirty thousand feet Roger and I sang a duet into a static-filled microphone. Then Roger invited everyone on board to visit Possum Holler when they were in Nashville.

Can you imagine what the Federal Aviation Administration would say about such carrying on today?

The original Possum Holler was open only a few months, but they allowed years' worth of good times.

The late Roy Acuff, even three decades ago, was the undisputed king of country music. He brought dignity to our industry, and everybody, fans and performers alike, knew it. I don't think I ever saw him when he wasn't wearing a coat and a necktie.

Everybody called him Mr. Acuff. None of the other men ever called any of the other men in country music "Mister."

One floor below Possum Holler sat Mr. Acuff's famous "Roy Acuff Exhibits," a museum containing his first fiddle, photographs from his Hollywood movies, posters from the time he ran for governor, and much more, including shining trophies galore. Mr. Acuff was so proud of that place that he was known to hand-polish the exhibits himself.

Then a commode backed up inside Possum Holler and leaked into one of Mr. Acuff's trophy cases below.

Mr. Acuff had visited Possum Holler as much or more than anyone else. He was always great about signing autographs for its customers. I'm positive he hated to see it close. But he owned the building, and he owned his prized exhibits.

He was as calm as calm could be when he told Billy that we would have to close the doors to Possum Holler.

"But why, Mr. Acuff?" Billy asked. "You love this place."

"I know it, son," he said, "I know it. But we just can't have turds inside my exhibits."

The doors were locked forever that very night.

My touring continued before, during, and after my ownership of Possum Holler. I've told millions of people in thousands of crowds that as long as the fans want to see me, I'll be on the road. That, and the fact that I haven't wisely managed my money, is why I'm still out there today.

I look at guys like Buck Owens who were smart in investing their money. Sometimes I envy the way they stay home. I'd be lying if I told you that there aren't plenty of times when I'm bone tired and, at sixty-four, want to spend my evenings listening to a crackling fire at home instead of the whine of bus tires a thousand miles away.

But in the same breath I'd have to tell you that the music I make for the people can't be any better than the music of their applause. There is nothing like twenty thousand people rewarding you for a three-minute song. It is the world's highest natural high.

That's why I was in Kansas City, Missouri, for still another show in still another town less than twenty-four hours after the Possum Holler closing. We drank a lot during the club's last night of business and kept right on during the all-night and next-day drive from Nashville to the show.

I was plastered when I went onstage.

The Jones Boys and I were part of a package with various big country stars. I had sung three songs when I decided to do some impersonations. I used to like to do them when I'd been drinking.

On this particular night, I impersonated Johnny Cash. I told the crowd that Cash would sound like this if he were drunk. Then I proceeded to lower my voice and stagger around the stage, acting like I was Cash and drunk.

The drunk part required no acting.

I intentionally reeled toward the drums and unintentionally got my feet tangled. Drunk, I fell over an amplifier and off the back of the stage. Thousands of people saw me.

The crowd knew I had pretended to be drunk to cover the fact that I was.

Backstage people were running to help me as I picked

myself off the concrete floor. I was hurting. Because of the curtain I couldn't see, but I could hear, the audience. People were laughing at me.

So I didn't go back out.

People began to boo and holler for George Jones, and the Jones Boys tried to settle them down by playing an instrumental. It didn't work. James Hollie, who played bass guitar for me for fourteen years, came backstage, and I spoke before he could make a sound.

"Say one word," I told him, "and you're fired!"

"But . . ." he said, and that's as far as he got.

"You're fired!" I said.

By then the band was filtering off one member at a time. I stood there rubbing my injuries and fired each one as he passed me. I can't count the times I've gotten drunk and fired the band for a bad, or for no, reason at all. I always rehired them the next day, and they came to expect it. When a new player joined, he often asked if I had really meant to fire him when I'd been drunk. After a while, he stopped asking. He just knew that come the next day he was supposed to assume that my tantrum from the night before was forgotten.

"All of you sons of bitches are fired at once," I said to one group of players when the three Adams brothers were a part of the Jones Boys.

"No we're not," one argued.

"Yes you are, you're fired, now get out!" I hollered.

"Bullshit, you can't get rid of all of us like that," one said.

"The hell I can't," I stated.

"Oh yeah, well, then you have to whip us all," one said. "And even if you could whip us all, we'd show up at the next show. If you hire another band, we'll set up our equipment in front of them and play louder."

"Goddamn," I said, "I got a band I can't even fire."

I was drunk, of course, and one of them said I started to cry.

Through the years there have probably been about two hundred Jones Boys. Because we worked, traveled, and lived so closely together, they came to know me pretty well.

I don't think that was ever more evident than one night when the band and I played somewhere in Texas and then rode over to Houston. As you know by now, I sometimes got mean when I drank. I got meaner when I drank and took diet pills.

The band and I played Dewey Groom's Long Horn Ballroom, and I was drunk and full of pills. I felt like I could whip the crowd and offered to do it.

"And if you don't like it, piss on you," I said into the microphone.

The place was filled with drunk and tough cowboys. Two or three came over the footlights onto the stage, but I was long gone.

James Hollie and some of the other guys had already begun taking down their instruments, wanting to get out before the place erupted into a brawl. The band used the four chrome legs from the steel guitar to defend themselves against some angry crowd members as they backed off the stage and out the door.

Amphetamines were very popular among Nashville musicians in the 1960s. One variety was yellow, and we called those pills "old yellers." Another was speckled, and we called those "speckled birds." Another was black,

and we called those "black beauties." Another was nicknamed "L.A. turnarounds." The joke was that you could
take one in Nashville, drive to Los Angeles, and turn
around and drive back without sleep.

Those pills gave their user artificial energy, making
him feel peppy even if he was exhausted. One Nashville
doctor prescribed them for most of us. A lot of hit songs
were written, and a lot were recorded, by musicians taking those pills.

Ralph Emery said one time that half of Nashville's
songwriting awards should be shared with that doctor
who handed out those pills in the 1960s and 1970s,
before Nashville's amphetamine use was replaced by cocaine.

I fumbled in my shirt pocket and got two black beauties on that Texas tour that included the Long Horn.
James and some other guys begged me not to take them.
They had seen how violent I could become when I
mixed pills with booze.

I let them plead with me, knowing full well that I was
going to take the pills, no matter what they said. I was
too drunk to keep on drinking. I knew the pills would
"wake me up" enough to let me get a second wind and
continue drinking. I put the pills on my tongue, stuck it
out at the band, and swallowed.

"That's it!" somebody said. "Let's get off this bus before he gets crazy." They figured they had a few minutes
before the pills took effect.

The band got off at a Holiday Inn, and by then I was
feeling the black beauties. I was beginning to level out,
getting that new energy that was overtaking the alcohol-
heavy sleepiness. I stayed on the bus by myself and told

the driver to keep driving—anywhere. He just drove around Houston, and I just drank and let the pills do their thing.

It should be said that there is a big misconception about my notorious years of drunkenness. Some folks think I was on a nonstop party. They think the good times always rolled.

But drinking wasn't always fun. My life, at times, was miserable because of drinking. So I drank to escape the misery caused by the drinking. At that point the loneliness and emptiness would overtake me. It was as if I were running from something, but I didn't know what. As if I were running from someone, but didn't know whom. I used to tell interviewers that I'd felt that way for most of my life.

I was haunted by ghosts and demons of my own making.

When the effects of amphetamines begin to wear off, and the user starts to come down, he often gets depressed. He can take another pill, but a time finally comes when his body is too tired and won't respond to the stimulants.

That's what was happening to me as I rode in the dark with no one but the bus driver, passing Houston's flickering streets. In the back, by myself, I watched the houses go by like the wasted years of my life. I had a hundred crazy thoughts, but none of them helped. I had as many crazy questions, but not one answer.

I finally decided the answers were that there were no answers. So I said to hell with it. I loaded my pistol and fired six rounds into the floor, walls, and ceiling. I reloaded, emptied the pistol, reloaded, and emptied it again.

I was careful not to shoot near the driver, who never said a word. I always seemed to hire drivers who looked straight ahead and never stopped driving when my shooting started.

I ran out of bullets and no longer had noise as my only companion. I was tired and felt totally alone when I told the driver to take me to the motel.

He parked the bus, and he and I went to our rooms.

The Jones Boys and I were off work the next day. I had time to sober up before climbing back aboard the bus to head to the next show. I was the last one to get on board and was ready for all the remarks about the bullet holes.

No one said anything. I didn't know the band had come up with a strategy. Nothing they had ever said had prevented me from going out of my mind when I took a notion. If nothing spoken had worked, perhaps something visual would.

Across every bullet hole the band members had pasted a Band-Aid. They had found children's bandages, the kind with clowns and colors and happy faces on them. That many conspicuous Band-Aids made it look as though the bus had been through a firing squad. But it had only been through one of my fits. I couldn't look any direction without seeing a reminder.

Nobody would let me remove those bandages. So we sat there, me looking at the Band-Aids and everybody else looking at me.

"Where the hell is the driver!" I finally fumed. Somebody went to the front desk to ask about him and discovered that he had never checked into the motel. Clearly he had taken off after he got safely away from the bus and my shooting. None of us ever saw him again.

The band always had its own way of getting even with me when I embarrassed them or made them angry. Six or seven musicians, creative by nature, can come up with some original ways to get back at a man.

And remember that practical jokes have always been a big part of life on the road for country music players.

I remember playing a great one on Charley Pride, the first real popular black singer in country music. We were in Waco and went to the home of a disc jockey after our package show. Like most heavy drinkers, I wanted everyone else to drink when I drank.

I told Charley he'd have to match me drink for drink, and he argued about it. But I was insistent and told him he could keep pace with me or do his drinking somewhere else. Not having my kind of tolerance, Charley got drunk and passed out.

That's when the disc jockey and I crept out to Charley's car. I painted the initials of the Ku Klux Klan on its side.

Realize this was in the middle 1960s, not long after passage of the Civil Rights Act. Remember that a lot of country fans in those days were rednecks and didn't cotton to the idea of a black man singing their music. Charley, in fact, had had two hit records on RCA before the label would even let it be known he was black. Record executives were afraid that the color of his skin would hurt record sales, and they weren't too sure that a bigoted fan wouldn't try to hurt Charley.

Charley staggered out of bed the next morning with a head that would barely squeeze through the door. I told him the KKK had come for him during the night.

He went to the window and saw those white K's painted on his car. He put his hand over his heart and held his chest a lot before we could get him to have some orange juice. He figured out what we had done and called us some names. He would have figured it out sooner if he hadn't been groggy with a hangover.

My own hungover thinking was slow when the band decided to get even with me for perforating the bus with bullets. We rode from Texas to California with those Band-Aids before anybody even talked about taking them off.

I had seen enough Band-Aids and enough of the inside of the bus. I loved the Pacific Coast Highway and the California countryside. So I told the substitute driver to pull over when we rolled past a car lot somewhere in Los Angeles, and I bought a new Buick convertible just so I could absorb the sunshine.

I had pitched another good drunk between Texas and California. I had felt no pain when I laid down the cash for that new car. The next day I was hungover when the band went to the bus and I went to the convertible. I had decided that I would follow the bus in the car and be refreshed by the time we reached the place for the show.

People who have alcohol and drug hangovers are jumpy. They irritate and excite easily.

Unbeknownst to me, the band had fixed a bomb to each of the Buick's eight spark plugs. I turned on the ignition, and they all went off. The blast shook the car, and smoke boiled from under the hood.

There is no telling what went through my hungover mind—perhaps I thought I was in an earthquake. I leaped out of the convertible. I didn't open the door, I sprung over it.

The band members were bent over laughing at me. They had to raise the hood and remove those contraptions before the car would start. Then the George Jones Show went down the road with most members riding the perforated bus and me trailing in the convertible. To this day I've forgotten who drove me.

About this same time I had a week off and Billy Wilhite and I went to Winchester, Virginia, for some rest and relaxation. I think we knew some folks there through Melba Montgomery. We wound up doing some heavy drinking with the police chief and went out with him on his boat. Word got out in that little town that we were there, and soon the chief's house was filled with guests. An all-night party lasted for four days.

One guy got so drunk he mistook the bare yard for a swimming pool. He stood on the banister, about ten feet off the ground, and dove into the "water."

Billy heard the man's neck pop from inside the house, came running, and told me he was dead. A damper was put on the festivities until the guy began to moan.

An ambulance was called, and I went back inside, where no one was mistaking land for wet stuff. They knew the real thing. The next thing I knew, some ambulance driver had me by the arm and said the diver was going to die if he didn't go to the hospital. But the guy wouldn't go unless he was accompanied by George Jones.

A drunk I didn't even know had put his life in my hands!

"All right," I said. "Let's go to the hospital."

They put an IV in the guy's arm, a bottle in my hand, and we were off. I sat in the back with the patient and had no idea what to do. So each time he groaned I just took another swallow. His pain hurt me less than any I've ever felt.

We got to the hospital, and an intern started hollering, "Who's going to pay this man's bill? I can't look at him until I know who's paying the bill."

"How much will it cost to get him looked at?" I asked.

"Probably one hundred dollars," he said.

"Well, here's three hundred," I said. "Now fix him and buy yourself some socks." I'd never seen somebody in medicine work without socks. I thought right then that the intern would never become a brain surgeon.

Billy and I left there on a Wednesday for a Thursday-night show somewhere in New York State. We got to La Guardia International Airport and were supposed to take a connecting flight on Mohawk Airlines, a commuter service. I realized I had time to have a few drinks, catch a later flight, and still make the show on time.

So Billy and I went to the bar.

We eased onto our stools, ordered a round, and watched the plane we were supposed to be on crash. It took off, rose about a foot, twisted, and landed sideways. It flipped onto its side, breaking off a wing. There were no fatalities.

Billy and I stared at each other. I wondered if I was as white as he was.

"Jones," said Billy. "This is one time when your stop for a drink might have actually *saved* your life."

And so it went, the singing while soused from the drinking, drugs, and drudgery of it all. The women, nameless beauties in every town, were as easy as a three-chord progression. Those who visited rock 'n' roll stars were called groupies. Those who came to country shows were called snuff queens. I don't know why.

In 1995 Waylon Jennings was writing his life story, and his editor asked him to name all of the girls he'd slept with. He thought the request was a joke and said so. Any editor who was around the country music industry during the freewheeling 1960s would have seen that asking most male country stars to count the women would be like asking a bricklayer to remember all the bricks.

But there were some women who weren't that way. They had a sincere interest in the music business, a sincere interest in me, or both. Many came to Nashville with an empty purse and a million-dollar dream. They just wanted to make it.

I don't remember where I was the first time someone brought a girl singer who had recorded one song that was a small hit on Epic Records onto my bus. I had heard and liked "Apartment # 9." I'm not sure I even got the singer's name the first time I heard it. I might have been drunk. But very soon I'd join the world in coming to know Tammy Wynette.

Chapter 11

I've been divorced from Tammy Wynette for twenty-one years. During that time I've never said an unkind thing about her publicly. I hate to start now but guess I have to because of this thing about telling the whole truth in my life story.

The reporters hounded me for years after the breakup. I got to where I wouldn't even talk to them. I'm from the country, and in the country a man doesn't kiss a woman and tell, and he doesn't disgrace her reputation, no matter what kind of relationship he does, or doesn't, have with her.

By now you might have noticed that I haven't said many negative things about anybody in this book. I've tried to air no one's dirty laundry but my own. I figure folks have the right to their privacy and to their own freedom of speech. If they choose to use that freedom to talk about themselves, that's fine. They don't need me to do it for them.

I'll point out the obvious—that it takes two to make a marriage work—and after six years Tammy's and mine failed. It was a team effort for a team that went down in defeat.

My wife, Nancy, called Tammy's office twice during the writing of this book in 1995. Nancy, Tom Carter, and I agreed that we should give Tammy a chance to tell her side about our courtship and marriage. Nancy told Tammy's secretary how we felt. Perhaps Tammy could have remembered things I've forgotten. But Tammy never returned Nancy's calls, so I assume she didn't want to participate in reconstructing the history of our lives together. If she didn't want to tell the way she remembers it, I don't feel she has the right to complain about how I remember it.

My heavy drinking was largely responsible for our problems. You don't have to be Einstein to figure that out. But in Tammy's 1979 autobiography, *Stand By Your Man,* she wrote that she knew I had a drinking problem when she met me in 1966. I had made no pretense of slowing down when we were married. I never made a secret about my bouts with the booze.

A woman who married George Jones and complained that he drank would have been like a woman marrying the Reverend Billy Graham and complaining that he preached. I'm glad Reverend Graham is still preaching and just as glad that I'm no longer drinking.

Before I tell you what I did to damage my marriage to Tammy, let me tell you two things I didn't do. I never beat her (although I slapped her once), and I never shot her or shot at her.

There have been published and motion picture accounts claiming both as facts. The simple truth is they're simply not true.

Another story claimed that I once broke the heels off 150 pairs of Tammy's high-heeled shoes, then told her, "Now that will keep you from walking out on me."

Another said that I, while "high on cocaine," placed the barrel of a high-powered rifle in the small of Tammy's back and forced her to stand for hours while I continued to take the drug.

I suppose those kinds of lies sell newspapers and magazines.

But Nancy got in her licks against one of the writers who printed false information about my treatment of Tammy.

In 1983 I opened Jones Country, another theme park I'll talk more about later. This writer came to visit, and Nancy immediately devised a plan. She asked if the writer would like to tour the property on the back of a three-wheeled vehicle. The writer was eager.

The writer climbed on the machine behind Nancy, who handled the controls. Nancy drove the three-wheeler down to a creek and parked in shallow water. Then she took off abruptly.

The machine reared up, throwing the writer into the water.

"You did that on purpose!" the writer screamed at Nancy.

"That's what you get for that crap you wrote about

George Jones," Nancy said, and she drove off, leaving the wet writer on foot.

And now, almost a quarter century after our divorce, some folks still think I'm married to Tammy Wynette. Not a week goes by when one of the Jones Boys isn't asked about Tammy and me. Some folks are really out of touch.

Nancy and I were in bed in the summer of 1994 when the doorbell was rung after midnight. That itself was disturbing since I live behind a high fence with an electronic gate in a house that's several hundred yards from the road. I thought I had privacy.

Nancy went to the door to face a drunk woman. Her hair was messed, her dress dirty, and she had torn her nylons while climbing over our fence.

"I want to talk to George Jones," the drunk said.

"He's asleep," Nancy said angrily.

"Well, wake him up," the woman snapped.

"Hell no, I ain't waking him up," Nancy said. "What do you want? I'm his wife."

"You don't look like Tammy Wynette," the drunk said.

Nancy knocked her off of the porch and called the police.

Billy Wilhite was my road manager when I met Tammy. I asked Tom Carter to ask him and some of the former Jones Boys to refresh my memory regarding Tammy's and my courtship and marriage. Two decades, a river of booze, a bushel of cocaine, and open-heart surgery have done a great deal to eliminate my memory. The following is a reconstruction that is the product of several persons' many memories.

Tammy was married to songwriter Don Chapel when I met her. She was touring and promoting her first hit record, "Apartment # 9," while Don was the front man, or opening act, for her show.

Tammy and I were booked by the same agency, Lavender-Blake, so occasionally our paths crossed on the road. If I happened to play a package show with her, she often did her set, then came to my bus to visit.

At first the visits were innocent.

With repeated visits I came to respect Tammy. She was a country girl who had picked cotton, okra, and beans and had come up hard like me. A lot of folks don't know she was married to her first of five husbands before she ever finished high school. She dropped out and later earned her general education diploma. That's hard when you've got a husband and baby. She even carried water from a spring to wash diapers by hand.

She left her first husband to come to Nashville to try her hand in the music business. Her husband didn't think she had a chance and laughed at her out loud. She arrived in a junk car carrying three babies and a tricycle on the top. After I got to know her, she told me that one of her great motivations to pursue a career in music was having heard me sing duets with Melba Montgomery.

"I know I can do as well as she can," Tammy said. "I know I can."

I came to find out that Tammy had listened to me for years, knew all of my songs, and that her mother enjoyed me. I was drawn to Tammy right from the start.

I hung around Don and Tammy, and nobody seemed to mind. Other times I'd leave my show in a car with Billy while my band took the bus. Billy would drive me to my next engagement. If Tammy was headed for the same place, or perhaps someplace near, she sometimes rode in the car with Billy and me. Other times, I went to one of her shows as an unannounced guest, as I did on a benefit show she performed in Red Bay, Alabama. I liked her and was just trying to be nice.

She and I had worked together the night before the Red Bay show, and I asked her where she'd be the next day. She told me, and I asked Billy to drive me there. I surprised her by showing up, then surprised her more by walking onstage to wave at the audience.

After a show, Tammy would sometimes ride with Billy and me while Don followed in another vehicle with their band. Somebody might wonder why a man would let his wife ride away into the night with two men, one of whom had a reputation for drinking and carousing. I don't know how to answer that question.

But Tammy was not only Don's spouse, she was the star act in their show. In a way you might say she was his bread and butter or meal ticket. After all, nobody was buying tickets to their show to see him. They were coming to see her. And Don might not have wanted to get cross with me since I had recorded some of the songs he'd written, good songs, including "When the Grass Grows over Me." That tune peaked at number two for two weeks on the *Billboard* country chart, where it was listed for seventeen weeks.

Billy, Tammy, and I got a motel room in Woodbridge, Virginia. Tammy and I slept in one bed and Billy in the other. Nothing happened, but I don't think Tammy's old man would have been too amused if he'd known she was between the sheets with me.

In Clayton, Delaware, Tammy did her show, took her part of the money, then took off again with Billy and me. If I wasn't booked to perform on a show with Tammy, she would often introduce me and I'd step from the wings and wave. Then our traveling trio would depart again, leaving Don and Tammy's band to follow.

If I had been him, I wouldn't have let her run around with me.

About this same time Tammy and I first sang publicly together and quite by accident. Tammy had recorded a hit with David Houston called "My Elusive Dreams." I did a package tour with David and Tammy. She usually opened our show, David was the middle act, and I closed.

The schedule called for Tammy to come back onstage during David's set and sing their hit duet. One night David asked her if he could go on first because he had to leave early. Then he asked if she would come out and sing their duet without first doing her solo set.

Tammy refused.

I think she, David, David's manager, and the promoter got into a beef about the scheduling. I thought Tammy was right. She shouldn't have had to walk onstage and do a song with David, take a break, then be introduced as a soloist. That violates show-business etiquette.

David's manager wound up insulting Tammy, and I didn't like that. She refused to sing with David, so I sang with her. In other words, I took David's part on the song for the rest of the tour. That made him mad, but Tammy got to perform her half of their hit duet, and I was glad.

Tammy and her group needed a bus, so I sold her mine before I had another to replace it. I wound up having to lease one. I put myself into economic sacrifice so Tammy could ease hers. The irony is that neither one of us rode the bus I sold her or the one I leased for me when we could avoid it. We instead traveled in that car with Billy.

Tammy and I spent our traveling time singing, laughing, and the like. We weren't doing anything wrong—except for falling in love.

Billy said recently that he remembers my repeatedly asking him if he thought she really liked me, and was he absolutely sure that she did. I was like a schoolboy.

Still, her husband said nothing, at least not to me. And if he said anything to her, she didn't say it to me either.

The silence came to an abrupt halt.

I went by Tammy's house one afternoon when her husband and children were at home. I had had a few drinks and was probably about half drunk.

I went inside and sat down with Don while Tammy stood in the kitchen fixing supper. The next thing I knew she and Don were in an argument, and I was just sitting there quietly drinking. (I found out later that Don was jealous of me and knew I was sweet on his wife.) Their voices raised, and Don called Tammy a "son of a bitch."

That was uncalled for. I felt rage fly all over me.

I jumped from my chair, put my hands under the dinner table, and flipped it over. Dishes, utensils, and glasses flew in all directions. Don's and Tammy's eyes got about as big as the flying dinner plates.

A man should never get between a husband and his

wife, especially if the man has been drinking and especially if the husband has been too.

"Don't talk to her that way!" I told Don. "She's not a son of a bitch!"

"What the hell are you interfering for?" Don said to me. "She's my wife. What the hell business is it of yours?"

I still can't believe what I said next.

"Because I'm in love with her!" I blurted out.

Suddenly, the silence was louder than the breaking of dishes.

"And I'll tell you something else," I continued. "She's in love with me, aren't you, Tammy?"

I've never put anyone so much on the spot from that day to this. Tammy Wynette was at home with her husband and their children at the dinner hour and I had barged in, torn up the place, and declared our love without having discussed it with her. In other words, the first time I told Tammy I loved her I told her husband too.

"Why yes," Tammy at last gasped. "I do love you, George."

That's all I needed to hear. What followed was the first step on a six-year walk that took us down the aisle, through virtually every state in the union, overseas, and ultimately into a divorce court of our own.

"Well, you don't have to take this shit from him," I told Tammy, who was still pretty astounded. "Get the kids, and I'll take you out of here."

She did, and I did.

For years people have whispered that I took Tammy Wynette from behind Don Chapel's back. That's a lie.

I did it in front of his eyes.

Tammy packed enough clothes for her kids and herself for a day or two, and we all took off for a motel.

I left Tammy and her three kids there and went to my own house. I probably thought that Don would call the law on me, and I probably didn't care. I'd had plenty of brushes before.

I don't remember if I was asleep or pacing the floor with excitement when the knock came. I opened the door to face a few cops. They said they had heard I had kidnapped Tammy Wynette, and I told them there wasn't a bit of truth to that—she had come with me by choice. I said she had gone out.

I don't think they were satisfied with the explanation from a man with a cigarette in one hand, a drink in the other, and a reputation in the middle. I don't remember if they had a warrant, but I remember they came into my house. They searched the place for a missing celebrity and her children. I could have told them she wasn't missing. I knew exactly where she was.

The police left, and I called Tammy at the motel.

By daylight I had called my secretary at the time, Shirley Phillips. I told her to book Tammy and me on a flight for Mexico, where we would get her a quick divorce. Then I decided I'd better tell Tammy.

I think Tammy and I took one of her kids to the hospital later that same day. I think it was for an eye disorder. But that night I took them all to my house.

The kids slept in one room, and Tammy and I slept together. Now I don't think it's anybody's business whether or not we made love, and I never would have told. But Tammy chose to tell in her book that we did, so

I'll own up to it. I can't remember that much about it. She said it was the first time, so I'll take her word for it.

I think there is something to be said for the fact that I went all over the country with a man's wife and never touched her until I had the decency to run off with her.

Years later, in her book, Tammy said she loved our first night of lovemaking except for the fact that I had an open bottle of whiskey on the nightstand. Now what would anyone have expected at that time on a table next to George Jones's bed—lace doilies?

We got up the next day, and I confirmed our flight to Mexico. I'd arranged for somebody to deliver a new Lincoln Continental to my house. It sat in my driveway when Tammy and I walked outdoors.

I handed her the keys. I had no engagement ring for her, so I pulled a giant diamond ring off of my own hand and put it on hers. She had the car keys in one hand, the ring on the other; me on the string, and Don in a rage. Friends, it was romance straight out of Shakespeare.

I had given Tammy Wynette one of the most expensive American cars made and a giant ring after having been with her for less than twenty-four hours. Little did I know that I'd still be giving, and giving, and giving several years after a divorce that was still six years away. That thought never crossed my mind on that romance-filled morning. I might have been hungover from booze, but I was definitely drunk with love.

We flew to Mexico City, and Tammy was divorced from Don Chapel before sundown. We thought.

We were higher than the clouds on the return flight to Nashville. I was thirty-seven years old. Nothing is more exciting than young love at any age.

Tammy and I returned to a city that was waiting on us. The fact that two people had run away had been leaked to a few hundred thousand.

TAMMY WYNETTE LEAVES HUSBAND FOR GEORGE JONES, screamed a headline in the *Nashville Banner*. I was later told that the *Banner* was affiliated with the Associated Press and that the story of Tammy's and my escapade appeared in newspapers all over the country.

I hated seeing my private life splashed all over the press, but I'd seen it many other times. Besides, it didn't matter because Tammy was divorced by the time the story hit the streets.

"Oh no I'm not," Tammy cried.

She had called her lawyer to tell him about getting the divorce. He told her that wasn't legal in Tennessee. Tennessee, he went on, was one state whose courts didn't recognize Mexican divorces.

If I had known that, we could have spent another night dodging the law at my Nashville house. I had gone to Mexico as the first step toward getting a wife, and all I got was a plane ride and a few tacos.

"See if I'll ever turn over a man's dining room table for his wife again," I teased Tammy. "And the next time I run away with a man's wife she can walk."

If I'd had a crystal ball I'd have quit right there. I should have taken Tammy home, apologized to Don, and given him a gift certificate to a furniture mart for a dining room table. And I could have told Tammy there was no charge for the forty-eight-hour use of the Lincoln and diamond.

But not me. I was in love. I really thought I was.

I was served the legal papers naming me a defendant

in an alienation of affection suit. I didn't know what that was. I thought "alienation" meant "alien," which I thought was somebody from another country. Did they think I was from another country because Tammy and I had shacked up one night in Mexico?

I soon found out differently.

Tammy got her share of legal papers too. Don sued for divorce, naturally, and he sued on the most serious grounds of all—adultery. I didn't think that was fair. Tammy wasn't wearing his ring the first time she and I made love. I had taken it off her personally.

I hated the fact that my behavior, motivated by romance, was creating problems for Tammy. I had tried to come into her life to improve it. So far, she had undergone a year's worth of trauma during her first two days with George Jones. And I had wound up being publicly recognized as the boyfriend of a woman who was married but didn't want to be.

Then my manager at the time, Bill Starnes, came to the rescue.

He found a lawyer who knew Alabama's marriage laws thoroughly. As it turned out, Tammy's marriage to Don had been illegal. She had married her first husband in Alabama. A person who married in Alabama had to wait one year after his or her divorce before he or she could marry somebody else, unless a judge gave them permission to marry earlier. Tammy hadn't waited long enough, and she hadn't gotten permission from a judge before she married Don. So her marriage to Don was illegal.

She didn't need to get a divorce from a man she had illegally married. That gave the green light for us to get married.

I know all of this sounds like a television soap opera, but so does most of my life.

To put an end to the confusion, Tammy got the idea to tell folks we had secretly gotten married, even though we hadn't. Now wasn't that dumb? News of our "wedding" came out in the press, and people were sending gifts and congratulations. They arrived for Mr. and Mrs. George Jones, and I didn't know who they were for. I have a pretty common name.

Well, the plot thickened.

It seems that Don had made a hobby out of taking candid pictures of Tammy while she was nude. He then sent them to other men around the country, but didn't tell Tammy. She was performing a show one night when a stranger showed her a naked picture of herself. That really made her angry.

I don't remember how I found out about the pictures. But when Tom Carter was doing research for this book, Billy Wilhite told him that Don tried to use the pictures to prevent me from marrying Tammy. Billy said that Don had told him I wouldn't want to marry Tammy after I saw the pictures. I didn't know Billy had been told that. I also didn't know that I indirectly wound up buying the negatives, which were later destroyed.

Billy secretly paid for the negatives with my money and burned the pictures.

It's all so silly. It's all such old news.

Before we were actually married, Tammy was already tired of the press attention that went with being my companion. It seems as though the press was after us all of the time. And the rumors were hot all over Nashville that we might record together, so we were overwhelmed with songwriters wanting us to do their material. It got to where writers I'd never even met would come by the house unannounced. And each time I went to the mailbox there were more song tapes inside than letters. It seemed as though every songwriter in town wanted a cut on what he thought was going to be a George Jones/ Tammy Wynette album.

I told Tammy she could get out of the limelight by moving with me to Florida. I had owned a house in Lakeland for some time. It sat on a freshwater lake and wasn't that far from some fine restaurants and some wonderful deep-sea fishing. I told Tammy I'd take her down there and show her the place. She was glad to go.

I had leased the place to my friend Joe Asher and his wife, so Tammy and I stayed at a motel. I had told Joe that I might be asking his wife and him to move out so that Tammy and I could live there. He understood.

The night before Tammy and I were supposed to view the property, Joe surprised me by dropping by our motel. Now I thought old Joe had been pretty understanding, willing to move out of my house so I could move in. So naturally I said yes when he suggested that we have a drink. Then another. Then another.

I got drunk, and Tammy got mad.

We wound up having a hell of a fight, which we carried out of the room and onto the balcony. Tammy ran down the stairs, and I was right behind her. I was wearing high-heeled boots, which were fashionable at the time, and my heel got caught on about the third step from the bottom.

I fell, broke my hand, wound up in the emergency room, and returned to Nashville with my arm in a cast. I don't remember what excuse I gave folks, assuming I was still bothering to give excuses by then. A lot of folks didn't even ask questions if they saw me with a black eye or one of my limbs in a cast. They had seen that before.

Tammy, to my way of thinking, wanted to spend too much time with me during our courtship and marriage. If I went to the store, she wanted to go along. If I had to go to the studio to overdub a song, she wanted to be by my side.

There is such a thing as smothering a person.

I loved Tammy. I had proved that. But I needed a break. I remember deciding that I wanted to get away for a little while, so I told her I had to go out of town. The truth is that I checked into a Nashville motel. I called an airline to see what time the flight I was supposed to be returning on was arriving. I called Tammy and asked her to pick me up at the airport. Then I called a taxi and planned to get to the airport about the time the flight did.

There was no way Tammy would know that I wasn't on board, I thought.

Tammy went to the airport with James Hollie and heard over the loudspeaker that my flight would be delayed by thirty minutes. I wish I had heard the announcement. I came strolling down the hall with a piece of luggage.

"I'm back," I told her. "My flight has arrived."

"This is the first time I've ever seen a passenger get here before his plane did," Tammy said. "Where have you been for three days?"

The argument was under way.

Such was the stormy and passionate courtship of George and Tammy. And just think, all of the above happened to us even before we were legally married.

Chapter 12

Tammy and I were booked for an extended engagement in Atlanta, and I suggested that we slip over to Ringgold, a tiny town on the Georgia-Tennessee border where they provide quick marriages to out-of-state residents. Marriage is one of the town's principal industries.

Other Nashville acts wanting to avoid publicity have gotten married there. Dolly Parton was recording for producer Fred Foster on Monument Records when she married Carl Dean in a quick ceremony at Ringgold. Foster had told Dolly he didn't want her to get married because the publicity would jeopardize her recording career. So she and Carl sneaked off, and the press and Fred were never the wiser for a long time.

Tammy and I had that same kind of secrecy. We tied the knot on February 16, 1969. The problem was that everybody in Nashville thought we had been married for months. We drove back to Atlanta for our show and broke the news to the Jones Boys.

"We're married," I told the band on the bus.

"We know," they said. "That's why we gave you gifts last August."

"Yes," I said, "but we were just kidding. We've actually been playing house. But we really did get married today."

It was so outrageous that it seemed totally logical to my band. We did the Atlanta shows, and Tammy and I went to our room. We were still in Georgia when she had some additional news for me.

She was pregnant.

I remember that her announcement made me feel we were starting the marriage on the right foot. I was going to be a dad again at thirty-eight. Maybe, I thought, I could be a real father, instead of an absentee one, as I had been for my boys by Shirley and my daughter by Dorothy.

I walked on air for a few days but then had an abrupt letdown when Tammy miscarried.

Not long afterward we moved to my house in Lakeland, which I had been using as a vacation home and a place to get away from the music business. We became friends with Cliff and Maxine Hyder, our next-door neighbors, and Billy Wilhite immediately went to work hustling a deal that would enable Tammy to own her own trailer park. Our intention was twofold: First, we wanted a place for some of Tammy's folks to live. Second, we wanted an investment in Florida's tourist industry and retirement community. I thought we could do well financially by providing some of those folks a place to live. My hunch proved to be right.

Billy cut a deal with a mobile home manufacturer whose terms said that Tammy and I would do a show for him on Monday or Tuesday night, our usual free nights, and he would give us a mobile home as compensation for each show we played. We put the trailers on fifteen acres that I bought for $100,000 and called the park Tammy's Courts.

Billy had pictures of him and me digging a ditch for sewer pipes and water lines by hand, but he lost them in a house fire a few years ago.

But there we were working, building, and investing. The press called Tammy and me "Mr. and Mrs. Country Music." I felt like "Mr. and Mrs. Suburbanite."

We owned residential and commercial real estate. We became a fixture of the neighborhood, whose residents treated us like people, not celebrities. I loved that.

I went to a sporting goods store and bought bats and balls for every kid in the neighborhood. We had exciting softball games with stiff competition. I became the kids' buddy, and I don't think half of them even knew, or cared, what I did for a living.

Cliff, who has Lou Gehrig's disease, had been withdrawn before Tammy and I moved next door. He is a former naval officer who was apparently demoralized when he lost some of his physical fitness. But he really came out of his shell after we became friends. He even became the starting pitcher for my softball team.

Later, he, Maxine, Tammy, and I regularly went deepsea fishing or out to eat. Cliff designed personalized boards for a parlor game called Aggravation, and the four of us became regular opponents.

Dog racing is a big deal in Florida, and we frequently went to the track. I even started an antique car collection.

It was so wonderful to be out of Nashville and have a life that bordered on normal. More and more I temporarily drank less and less. I might have a glass of wine or two with a meal. Maybe a beer now and then. Except for a rare binge, I wasn't drinking heavily and for the right reason: I didn't want to.

At that time, I was happier than I'd ever been.

Contentment wasn't the only reason I was sober more often. Billy, while reminiscing for this book, talked about a trick that Tammy and he played on me to curb my drinking on the few occasions when they saw a bender approaching. I never knew about their conspiracy until years later.

I didn't especially like for Tammy to drink, and I hated for her to get drunk. A couple of times when I was starting to get loaded, Billy and Tammy cooked up a scheme with airline flight attendants. The attendants, who were in on the trick, served Tammy a soft drink, although Tammy had faked an order of vodka and a mix. She began to belt down the decoy drinks, and I became worried about her. My concern put an abrupt halt to my own drinking.

"Don't serve her anymore," I ordered the stewardess. I never failed to look after Tammy on the rare occasions when I thought she might be getting loaded.

That scheme didn't work so well when we traveled on our bus, where I could see what was being poured into

Tammy's glass. So Billy and Tammy put a plant next to her. When I started to get drunk, Tammy would order a mixed drink and Billy would mix the real thing in front of me. He'd hand it to Tammy, then say something to me so I would look in his direction. While I wasn't looking, Tammy would pour her drink into the plant pot.

"I'll have another drink," Tammy would say, and Billy would fix her one. I thought she was belting them down awfully quickly for an infrequent drinker and became afraid she was going to get sick.

I'd order Billy to stop serving her, and I wouldn't drink myself since I had said she couldn't. Looking back, I wonder why Tammy didn't use those tricks more often if she really wanted me to lessen my drinking.

My happiness reached its peak when Tammy told me she was pregnant again. I was a husband and potential father living the sane life. I loved being concerned about the things that never concerned me before, such as how to rid the lawn of weeds or whether it was time to clean the shutters.

I don't think I threw a doozy of a drunk until the fall of 1969, when Cliff, Maxine, Tammy, and I went to Nashville so Tammy could appear on the national Country Music Association Awards show telecast. She was nominated as "Female Vocalist of the Year" for the second consecutive year, and she won. We saw old friends before the show, and I had a few drinks. And then a few more, a few more, and you know the rest of the story.

Alcoholics Anonymous teaches that the alcoholic must "change his playmates and playground" if he is to become sober. In other words, a person who is trying to give up alcohol can't hang around old drinking buddies.

I had been away from them in Florida but fell in with them again during that return to Nashville. I thought I could take a drink or two, but the drinks quickly overtook me.

I wound up getting soused, but I went to the awards show at the old Ryman Auditorium anyway. Tammy wouldn't sit with me, and I don't remember who I eventually sat beside. But I was on my best behavior, and I don't think anybody knew I was drunk. I didn't want to spoil the evening for Tammy, and besides, I was eager for her to accept her award so I could get back to my good life in Lakeland.

Later, my band came to visit Tammy and me in Lakeland. I got drunk and fired them all. Most of them didn't take me seriously because they remembered when I used to get drunk and give them all the boot. They figured I'd hire them back the next day. So they got into the bus and drove back to Nashville and, because I was drunk, I got mad.

I called the police and reported a stolen bus.

The cops picked them up somewhere out of state. I guess it's not hard to find a forty-foot-long, two-tone bus bearing a sign in four-foot letters that says, MR. AND MRS. COUNTRY MUSIC.

I never filed charges, and the whole thing was forgotten as soon as I got sober.

Now it had gotten to where drinking, which had once been so important to me, became an intrusion on my personal happiness. I was having too good of a life on a natural high. I didn't want to interrupt it with booze.

And then I found our dream house. It took a lot of renovation and remodeling, but I have to say that it became my favorite of all the houses I've ever occupied (until the one Nancy and I built in 1994).

The Lakeland mansion, and that's what I eventually made it, had sixteen rooms, including six bathrooms. It, and five acres, were priced at $100,000. I got it for less. (Later, I picked up some land next door, which expanded our holdings to forty-two acres.)

The place had been vacant for a while, so it was in dire need of repair. I told Tammy I'd have it in tip-top shape by the time the baby was born, and I went to work. I tore almost everything old out of the house and replaced it with new. Billy and I rode bulldozers to change the landscape.

And once again, my dream to own a major country music park surfaced. I determined that I would have one like the one I had while married to Shirley, except that it would be bigger and better. I planned to feature the biggest names in country music and figured I'd draw enough people to the theme park to pay for the house while turning a tidy profit.

A lot of folks would be surprised to learn that I enjoy interior decorating. I can walk into a shell with a roof and tell you what it would look like after six months of work. Then I can walk through a furniture store and tell you just what would go with what and in what room.

That's the kind of personal interest, or passion, that I took in Tammy's and my Lakeland home.

At first, she didn't seem too keen on the place, but I didn't mind. I planned on doing all the work and knew that when the place was finished she'd fall in love with it. As far as I was concerned she could lie by the water at our old house, which she loved to do, while I built the new one.

So Billy, some employees, and I worked while Tammy's pregnancy progressed. I vowed that our new child would come home to our new house.

Tamala Georgette Jones lived at our old address only a few days. Then the three of us moved into the big house, which I had named the Old Plantation. By the time we arrived, I had personally overseen the painting, papering, carpeting, and all the rest for every room in that sprawling house.

Tammy and I were still working our one-nighters and extended engagements during this time, as I had to keep up our cash flow to pay for all the physical improvements to our lives. Our booking agent put us into Las Vegas for a week.

We had never worked a swanky Las Vegas hotel as a duo. I wasn't crazy about the engagement because I didn't know how Vegas would accept country music. Remember, this was 1970. I was afraid they'd make fun of the music and of us.

Folks have a right to their opinions, and I could always handle it if they didn't like country music. But I could never handle it if they made fun of it. I took that personally.

Tammy and I had a comedian in our road show at the time named Harold Morrison. He was good. The only time I ever saw him fail to make people laugh was when we played an Indian reservation somewhere in the Southwest. No matter what joke Harold told, the people just stared at him.

After the show, when all of us were signing autographs, an Indian walked up to him and looked him straight in the eye.

"You know," he said, "I watched you and listened closely. I want you to know it was all I could do to keep from laughing at you."

The guy had no idea he was *supposed* to laugh. Harold fell out cackling at the man.

I was more confident in Harold's ability to go over in Vegas than I was in Tammy's and mine. So on the afternoon before our opening night I eased into a casino next door and had a drink to settle my nerves. I eventually got so settled that I couldn't move.

I sat there in a crowd of hundreds all by myself. My name was in six-foot letters on a marquee next door, but my spirits were lower than the casino floor. Slot machines were ringing, and people were laughing and carrying on. There is a special sadness that goes with feeling alone while those around you are having a big time. Then, because you feel alone, you drink to ease the loneliness. That makes you more lonely.

God, I'm glad my drinking days are past.

On this particular afternoon, as the Nevada sunset turned Las Vegas into a flashing wonderland, I knew I was too drunk to go onstage anywhere, especially in a major entertainment center inhabited by the world's best acts. So I stayed at the neighboring casino until after Tammy had started our show without me. Then I slipped into our hotel, up to our room, and went to sleep. I flat-out missed the opening night of a very important booking for Tammy and me.

One Vegas reporter, familiar with my reputation for getting drunk and missing shows, called me "No Show

Jones." I wonder if he thought he was being original. My head was throbbing the next day when Tammy woke me up complaining. Tammy never needed an excuse to nag me about my drinking, and often that was all the excuse I needed to drink.

She went on and on about how I had embarrassed her in front of the hotel manager and some very important press. To make matters worse, the show I had missed was on her birthday.

I let her pitch her fit and went on that night. I made every show for the rest of what became a very successful run.

On the last night, I played blackjack all night and won several thousand dollars. Tammy later said that I got drunk at the table and into a hassle with the pit boss. She said I had a physical struggle with the guy and had to be evicted from the casino.

I don't remember that and am skeptical about the story.

Tammy and I performed mostly one-night shows for the rest of the year. During that time I was able to finish my Lakeland country music park. The mere opening of the park was a victory in itself because I had had to fight city and county officials so hard to get the commercial zoning I needed. Some of the city and county fathers didn't want the park. Their city was growing fast enough as it was, they thought, and they didn't want the additional commerce that eleven thousand visitors would bring every weekend.

I thought their thinking was selfish and backward, and my lawyers had many heated battles with the Lakeland power brokers. Many times I was convinced that they were going to keep their little town the way they wanted it and no country music singers from faraway Nashville were going to improve it. They'd see to that.

I won't bore you with all of the details of the legal wrangling. But the day of the grand opening came at last. I remember standing spellbound in front of a giant sign that said, OLD PLANTATION MUSIC PARK. With the land, construction, landscaping, and legal fees, I had invested a quarter million dollars, a sizable chunk of change back then.

My house, which fans could see from the park, had white antebellum-style columns on the front porch. I put similar columns on the stage of the Old Plantation Music Park. The stage also had red carpet and was illuminated by a chandelier shaped like a wagon wheel.

I wanted the park to be a place where all of my friends in the country music industry would want to play. So I built nice dressing rooms. Most, like me, were accustomed to the cramped and worn dressing rooms of the old dance halls where we often played. And none of us ever had dressing rooms when we worked outdoor shows. So my addition was a nice touch.

The weather is nice year-round in Florida, which is one reason I decided to build the theater there. But I wanted to take no chances on a show being rained out, so built a flat roof over the eleven thousand seats.

I had planted every kind of shrub that grows in Florida, and I had other plants imported that would thrive in the climate. Flamingos and peacocks strolled the grounds. I had small carnival-type rides for the kiddies and concession stands and hot dog and hamburger restaurants around the grounds.

Tammy, by then, had more relatives living at her trailer park, and I moved them off of that property and onto the grounds of the Old Plantation. Some guys have their relatives under one roof. I had mine under several.

Billy Sherrill, one of the most successful record producers in Nashville history, was producing Tammy and me at the time. He flew down for my grand opening, and I was proud for him to see where I was showcasing the music that we made in a Nashville studio.

I'm going to confess that I was worried about opening day. As I indicated earlier, Lakeland, Florida, had never seen anything like the Old Plantation Music Park. And we didn't sell a lot of advance tickets. Country music used to attract mostly working people to its concerts. Many of those folks lived from paycheck to paycheck and had no spare money to buy tickets in advance. They bought tickets to a country show on the day of the show. Promoters called them the "walk-up" crowd, and they comprised the majority of any country music audience in the 1960s and 1970s.

Well, we had about twenty thousand walk-ups. That meant we turned away about ten thousand people, not counting the few advance tickets we had sold. Traffic to get into the park was backed up for miles. The sheriff's department had to call off-duty deputies at home to help with traffic control. Television helicopters flew overhead for news coverage.

After all the seats were filled, arrangements were made to put people on the ground. The crowd had anticipated that. Many had come with blankets and playpens. One or two had mattresses strapped on top of their cars.

There were lawn chairs and ice coolers as far as the eye could see.

We sold every scrap of food, and every ounce of liquid, from every outlet on the place.

My country music theme park was a runaway hit!

Conway Twitty joined Tammy and me for the grand opening. He had recently held the number-one slot on the country chart for four weeks with "Hello Darlin' " and had been a pioneer of rock 'n' roll in the 1950s. Conway had had two glorious careers, and folks couldn't wait to see him live at my park.

Then Charley Pride showed up as a surprise guest. Charley was riding high with "Is Anybody Goin' to San Antone," a number-one song that became the biggest of his many hit records. Can you imagine how big the crowd would have been if he had been an advertised guest?

Tammy sang her songs, I sang mine, Conway did his, and then Charley. The four of us, with the Jones Boys, wound up doing gospel songs together, and the crowd loved it. What had been planned as a two-and-a-half-hour show stretched into four and a half.

No one left his seat.

And best of all, I was drunk with success and pride and nothing else.

Eventually, Merle Haggard, Charley Pride again, Johnny Cash, the Carter Family, Loretta Lynn, the Statler Brothers, Tom T. Hall, Jack Greene, and Jeannie Seely played the park, among others. Tammy and I worked it regularly.

I opened my antique car collection to people with paid admission to the park. I had a 1929 Model A Ford, a German Steyr that had been used by Adolf Hitler, a 1936 Chevrolet, a 1940 Lincoln Zephyr, and a 1923 Cadillac that had hardly been driven.

Webb Pierce, who had been one of country music's biggest stars in the 1950s and 1960s, had owned a gaudy convertible that he featured on a record album cover. I forget what kind of car it was, but he paid Western fashion designer Nudie of Hollywood to cover the car's interior with silver coins, sequins, and the like.

I bought a Pontiac that Nudie had also converted. It was a white convertible, and there was a plastic dome to shield the interior. The dome was in the shape of a bubble top like those used by presidents seeking protection from assassins. (Mine wasn't bullet-proof.) Nudie embedded four thousand silver dollars in the dashboard, console, doors, and a part of the floor. The console was actually a saddle.

There was no part of the park that wasn't a hit. And the city and county officials who had fought me while I built it suddenly became my allies. The park was listed in literature published by the Chamber of Commerce. It was touted by the Florida Department of Tourism. Everybody suddenly was in favor of my park. People who hadn't wanted to cook the experimental meal wanted to dine at the banquet of success. But that was fine. I had felt alone while I pursued my dream, and it was refreshing to at last have supporters.

I think that, by now, you get the point of how much I loved the estate that I worked so hard to build. It was my home and a big part of my livelihood.

So why would I destroy it? It makes no sense to me,

and I don't think I did destroy it, not in the manner that's been portrayed in books and motion pictures.

Those accounts indicate that I had been sober for months when, for no reason, I got deliriously drunk.

I don't think so.

I hadn't quit drinking entirely, but when I got drunk, it was always for a reason. Perhaps a bad reason, but a reason nonetheless.

Some accounts have it that I got up one morning in a great mood, went to town, and came back as a raging maniac. Again, I don't think so, although I might have come home with liquor on my breath.

In *Stand By Your Man*, Tammy wrote that I leaped from my bed after having passed out from drunkenness. She said that she and an employee had laid me down. She went on to say that she and the employee fled the house in fear of me but that "for an instant I froze in my tracks." She was referring to a .30-30 rifle she said I had aimed at her back.

"You may run out on me, baby. But you won't run out on this," she quoted me as saying. In the next paragraph, she said she heard the sound of a "loud click," the gun's safety being released.

"Even as I was running the flesh was crawling on my back in terrified anticipation of a shotgun blast," she continued.

Now which was it—a rifle or a shotgun? One sentence claims I was aiming a rifle, and another claims I was aiming a shotgun.

Tammy is from the country. She knows the difference between a rifle, which shoots one bullet at a time, and a shotgun, which shoots hundreds of pellets. Not knowing the difference is like not knowing a BB gun from a water pistol.

Then Tammy claimed I fired a gun at her as she ran across our backyard. Nonsense.

A 1981 TV movie adapted from her book showed me shooting up the interior of the house that I had worked so hard to remodel. The movie showed fixtures splattering in all directions from the force of a shotgun blast.

Folks, it didn't happen.

Tammy also claimed that she sought the help of a two-hundred-pound man with biceps bigger than her waist. I don't think so. If biceps were that big on a man that small, his head must have been the size of a watermelon.

I don't think so.

In actual fact, men in white coats came to the house. They wouldn't listen to a thing I had to say. They had the law on their side. I had my reputation against me.

They put me in a straitjacket in the driveway of my dream home. Some of my employees watched. Thank God the authorities didn't come on a concert day. No telling how many fans would have seen.

I was placed in a padded cell, as if I were a mental patient, for ten days. For the first few days I wore that straitjacket and was fed with a spoon as if I were an infant. Someone helped me use the rest room. You can imagine the humiliation.

Tammy went off on a tour with my band. I couldn't reach her by telephone, and she never came to see me.

I don't remember much else about the time in the hospital, except that I was given a lot of literature about alcohol and intoxication and I took a few tests that made little sense to me. When they let me out, I went straight home. The place was a total disaster.

Remember, there had been ten days for our maids to tidy up.

I returned to broken dishes, glasses, and shattered fixtures of every kind. You'd have thought a tornado had struck the place.

In January 1995, Cliff Hyder, who Tammy says in her book is one of her best friends, did a tape-recorded interview with Tom Carter. Cliff said he wondered if Tammy had ordered our staff to tear the place up so I would think I had made the mess.

I don't know.

I know Tammy would have done almost anything to keep me from drinking, and, as I've admitted, I had been drinking the day she had me hauled away.

I won't hide the things I've done. I think this book's honesty so far has indicated that. But I hate to be blamed for things I didn't do. And I didn't destroy our Florida mansion or shoot it full of holes. And I've never fired a gun at Tammy Wynette.

Chapter 13

The thing I remember most about my ride home from the hospital was that I traveled alone, except for a taxi driver who I'd never seen before and haven't seen since. I paid him and walked by myself into the giant and empty house.

Being by yourself, when you're lonely, is hard anyplace. But it's harder in big surroundings, especially if those surroundings hold memories of better times. My spacious home felt like a hollow mansion made for one.

I missed Tammy and the baby. I missed Tammy's relatives. I missed the staff. I knew I had done wrong in getting drunk, but as I just said, I knew I hadn't destroyed the interior like it was when I returned. I felt like the horrible mess was intentional and wondered how people I trusted could tear up something I loved so much. I had put my money, heart, and soul into the restoration of that house. Then I realized the wrecking had been done to try to teach me a lesson.

"If you get drunk and hurt your loved ones, we're going to hurt the house you love so much" was the unspoken implication.

I'll never know who actually did all of that incredible damage. But I know I didn't, not to that degree.

I wondered why no one was there to meet me. I'd been gone for ten days. My life had been on hold, but everyone else who lived there had lives that went on and largely at my expense. Even from inside the hospital I was the family's principal supporter. On the day I came home, I felt like little more than a walking and talking meal ticket for some folks.

Slowly, by myself, I began to clean the mess. For days, I swept and picked up and repaired quietly.

I bought new lamps, fixtures, and art. I shopped for furniture. I patched the holes in the Sheetrock and painted the patches.

By the time Tammy returned from Canada, it was as if nothing had happened to our beloved estate. The place looked new again. I thought about telling her that I suspected the place had been torn up to make me think I had destroyed it while drunk. But I knew that would only start an argument.

So I welcomed her back to the Old Plantation and told her I was sorry I didn't get to accompany her on her trip.

I was sober for several weeks, and then I pitched another drunk for two or three days. My point is that although I continued to drink, I was drinking less quantity, and drinking less frequently, than I had since my first swallow as a teenager. I failed to see why Tammy didn't encourage me when I was sober instead of pouncing on me when I slipped. Old habits die hard. I was putting mine to a hard but definite death. I really think I could have quit altogether if I'd had proper support. After all, I eventually did.

But my gradual weaning from the bottle wasn't good enough for Tammy. She wanted me to be instantly sober forever.

So she left me.

I came home one day, and she and the kids were gone. The staff acted like they didn't know where they were. Then the Lakeland newspaper reported that Tammy Wynette had returned with her children to Nashville, where she had sued George Jones for divorce.

If somebody hadn't pointed out that story to me, I might have been the target of an uncontested divorce. I was never served divorce papers. Maybe Tammy could have convinced a Nashville judge that she didn't know my whereabouts. Tammy was a persuasive person who enjoyed the good reputation in our marriage. I had the reputation of being the undependable drunk.

I traced Tammy to the house we had in Nashville. I flew up there unannounced and knocked on her door. I thought that would prove how sincere I was about someday quitting liquor forever, if she would help me. And I thought it would show her how much I loved her, Georgette, and Tammy's daughter, Tina, who I had adopted.

Tammy showed me off the porch. I don't think I even got inside the house before she told me to go away. So I did, to a bunch of Nashville bars, while Tammy went back to Lakeland.

Many doctors and counselors would tell me during

the upcoming years that I was sick with a disease called alcoholism. As I indicated earlier, I had always thought that heavy drinking was a moral failure, not a physical or mental sickness.

To this day I'm not ready to take a stance either way. Maybe some folks are alcoholics and others are just voluntary drunks. Maybe some folks drink due to body chemistry and others due to their lazy characters. Maybe some have drinking problems, while others have problems enough to drink.

If you have someone in your life with a drinking disorder for whatever reason, you're not going to help that person, or yourself, by being insensitive. Or by nagging the person. Or by leaving when he or she is down.

That's hateful behavior.

I've seen hate change many things for the worse. I've seen love change everything for the good.

I didn't need to hear that I was a drunk, not when I was trying so hard to quit and not when I was going through extended sober spells. My self-esteem was already low from the guilt I was constantly heaping on myself. I had watched my daddy damage his family by boozing, and I resented him for it. Here I was doing the same thing. But he never tried to quit like I was trying. All I needed, I know now, was a dedicated helper.

I returned to our Nashville home, but Tammy was still in Lakeland. I followed her again.

I walked into the Old Plantation, and before Tammy could say a word I told her I'd try harder than ever to quit drinking forever. I pleaded some more, and in a day or two she withdrew her divorce petition.

After that, I'll bet I was totally sober for a year.

For George Jones to be sober for a year was incredibly significant. I'd never dreamed I'd make such a giant stride toward the end of my boozing. I actually thought I had it whipped. After a month or two, I didn't even think in terms of getting drunk. If I got upset, I might get angry, sad, depressed, or whatever. But, thank God, I didn't get drunk.

I was making all of my personal appearances with Tammy, and I even gained some weight. I looked healthy. Smoking was my only bad habit.

And I didn't drink for the right reason—I didn't want to. I've talked about the damage I had done to my career, marriage, and fatherhood. But I wanted to quit for yet another reason. My drinking had hurt virtually every friendship I'd ever had.

I got drunk once and threatened to whip my buddy Cliff Hyder. Another time I was drunk and showed up on Ralph Emery's radio show unable to speak without slurring my words. Ralph and I had been friends for years, during which time he had helped my career. I regretted the way I had embarrassed him and myself. I once promised Merle Haggard that I'd do a show for him if he'd do one for me. He did his show, and I missed mine because I was drunk. I could go on and on about how drinking had hurt my personal and professional relationships.

One of the worst things I ever did was against Porter Wagoner.

Tammy and I were playing the Grand Ole Opry. The show is run in segments, and Porter was the host of our segment. My mind became extremely altered when I mixed liquor with diet pills, and I often got very aggressive and hostile. Flat-out mean. I was drinking and taking pills when I saw Porter head for the men's room at Ryman Auditorium.

I had gotten it in my head that Tammy and Porter were seeing each other romantically. I followed Porter into the rest room and saw him standing at the urinal.

I walked up behind him and shouted, "I want to see what Tammy's so proud of!"

Then I reached around and grabbed his dick. I twisted hard.

Porter began to jump and wave his arms. His sequin suit made him a blur of shimmering silver. He doesn't move much onstage. He moves a lot when you pinch his penis.

He peed on himself and had to change clothes. Somebody said he missed his next segment and Ernest Tubb had to substitute.

The next time I saw Porter I was sober, apologetic, and very humble.

"Hey, man," he said, "that behavior wasn't you. That was a drunk man. I forgive you."

He was trying to be nice. He was trying to excuse behavior that was inexcusable. He said he forgave me, and maybe he did.

But he didn't forget.

Almost a quarter century later, when Porter was asked to recall his interactions with George Jones, the only specific story he told was about the dick twisting. He told it to Tom Carter backstage at the Friday-night Opry and said he would call on Monday with additional recollections about our years together.

He still hasn't called.

Imagine having a friend for four decades whose only pointed recollection for publication is that you twisted his dick.

People always remember the worst. I know now that I exhibited some of the worst behavior imaginable during my days of heavy drinking.

Unfortunately, the truly heavy drinking was yet to come.

Despite our success as a touring duo, Tammy and I did not record together until 1971. Our first single was a remake of my 1965 hit "Take Me." We had been doing the song on our show and decided to put it out as our first record.

It was on the *Billboard* survey for thirteen weeks and peaked at number nine. The decision to record together was mutual between Tammy, our producer, Billy Sherrill, and me. I was still under contract to Musicor, and its executives wouldn't let me record with Tammy on her label, Epic, unless I bought out my contract.

I paid $300,000 to get out of one contract so I could enter another. Had I not paid the money, which I borrowed against royalties, there might never have been any duets by George Jones and Tammy Wynette. We recorded from 1971 through 1980 (five years after our divorce) and had thirteen single records. Three went to number one, including "We're Gonna Hold On," "Golden Ring," and "Near You."

Two of the hits were largely the result of shrewd marketing.

Rumors circulated about our pending divorce during the entire time we were married. We played into the hands of those rumors when we cut "We're Gonna Hold On," a song that sounded like our personal vow to hold on to our marriage no matter how difficult. The same was true of "The Ceremony," a song that topped out at number six after fifteen weeks on the chart. That tune incorporated a spoken part that was supposed to be the voice of a minister performing a marriage ceremony. Then Tammy and I said our "vows" to each other.

It sounds cheesy now, but it was a show-stopper for two people whose divorce was often the subject of tabloid speculation. People went crazy when we did "The Ceremony" live.

With the records' popularity, the fact that I was making all of my personal appearances with Tammy, and the success of the Old Plantation Music Park, Tammy and I were doing well financially. I was making more money than I ever had.

But with success went demands—demands I could meet since I was sober. I just couldn't be every place I was wanted at once.

I had opened the Old Plantation Music Park to fulfill a lifelong dream. It had been a three-year runaway hit. But something in my life had to give, and I decided it would be the park. Besides, our music careers were too hot for us to be living in Florida. We needed to be in Nashville. So I sold the park, estate, and all of the land that went with it.

That was not a decision I made easily.

The profit was enough to buy a home on Old Hickory Lake in Hendersonville, a Nashville bedroom city, and a farm with about 350 acres in Springfield, Tennessee, a small town about thirty miles north of Nashville.

I put a herd of cattle on the farm and commuted back and forth to Hendersonville. Tammy and I went out for short tours with the band, then I went to the farm and fed cattle, mowed hay, and did anything else I could do that was rural and had nothing to do with country music.

Then I bought a third house, this one on Tyne Boulevard on a hill overlooking Nashville. As you know, I've never had an aversion to spending money. I've gotten into trouble because I've spent it when I didn't have it. (I was always better at making money than managing it.) But in the early 1970s, it seemed as if my buying power would be forever unlimited.

Besides my hits with Tammy, I had come out with "A Good Year for the Roses," a Jerry Chesnut song that rose to number two in 1971, "We Can Make It," which peaked at number six in 1972, "Loving You Could Never Be Better," which topped at number two in 1972, and "A Picture of Me (Without You)," which rose to number five in 1972.

Tammy, in 1968, had recorded "Stand By Your Man," a song that remains the biggest hit of her career twenty-eight years later. She had ten number-one songs from 1968 through 1972, including "D-I-V-O-R-C-E," "Singing My Song," "The Ways to Love a Man," and "Bedtime Story," just to mention a few.

Making money was as easy as going up on our performance fee. So many promoters wanted us for so many shows, we hired someone whose job was more concerned with rejecting offers than accepting them. We didn't have to take more shows, we simply had to accept more money for the ones we took.

And I was still sober.

On September 12, 1971, Tammy threw my fortieth birthday party. I didn't take a sip.

I might have gotten overconfident. Not long after that, I pitched a drunk, and it was as if I was making up for lost time. I stayed wrecked for about three days. You have no idea how I dreaded facing Tammy. As I recall, I went to our house on Tyne Boulevard because I thought she'd be at one of the others. But she wasn't.

Then Tammy did something that, despite my drunkenness, I still remember. She agreed to cook for me, and I thought that was awfully nice of her, what with me coming in loaded and all.

I probably had no business eating because I was so full of booze. My stomach was probably too upset to hold normal food. It certainly couldn't have held rotten food.

And that's what Tammy served me.

I don't know where she got the stuff, but she actually put moldy and decayed food on my plate. The meat was brown because it had started to spoil. The green vegetables were brown.

I took one bite and, even in my drunkenness, knew what she had done. I accused her of serving me spoiled food and maybe even accused her of trying to poison me.

Much to my surprise, she admitted that the food was spoiled. It was her way of getting back at me for getting drunk. I'm thankful I didn't eat it. Can you imagine putting food poisoning on top of a hangover from a three-day drunk?

Tammy found another house she wanted, this one on Franklin Road, and I bought it for her. I had to borrow against my royalties from my record label again, and I did. I tried to buy her anything she wanted, and Tammy had expensive tastes. Maybe I was trying to ease a guilty conscience from all of the times I got drunk.

A lot of folks think that if it hadn't been for my drinking Tammy and I would have had a storybook marriage. But that isn't true. We argued about things other than the bottle. Tammy, I suspect, has changed a lot since our divorce in 1975. But there was a time when she was a high-spirited and opinionated woman. I was always more passive, especially when I was sober. Tammy used to worry about things, while I had a policy of letting things ride. Sometimes she'd get worried when she thought I wasn't getting worried.

Tammy used to lose her temper and physically attack me. The band used to love to watch that because I wouldn't fight back. I couldn't bring myself to hit her when I was drinking, and I sure couldn't do it sober. Tammy, more than once, got me down on the floor of the bus while pounding me. I didn't know what to do except take it. It sounds funny, but it hurt nonetheless. Even a little kid can hurt you if you just lie there and take it without fighting back.

"Get this woman off of me!" I shouted, usually to James Hollie. After these attacks I would routinely ask to be let off at the next town that had an airport. From there I would fly to our next show or to our home if that was our destination.

Despite Tammy's temper and her nagging about my drinking that often drove me to drinking, she could be a compassionate human being to members of my family. My two sons stayed with us one summer in Lakeland,

and she treated them like her own children. My mother loved Tammy, and Tammy and I never told her we had marital difficulties. It would have upset Mama tremendously.

Mama used to visit Tammy and me in Lakeland, and we would take her to the dog races. She was a lifetime Pentecostal and didn't believe in gambling, but she'd tell Tammy which dog she thought was going to win. Tammy would fuss over her and sometimes bet on the dog Mama favored. If it won, Tammy would try to give Mama her winnings, but Mama thought it was sinful to collect.

Mama got sick, and I'll bet that Tammy flew with me to Vidor to see her at least four times. Sometimes my sister Helen would call and say that Mama was bad off and that we'd better come quickly. We might have to cancel a show or leave in the middle of the night. Tammy was always by my side and never complained once.

Tammy, the Jones Boys, and I went to the International Festival of Country Music at Wembley Stadium in London on April 12, 1974. It was after midnight when the phone rang in our suite. I answered and heard the static-coated voice of Helen in the United States, where it was daytime. Helen didn't think Mama would live until nightfall.

Tammy and I got up, packed, and caught the first flight to New York City, on to Houston, then rented a car to drive the ninety or so miles to Vidor. We traveled for twenty-four hours with no sleep and lots of jet lag. But we were too late.

Mama died on April 13. She was seventy-eight. She

spent the last two weeks of her life in a coma inside a hospital.

Mama had suffered a heart ailment when she was seventy-two, and her body resisted a pacemaker. So surgery was performed that threw her body into shock. She never fully recovered in the six years before her death.

Tammy and I, my brother, Herman, and my sisters went to her funeral at the Memorial Funeral Home in Vidor. It was a simple ceremony for a wonderfully simple woman. Someone sang "Precious Memories," and as I stood there, my mind was flooded with them.

I had bought my parents a house about two miles from mine when I was married to Shirley. I'd get on a drunken rampage and Shirley wouldn't know what to do, so she'd call my mama.

Mama was the only one who could settle me down. She'd hold my hand, call me Glenn (she always called me by my middle name), and tell me that she and Jesus loved me. I might have been filled with rage, but the sight of her presence and the sound of her voice never failed to soothe me. Like a child, I would often fall asleep.

"I've seen him so drunk he couldn't talk," Helen would say years later. "But I never saw him say a cross word to Mama. She could always put him to peace."

In the wake of our divorce, Tammy took a Bible that Mama had given me. I got it back years later, and Helen found a note inside written by Mama to her children, mostly to me. The note referred to Carolyn, a woman who had tended Mama in her final days. Its handwriting was crooked and its English broken. I can't read the letter to this day without crying.

"You all know I love you all dearly," Mama wrote. "I done the best I could for you. Carolyn gets the Bible, got her name in it. You all be sure and keep flowers in our vase on the graves. I want George Glenn to have my new Bible and for him to be sure and read it for my sake and his. I love him so much. I made a failure, but I hope we all meet in Heaven."

Those were Mama's final words to her children in care of the one child who didn't find them until years after her passing. Mama, I know, thought she had "made a failure" in me because of my drunken ways. My lifestyle broke the heart of an old woman who never gave anything but kindness to others. I want to see her in Heaven. I want to tell her I'm sorry.

During her funeral I thought of Daddy and how he was so upset by something indirectly involving me that he was thrown into a stroke on a Thursday and died on a Saturday.

Because Shirley was frequently angry at me about my drinking, she decided to take it out on my parents. She neglected to make the payments on their house, even though there was money to do so. My parents were caught totally off guard when a man from the sheriff's office showed up to evict them. Daddy argued that the payments were current. Then he asked why, if they were behind, he hadn't received any past-due notices.

Shirley had thrown all of them away.

My folks had been given their final notice to make a house payment and didn't even know it. The sheriff's deputies set their belongings in the yard before their very eyes and for all their neighbors to see.

That was the nicest house Daddy had ever lived in and

the only one I'd ever bought him. His simple mind couldn't handle seeing strangers in uniforms take it away.

I had no idea any of this was going on and couldn't be found, of course.

After Daddy died Mama lived with her children. She finally moved in permanently at Helen's place, where I built a room on to the house. Eventually, we hired a woman to help Helen.

I was feeling so much remorse at Mama's funeral. Celebrity, wealth, hit records, travel, and all the rest mean nothing in the wake of the death of blood. Tammy understood my pain.

We worked our personal appearances throughout the summer and fall. That year I had three records that together spent forty-two weeks on the *Billboard* country chart, including "The Telephone Call." "The Grand Tour" and "The Door" went to number one. Tammy and I released two more songs that together spent twenty-five weeks on the chart.

My career was red-hot, and our duet career was pretty warm.

But Tammy's solo career didn't fare so well that year. She had only one record, "Woman to Woman," make the *Billboard* country chart in all of 1974. It peaked at number four. Previously, Tammy had recorded fifteen number-one songs in six years. So she thought the fact that she only had one hit in one year, and that it failed to top the chart, meant her career was getting cold. She didn't handle that well.

Tammy fell apart one December night as we lay in bed. She cried and complained literally all night. She said she was afraid she'd never get another hit. She was going through disputes with Epic, our record label, and even wondered if the decision-makers there intended to release any more of her records. It was a ridiculous concern from a woman who'd made so much money for them. Besides, she and I had recorded a duet for Epic only the night before.

Nothing is harder than a lack of rest on someone with a drinking problem. In Alcoholics Anonymous recovering alcoholics are warned against getting too tired. Tammy's crying binge simply wouldn't stop. By sunrise I was exhausted.

Shorty Lavender, our booking agent, was building new offices. I was helping with the work. I'd promised him I'd come by about 10 A.M. I had probably been up since about eight the previous morning. That meant I had gone through a full day's activity, a recording session (which had gotten stressful), and an all-night pity-party with Tammy.

I had virtually been without sleep for about twenty-six hours. Anyone's nerves would have been shot. The nerves of someone who used to drink heavily for weeks were shattered.

When I headed toward Shorty's office my hand was shaking on the steering wheel. So I stopped at Ira's steak house before 10 A.M. for a double shot. In fact, I had four double shots, eight ounces of liquor, in the space of twenty minutes, on an empty stomach.

I was drunk in no time flat. And I drank all day.

I didn't want to go home in that shape. Tammy had seen me like that plenty of times before, but she hadn't seen it lately. I had vowed she'd never see it again. I had no defense. Anything I'd say was something I'd said before.

So I drove to Franklin, a neighboring city, and got a motel room. I slept it off and called Tammy the next morning. I told her truthfully what I'd done, told her I was so glad I no longer did that routinely and that I'd be home in a little bit.

"No," she said, "you won't be at this house, you son of a bitch. Not in a little bit or not ever. Don't you ever come around me again."

And she meant it.

I went to see my friends Peanut and Charlene Montgomery in Florence, Alabama, and stayed drunk. I called Tammy a couple of times. She hung up or told me again not to ever come around.

A couple of weeks later, I found out that Tammy had put my clothes on a boat we kept on Old Hickory Lake. She had put them in garbage bags and hadn't tied them shut. When the bags were thrown onto the bow they opened and clothes went in all directions. They lay on the deck, absorbing sunshine and rain. Many were designer clothes that had been made for the stage. Many were ruined forever.

I had my car and perhaps two thousand dollars with me. I owned a lot of other things, but they were in our joint names.

And I also had a knowledge that I'd never had before. I *knew* that Tammy wasn't going to let me come home. Maybe it was the way she totally refused to talk about making up. Or the way she wouldn't listen to an apology for one of the few times I'd ever gotten drunk for one night only.

It was nine days from what was to be a very lonely Christmas. My body was with Peanut and Charlene, but my mind was with Tammy, and my heart was with our little family—a family I would never see as mine again.

So I did what drunks do best. I drank.

In the midst of it all, I got word that Tammy had been hospitalized for a drug overdose. Was it accidental? Was it done to ease hurt she might be feeling about our separation? If so, I thought, then why not get back together?

But Tammy never answered my calls; instead, someone always said she didn't want to talk to me.

Our net worth together was into seven figures. But our divorce decree, finalized on March 21, 1975, was a mere six pages.

The divorce was not complicated because I didn't contest it. I didn't even go to court. I told my lawyer to tell Tammy's that she could have whatever she wanted. She wanted most of all we had.

I wasn't thinking right and assumed that if she got the house we had on Franklin Road she would also get the payments. I found out years later that those house payments were being deducted from royalties Epic Records owed me. We had paid about $1 million for the place.

Besides the house, which Tammy lived in until 1993, she took our children, our touring bus, our real estate in Alabama, my stock in the Shorty Lavender Talent Agency, and one thousand dollars a month in child support for Tamala Georgette, who Tammy agreed to let me see two days a month for eight hours a day. (I made the first child support payment, and when I wasn't allowed to see Georgette I stopped. Tammy eventually sued me

for forty thousand dollars in back child support and
won.)

I got the house on Tyne Boulevard. Tammy and I owed
seventy-five thousand dollars to the Commerce Union
Bank. The divorce decree said I had to pay off half of that
when I sold the Tyne house.

Tammy might argue that she lost during our marriage.
There is no argument about who won during divorce.

I'm glad the telling of this part of my story is finished.
Tammy and I have had a quarter century in which to
mellow, and I feel we've done that. We recorded together
in 1994 and 1995 and toured together the following
summer. Fans and critics were astounded. I'll tell you
more about that later.

I have no regrets about my marriage to Tammy except
for my heavy drinking. And I regret that period.

Tammy's life has been difficult since the divorce, and
she's stood up bravely. She's been in and out of hospitals
perhaps twenty times or more. I actually thought we
were going to lose her when she contracted still another
ailment in 1993. Nancy and I were fortunate enough to
be among the first to her bedside. That time, Tammy
suffered a bile duct infection that left her in critical condition for a week.

Once again, her tremendous inner strength domi-
nated, and she pulled through when some doctors had
written her off.

She made big news with that one.

After me she married another guy, and that lasted only
a few days. She married George Richey in 1978, and they
had their problems, some of which were financial. Those

were made public in the early 1990s. Tammy had always hated seeing her personal life spread out for public viewing.

Tammy Wynette has sold more than thirty million albums. She became the first female country singer, in fact, to record an album that sold more than one million copies.

I have nothing but respect for her artistry and the woman, indeed the lady, behind it. The things I've talked about in these pages are old news. Very old.

Concert promoters were reluctant to book Tammy immediately after our divorce. They wanted the two of us, as we had become an established act on the country music touring circuit. One of Tammy's first acts after the divorce was having our bus repainted to cover the sign that once read, MR. AND MRS. COUNTRY MUSIC.

Tammy toughed it out and went right on working.

I went right to the bottom. I had no idea the bottom could be so low.

Chapter 14

I opened my second Possum Holler club the day my divorce from Tammy was granted.

The divorce had triggered my renewed drinking, and I drank during the entire day it was granted. Everyone predicted I would miss the grand opening, a gathering of the most important music industry people in Nashville. I fooled folks by showing up and even more by performing.

It had rained all day before the opening. Streets were flooded throughout Nashville. Everybody thought the first-night festivities would be a flop. But so many folks turned out you couldn't have stirred them with a stick.

A lot of country stars were on hand, and they jumped onstage. The club, located in historic Printers Alley, the hotbed of Nashville tourism during the 1970s, had the spirit of the Possum Holler of a few years earlier.

And its layout was very clever. A VIP Lounge was built at the same level as the stage. That meant that if a celebrity was sitting in the lounge he or she had to do nothing but take a few steps in order to be onstage. The stars usually sat together, so it was tempting for several to make their way to the stage after the first one broke the ice. Once again I had a place whose customers were the Who's Who of Nashville entertainers.

I didn't actually own it. Once again I simply put my name on it and was supposed to be paid for that.

As so often has been the case in my life, I didn't get my money. People have asked why I haven't hired people through the years to handle my money. I have. And some of the handlers turned out to be some of the biggest thieves. I don't have the greatest financial mind myself.

The new Possum Holler was intended to be a place where my band could perform on the nights we weren't working the road. That was a lot of nights.

I missed more personal engagements than I kept from 1975 through 1980. The nickname "No Show Jones" really became solid. I now go along in stride with my old reputation, which I'll never live down in some folks' minds.

Today I own several cars and trucks for Nancy, my staff, and me. Each has a license plate that reads NOSHOW1 or NOSHOW2 and so forth. A lot of country stars put their names on their touring bus. Not me. I simply have NO SHOW on the front of mine. Traffic directors at my concerts always know it's my bus, and I'm waved right through.

Most of my concert promoters and disappointed fans

in the middle to late 1970s blamed my absence on alcohol, and they were right. I had drunk heavily for years and had pitched benders that might last two or three days. But in the 1970s I was drunk the majority of the time for half a decade. If you saw me sober, chances are you saw me asleep. It was a five-year binge laced with occasional sickness from sobriety. The hangovers start to hurt real badly when you pass forty.

Some folks think they're in pain if they've had one too many cocktails the night before. They have no idea how it feels to have one too many pints. It's like going through a violent food poisoning with an ax in your skull.

The second Possum Holler was managed by Alcy Benjamin "Shug" Baggott, a veteran Nashville nightclub operator who had owned five or six clubs before Possum Holler. Shug decided he wanted to open a country music nightclub that catered to tourists. That might not seem like an original idea in Nashville, but, in 1975, it was. Tourists used to complain about the absence of live country music in Nashville. It's largely absent to this day. With the exception of the Grand Ole Opry and the concerts staged at Opryland during the summer, there is little live country music in the capital city of country music.

Maybe I should open another Possum Holler. Not a chance.

Shug, by his own admission, didn't like country music. But he liked the money he thought he could make off of it. He asked a friend whose name he should put on the marquee. The guy suggested Faron Young, Webb Pierce, or George Jones.

I wish Faron or Webb had gotten the deal.

I got it not because I had sold a certain number of records, and not because my shows drew a certain amount of people, but because Shug and I had the same barber.

I didn't know Shug, and he didn't know me. But whenever I went for a haircut, which I've done almost weekly for many years, the barber would play my records. Whenever Shug was in the shop he had to hear me sing, and he didn't like it. If I left the shop before Shug, he always asked the barber to take my records off.

Shug had gone to a benefit show for Ivory Joe Hunter at the Grand Ole Opry House in 1974. Tammy and I were on the bill, one of the last we worked before our divorce. Shug later told a lot of folks, including me, that Tammy and I were his favorite part of the program. He even said he became a George Jones convert.

I had no idea, at that point, that Shug and I shared the same barber or that he had seen me perform. I still hadn't heard his name.

I went into the Hall of Fame Motor Lounge one night with Billy Wilhite, and Shug sat down at our table uninvited. He introduced himself and explained what he wanted to do with a nightclub and me. But I was too drunk to talk business, he said later. I know I was too drunk to remember.

Shug suggested that Wilhite, he, and I meet the next day when I was sober. Little did he know.

I made the meeting but not the sobriety. Once again I was too wasted to talk seriously about anything. That happened about four times.

Shug finally caught me sober, and we struck some

kind of handshake deal. Nothing was ever put in writing. I've always been overly trusting of people. And I've often been taken to the cleaners. Possum Holler Two proved to be no exception.

I'll never know how much money was made or who got it all from a watering hole bearing my name. The power of endorsement has always been strong. And George Jones endorsing a tavern in the 1970s would have been like Michael Jordan endorsing a basketball in the 1990s. It couldn't miss.

Shug took me to the club's intended location, and I started walking through the place. It had previously been a nightclub under another name, and I started telling Shug how he should remodel.

"Take out this wall here," I said. "Put up a wall there. Paint here, and lay some red carpet here."

I was full of ideas, and Shug loved them. He just couldn't afford them. He estimated that my ideas would cost about $100,000 and said he didn't want to spend that much money.

I told him I'd put up half. I didn't tell him I was broke.

I sent him to Jerry Jackson, my accountant at the time, and told him Jerry would write him a check off my account for $50,000.

Shug went to see Jerry, and Jerry laughed at him.

"George doesn't have any money," Shug was told. "He's broke."

Wilhite pointed out that I had never contested any of my three divorces and that I had never gotten a fair settlement out of one. I don't know why I always did that, except that I don't like to argue with people about money, especially folks who used to care for me. At the time of my divorce from Tammy, I was still in love. I thought if I gave her everything in the divorce she might give me another chance.

So I had no money except the cash in my pocket, perhaps a couple of thousand dollars. I could have gone out and worked a road date and picked up a few thousand, and occasionally I did that. But I was usually too drunk to make the trip or too drunk to perform after I arrived. I blew off more shows during the 1970s than most country singers were offered.

All of my life I hid when I hurt. At that time I hid in a bottle.

Since I wasn't traveling to a lot of shows, my old bus was parked outside the Possum Holler club. Tourists saw the bus, saw my name on its side, saw my name on the marquee, and assumed that if they came inside they could see me. We had a lot of human traffic. After a while, I decided that Shug Baggott, who had walked into my life through a barbershop, was a pretty smart guy.

I asked him to become my manager. He said no.

I said I would pay him five hundred dollars a week plus expenses, not bad money twenty years ago. He asked if I was going to pay him out of the money he was loaning me. I got his point.

My business affairs were in as much of a mess as my personal life. My band hadn't been paid in about fifteen weeks. Shug had no eagerness to jump into my personal and career management for me. But I was vulnerable, and perhaps he recognized that. Shug could be very persuasive, and he was obsessed with getting cash.

"At that point in my life my first priority was making

money," he said in 1995. In time he made a believer out of me.

At first, things between Shug and me were fine. He eventually became my manager. His brother, Sandy Baggott, became my road manager and got me to some of my dates. I went several weeks without missing a show. I often arrived drunk, but I arrived nonetheless. Then Shug came up with a rich guy who wanted to invest in my career. He offered me one million for a one-year exclusive performance contract on me. I was already under a booking agreement to AQ Talent, owned by Queenie Acuff, an old friend, and Billy Wilhite. Queenie and Billy graciously tore up their contract with me so I could take the million-dollar deal, which offered a quarter million dollars up front.

I got my $250,000. But I was heavily in debt to my band, accountant, lawyers, and others. My quarter million dollars didn't last long.

Before long it was the same old story. I'd work, but I never had any money. My band and my creditors weren't paid in full, just enough to keep them hanging on. The people who handled my money had explanations, but never any I could understand. There are a lot of ways to confuse a simple man who is as trusting as he is drunk.

Given my intoxication and state of mind, it took all of my strength to work. Since I wasn't getting ahead, I again didn't care if I worked or not. It was all a vicious circle on a downward spiral.

And so I drank more.

Realize that alcohol, if consumed enough, will lessen hunger pangs. The hardened drunk will not realize how hungry he becomes. I had become like that, so it wasn't overly hard for me not to eat for days. The little nourishment I had came from the few vitamins that hide in blended whiskey. Without anything close to a proper diet, I lost a lot of weight and I was extremely weak most of the time.

I was booked one night into the Possum Holler club and arrived staggering drunk and exhausted. I told Shug I simply couldn't go onstage. He reminded me that my appearance had been advertised. He also reminded me that I had missed other scheduled appearances at my own club. I had no credibility left in Nashville, he insisted.

He was right.

"But I just can't go on tonight," I said, pleading. "I'm too tired to stand up, much less sing. I'd do it if I could, but I can't do it tonight."

Shug is a tall and forceful man who had a way of getting his way. Perhaps that's why he's been so successful in the cutthroat world of nightclubs.

"You can go on, George," he told me. "You just need some energy."

With God as my witness, I had no idea what he meant.

He pulled a small bottle of white powder from somewhere and dipped into it with an extremely tiny spoon. Up to that point in my life, I had only *heard* of cocaine.

He held the spoon under my swaying nostril and told me to inhale hard. I had no idea what I was doing. I must have done it too hard. I breathed forcefully, the stuff burned the lining of my nose, and went immediately into my empty stomach.

I instantly began to throw up whiskey. The vomit streaked my jacket and trousers, and I didn't know it.

Something should be said about my clothes, and almost anyone who has ever known me will tell you it's true. Even in my lowest hour I dressed neatly. I got to a point where I sometimes didn't bathe or shave, but I almost always had a crease in my pants, a press in my jacket, and starch in my shirt. There were hundreds of times when I was too wasted to take clothes to the laundry or dry cleaners. So I simply bought a new outfit and left the worn one wherever I happened to take it off.

Jimmie and Ann Hills, who later became my personal assistants, reminded me in 1995 that I always left clothes at their house, where I sometimes went to change. Ann mentioned recently that the last pair of pants I left there, in the late 1970s, had a twenty-eight-inch waist.

"He got as skinny as a little boy," she said, " 'cause he simply wouldn't eat. I'd get up and he'd be gone and there would be his dirty clothes. I'd tell Jimmie that those clothes would be our final reminder of George. I knew each time he left that we'd never see him alive again. And then I'd cry the rest of the day."

On my first night with cocaine, I became so instantly high that I didn't care about clothes. I didn't care about any aspect of my appearance. I was overwhelmed by the artificial energy the drug gives. I was staggering drunk but felt like I could go twelve rounds with Muhammad Ali.

And so I went onstage.

In the front row I could see people pointing at my clothes. I looked down and there, in the spotlight, I could see dried puke on my jacket and trousers.

Embarrassment overtook me, and I couldn't wait to get offstage. I had found another hiding place in a much smaller, but much more effective, bottle.

My fondness for cocaine flourished instantly. Shug knew a guy who made runs to Florida to buy the stuff, so I had an unlimited supply. I shared the cocaine with others in the music business. All agreed I had the best in town. I used it heavily, off and on, for about seven years.

I'd get drunk and slosh it around, and I'm convinced I spilled thousands of dollars' worth. Then it was back to Shug to buy more drugs.

Staying messed up on cocaine made me more manageable, some folks thought. Cocaine accelerates the user's metabolism. It's a stimulant. It made me think I had drive, so I wouldn't pass out like I would when I was hopelessly drunk. Give me a blast of cocaine and I wouldn't think I was exhausted from days of drinking.

Cocaine also keeps the heavy user confused. It stays in his system for three days, during which he doesn't think as logically as he otherwise would. Since I was using cocaine almost every day, there was rarely a time when I wasn't confused. I was easy prey for those who wanted to take financial advantage of me.

Cocaine also makes the user extremely impulsive. If he sees something he wants, he wants it right then. I once traded a pair of Nudie Western boots, worth perhaps a thousand dollars, for a pair of used sneakers. The wearer took them off his feet, and I took the boots off mine.

I once needed some cash and tried to sell a forty-thousand-dollar boat to Velton Lang, former road manager for Conway Twitty, for five hundred dollars. (Velton could have taken advantage of me, but he didn't.)

Cocaine also makes the user irresponsible. Using cocaine makes the user want nothing except more cocaine.

Billy Wilhite, in 1994, said that he once gave me some chemical stimulants at a recording session because I had told him that taking them would eliminate my desire for booze. As it turned out, I took the pills, got drunk, then went home and had an argument with Tammy. The next day she showed people marks on her neck and said that I had strangled her. I hadn't.

So I was going merrily along in the spring of 1975 with cocaine, my newfound crutch, and released "Memories of Us" and "I Just Don't Give a Damn." Neither song did anything substantial. "I Just Don't Give a Damn" was my eighty-sixth single record. It was on the *Billboard* survey for only four weeks and peaked at number ninety-two on the Top 100. I had never released a record on a major label that did so poorly.

My counterparts, Merle Haggard and Conway Twitty, were setting the charts on fire. Haggard released "Always Wanting You," "I'm Movin' On," and "It's All in the Movies" the same year. Each song went to number one. Conway had "Linda on My Mind," "Touch the Hand of the Man," and "This Time I've Hurt Her More Than She Loves Me." Each song went to number one.

I constantly feared that my career, like my three marriages, was over. I had nothing left but my name, and my name was associated with missing personal appearances and not paying my debts. I truly began to feel that my reckless ways had caught up with me at last. Drinking and taking drugs had all but ruined the life of a man whose voice had been heard around the world.

I became so scared about the consequences of drinking and taking drugs that again I did what I always did when I was afraid—I drank more and took more drugs.

Shug today says that he had my career in mind when he made decisions about my recording and touring. I believe him. Why shouldn't I? He, after all, got a cut of everything I earned, so he certainly had the incentive to help me get back on top.

And he got no winning arguments from me about where my money was going. I was too wrecked to make much sense. If I had valid questions about why I had nothing left after I earned twenty thousand dollars in a weekend, he had answers. He could always beat me in an argument because my drug and alcohol use kept me mentally crippled.

Another reason my career was falling so dramatically was because I wasn't getting promotional support from Epic. A record label won't pump money into an artist who won't make personal appearances.

Jennifer O'Brien, who became a background singer and duet partner on the road with me about this same time, met a fan who told her she had bought a ticket to see me on seven different occasions. I missed every show, and to this day I don't know if that woman ever saw me perform.

I missed a New Year's Eve show with Johnny Paycheck in Tulsa, Oklahoma. The promoter promised not to sue me if I would do a makeup show for free. I have played millions of dollars' worth of makeup shows to avoid being sued.

I told the Tulsa promoter I would, but I got drunk and missed the makeup. Shug or somebody talked him into booking me for a makeup show for the makeup show, and I missed that too. On my fourth attempt I made it. But I was too drunk to sing and only did thirty minutes. I left the stage to a chorus of boos.

Because of my dwindling reputation in the United States, Shug thought I should play overseas, where I had not disappointed as many fans.

So I told him I'd go. But he didn't tell me that the first place he wanted me to play was Northern Ireland. The Catholics and Protestants were blowing each other up over there by the hundreds. It was the bloodiest religious war of the decade. It seemed as though every time I turned on a television set I saw innocent men, women, and children being slaughtered.

Then I found out that one of the places where I was booked had just been bombed. Glen Campbell had played a performance hall where he was escorted by military police with machine guns into an auditorium that was surrounded with a ten-foot-tall chain-link fence topped with barbed wire and razor blades.

My band, which hadn't been paid in weeks, was in no hurry to play a safe Iowa fair with me. The members had a fit when asked if they'd wait on their money while playing a war zone, and we had a serious discussion about wearing bulletproof vests onstage.

Northern Ireland could give us no guarantee of protection. Its officials even urged us not to come, saying our lives would be in danger. I wouldn't have wanted to play that tour if I had been sober. I certainly didn't want to play it while living with the paranoia that every hard-core drunk and cocaine user has. I told Shug I wouldn't go. He demanded that I did.

The promoter sent the band airplane tickets. They were told they were going to England but, when they got in the air, learned they were en route to Dublin and then war-torn Belfast. There was no turning back. Six of them got so drunk that they consumed every bottle of wine on the Boeing 747. Not one other passenger got one drop.

Back in the States, I'd told Shug I'd meet him at Nashville International Airport. He thought I was going to fly with him to Ireland.

"Just let me stop by Tammy's house so I can see my daughter, Georgette," I told him. "Then I'll be along to the airport in plenty of time."

He believed that, and I got in my car and tore out for Florence, Alabama, to Peanut and Charlene Montgomery's home. Florence is about two and a half hours from Nashville. I figured Shug would never find me.

I had always told him that I was never late. "If I'm not there on time I'm not coming," I had said.

I was supposed to meet him at 3 P.M., and at 3:15 P.M. he remembered my words. At 3:45 P.M. he was in his Music Row office, and he launched a telephone search for me. Between those calls, he called the overseas promoter and told him that *he* didn't want to bring me to Ireland because it wasn't safe.

The next day Shug called the promoter again and told him I was ill. He asked the promoter if he could send Merle Haggard as my substitute. The guy didn't go for it.

"Jones is drunk, isn't he?" the promoter said. "That's why he isn't coming."

I probably was drunk, but that had nothing to do with

my absence. I was holed up in Florence, where there was strong whiskey, cool air-conditioning, and no gunfire or grenades.

Shug found out that I often visited the Montgomerys, and then someone reported having seen me on a street in Florence.

I still can't believe what happened next.

Shug gathered his cronies, enough men to fill eight limousines. The cars, accompanied by an airplane that flew on ahead, drove in a convoy from Nashville to Florence to find George Jones. It became a full-blown manhunt.

After Shug arrived, he enlisted additional people from Florence along with a helicopter. I was the target of a search that couldn't have been any more intensive if I had been on the FBI's Ten Most Wanted list.

And all I wanted to do was go fishing with friends in Alabama.

Shug set up a command post at the Florence Holiday Inn. He put a stakeout on Peanut and Charlene's house, my barbershop (I sometimes used to drive there from Nashville just for a haircut from Jimmie Hills), at the grocery store where I shopped, at the liquor store, and at every bar I had ever visited. Shug gave a description of my car to anybody who would listen. That helicopter flew all over Florence looking for it.

I had a citizens band radio and listened to searchers as they unfolded their dragnet. Some of Shug's associates were big and muscular. They were driving Cadillacs and Lincolns. They resembled the Mafia, and someone called the Florence police thinking that's who they were.

So the cops raided Shug's command post.

Officers bearing guns charged into their motel head-
quarters and demanded to know what was going on.
Shug, like many nightclub owners, had friends in high
places. He called someone with the highway patrol, who
overruled the Florence police. The officers were pulled
off of their investigation of Shug Baggott.

I had swapped cars with Peanut and Charlene, and
they had swapped with someone else. Searchers didn't
know who was driving what. By late the first night I was
tired. Knowing that I'd be spotted at the Montgomerys',
I tried to get a motel room. Each time Peanut, Charlene,
and I pulled into one of Florence's few motels we saw a
limousine with Tennessee tags. I was running, but I had
no place to hide.

And so we got a tent.

The three of us fled to the woods, where someone had
the idea to send up a decoy. Charlene or Peanut sneaked
to a pay telephone, called long-distance directory assis-
tance, and asked for the telephone number of any Laundromat in Chattanooga, Tennessee. A Laundromat was
called, and whoever answered was asked for its street
address. Then Charlene placed an anonymous call to
Shug's command post.

George Jones is at such and such Laundromat, she
said. It's at such and such address in Chattanooga, she
added.

"He won't be there long, and he's in pretty bad shape,"
she said. "I don't think you can take him by yourself."

Within seconds a helicopter lifted off from Florence,
and a few limousines raced under it. Shug continued to
direct all the activity on his CB, and I continued to listen

on mine. He and his searchers had no idea that I was hearing their every move.

I guess the helicopter pilot landed his craft on the lawn or in the street next to the Laundromat one state away. I was listening when Shug got on his CB to all of his units and told the searchers they had been fooled. I laughed out loud and then decided to increase my fun. I got on the CB.

"You guys are looking for me, but you can't catch a Possum," I said. (My other nickname, after "No Show Jones," was "Possum," as it is to this day.)

"George!" yelled Shug. "Where are you? You'd better get in here right now!"

"You guys are looking in the wrong place," I said. "You need to be about five miles to the northwest."

From a vantage point on a hill, I could see men running out of the motel and jumping into limousines. They burned rubber racing to where they thought I was.

It was a circus, and by now Florence radio and television had picked it up. For all I know Shug had enlisted their help.

"Anyone who has seen country music star George Jones, believed to be in Florence tonight, is asked to call this number," the newscasters said. Digits were flashed at the bottom of the screen.

By the second night of the second day I weakened. I had been awake the entire time. Our tent leaked, and we had gotten drenched in a blinding rain. We were hungry but couldn't go for food. My picture had been plastered all over television, and a lot of folks knew me by sight anyhow.

Peanut and Charlene had lived around Florence all of

their lives, and Peanut was a local recording artist. They would also be spotted if we left our tent, which was hidden safely in the Alabama woods. We had no food or water. The ground was our bathroom.

Cold, wet, filthy, and mentally spent, I called Shug. He had beaten me down. I could hardly speak for crying. I had run to Alabama to keep from going to Ireland. All I could think was that Shug was going to run me to death in the United States instead of me being shot overseas.

I asked Shug if he would hurt me if I came in. He said he wouldn't. (Someone, not Shug, later beat the shit out of me as punishment. I won't say who.)

And so I gave up. More accurately, I turned myself in to my manager. I promised Shug I would meet him at the Nashville airport if he would call off his dogs.

"Just let me have a shower and a meal and a night's sleep and I'll be there tomorrow," I said.

Everybody in his group urged him not to believe me, he said years later. I'll bet they did.

But he could hear the fatigue and fear in my voice and knew I wouldn't try to run from him again. He told me he'd take his people and leave town and would see me the next day at the airport.

Remember the television footage in June 1994, when thousands of people were standing along Los Angeles streets waving at O. J. Simpson and the police who were chasing him? That's what Florence looked like when Shug took his henchmen and their convoy out of the city of thirty thousand. That chase seemed to have tapped the fascination of everyone in the community. People stood along streets and cheered the limousines as they eased out of the city.

Reporters and others who had participated in the search probably thought they had done a good thing. I don't know what they were told as to why I was "missing." I'm sure they weren't told that I was hiding from a manager who was going to make me go into a battlefield. But by fleeing to Florence, I had missed the shows I wanted to miss in Ireland.

So the limousines went on to Nashville, the people of Florence went to their homes, and I went to bed.

The next day I went to Nashville and then on to the safety of England. My overseas tour, late though it was, was finally under way.

Chapter 15

The band had gone abroad without me, thinking they were going to England. They were. They didn't know they weren't immediately *destined* for England but routed through it on the way to a war zone. They were halfway over the Atlantic Ocean before someone noticed the last ticket in his ticket book. It said: BELFAST, NORTHERN IRELAND.

Everyone in the group had shared my position, agreeing to go to England but not to Ireland. They had insisted on a promise of no Ireland dates before they boarded the aircraft.

The top tickets in their books all pertained to English shows. The band was furious when they found the bottom ticket. They had been fooled.

The band's midair discovery prompted their excessive drinking. They not only reproduced my music but also my personal behavior after learning they were preparing to enter war-torn Northern Ireland. I heard about some of their escapades later and even received some of the blame, although I was on the other side of the ocean. Most of the guilty band members weren't identified by name but just as "George Jones's band." But in light of the way they were tricked, I don't blame them for anything they did.

The band staggered off the airplane at Heathrow in London and went noisily to the baggage claim. Their instruments were steered down a shoot onto a baggage carousel. Ralph Land, my drummer, noticed that a man assigned to catch the luggage was simply letting bags slam into each other. Ralph became concerned about his drums.

"Are you going to catch my trap case when it comes down?" Ralph asked the guy.

"What's a trap case?" the baggage handler wanted to know.

"It holds my drums and cymbals and everything else," Ralph answered.

"How much does it weigh?" the man asked.

"About one hundred and twenty pounds."

"No," the man yelled above the crowd and loud machinery. "I'm not going to catch it."

"Then get out of the way!" Ralph ordered.

Ralph, who was still drunk, climbed on top of the baggage apparatus. His drums sped down the steep chute almost with the force of gravity. He braced to catch them, but the impact was overpowering. He spun around and around, and because he was slightly elevated, people throughout the terminal saw him. He just about threw up from spinning while drunk. What he did next resulted in total chaos.

Ralph Land, key member of my band, single-handedly shut down the baggage flow at the world's busiest airport. A whistle sounded the instant Ralph picked up his bag. Ralph had performed the job of a baggage handler, who belongs to a union. Only members of that union were allowed to touch luggage.

The entire union membership stormed out on strike. Thousands of passengers and their bags were left behind.

The Jones Boys had arrived.

Baggage handlers carrying suitcases for old ladies instantly dropped their bags. Electric conveyors transporting bags from airplanes were turned off, stranding luggage in the depths of Heathrow.

The Jones Boys hurriedly grabbed their own bags and walked quickly out of the airport to taxis. Thank God they didn't offend the cabdrivers or they might have brought the entire country to a halt. A few more minutes inside the airport and they might have found a way to trigger an international incident!

My band was met with astonishment everywhere they went in Ireland. Residents couldn't believe that Americans had come to entertain in the sensitive political climate. Taxi driver after taxi driver told my musicians about musicians who had been shot from the audience while performing.

Ralph and my fiddle player, Zeke Dawson, were Vietnam veterans who were leather-tough and didn't frighten easily. Neither did the other players, who had worked many rough-and-rowdy honky-tonks with me. But after the third soldier carrying a rifle warned my boys that they might not leave the country alive, they became believers.

In Belfast, my band saw soldiers with .50 caliber machine guns posted on rooftops. Zeke was carrying his fiddle case, not knowing that military rules didn't allow that.

All of a sudden a soldier put Zeke up against the wall while others pointed their rifles at him. They thought he had a bomb inside the case. When Ralph saw how Zeke was being roughed up, he tried to help him. Instantly, another soldier hit Ralph in the back of the head with the steel butt of a rifle.

But the Jones Boys were troupers and went forward with plans to perform.

"Whatever you do," they were repeatedly told when they were in Belfast, "never talk about the war between the Protestants and Catholics. Just keep playing no matter what happens. In fact, don't even *mention* Protestants and Catholics."

Wanda Jackson was on that tour. My band had agreed to play behind her. The first night during the first show after her first song, she told the capacity crowd that she had a question.

"Why can't you Protestants and Catholics get along?" she asked.

My band dropped their instruments and fled for the wings. They feared machine-gun fire at any second.

Wanda was enthusiastic to share the message of Jesus Christ as she saw it. Ralph said she began to preach the Bible to the hostile crowd. The boys began to look for more wine.

If they hadn't found it, they probably would have been converted themselves just to ask God to repeat a New Testament miracle and turn water into it.

The boys eased nervously back onstage and backed Wanda on another song. She began to preach again. Once more, they sprinted off stage and out of sight. Wanda may have finished singing with only the shouts from the crowd.

After the show and back at their hotel, the band was met by members of the British Broadcasting Corporation, who told them how much they appreciated their bravery in coming to Ireland and said they couldn't persuade Irish musicians to get in front of an armed crowd to sing.

Ralph asked reporters if they were covering the war.

"Not really," one told him, "we're just up here counting cadavers."

Ralph went right back to drinking.

"Are you guys going to Dublin tomorrow?" Ralph was asked.

"Yes," he said.

"I don't think I would," Ralph was told.

The reporter said that several musicians from Belfast had recently tried to enter Dublin where they were taken off a bus, lined up, and shot. My band forgot their bus, forgot the Dublin show, and took an airplane back to London and safety. All the time my band was working hazardous duty they weren't getting hazardous duty pay. In fact, they weren't getting any pay.

My money continued to be mismanaged, and my band still had not been paid for weeks. They had refused to go overseas until they received back pay and payment in advance for the upcoming shows. So each player was given enough money to entice him to go overseas.

And each check bounced.

Those guys were thousands of miles from home and calling collect to wives who were threatening to leave because they couldn't pay household bills or buy groceries. The promoter had paid my manager half of the money before the band's departure and had made good on the rest each time they performed. So management got its money, but my players only got deeper into financial trouble. Two of the musicians were later divorced and blamed their marital problems on financial pressure from not getting paid while working for me.

Ralph was talking to his wife from Belfast, assuring her that the bounced checks would be made good and that he was in no danger. She tended to disbelieve him after a bomb exploded and cut the telephone line, which did little to ease her fury.

I didn't handle the money and, too often, didn't get paid myself. But I was too drunk, too filled with cocaine, and just too tired to sort it all out. I wanted to believe my management would handle things.

In the middle of all of this, Shug, or someone in his group, decided I would be more comfortable if I had a female traveling companion. She wasn't a prostitute. She was a Nashville woman hired to fly to England to finish the tour with me. Shug apparently thought that would calm me down and make me more willing to perform.

Imagine what that did to morale! My guys couldn't get paid, but my front office somehow had the money to hire this woman, pay for her round-trip airfare overseas, and even buy her a fur coat!

The guys bitched each time she got on the bus. I didn't want her there either and wound up sending her home.

We returned to the United States, where my life and money continued their downward fall. I discovered years later that, once again, I often was told I was working for one figure when I had been hired out for a higher fee. I never saw the difference. I learned, once more, that I was being booked into several cities on the same night. As I could only be in one place at a time and thus didn't show up at the others, my managers told promoters that my absence was in keeping with my reputation for drinking and missing shows. Promoters were again filing lawsuits against me for missing dates I didn't even know I had.

People wonder why I didn't put my foot down and take hold of my career and personal affairs. It's hard to answer that except to say that life had become a vicious cycle and I couldn't see any way out. I knew that most of my problems were caused from drinking and taking drugs. Because I couldn't handle what drinking and taking drugs were doing to me, I drank and took more drugs. I had quickly become addicted to cocaine, and Shug saw to it that I got it easily. It gave me an artificial high that kept me from complaining about the way he was handling my money and other affairs.

I actually worked a few shows for no money at all. Somebody else got my performance fee, and I got cocaine. It kept me high and, more important to management, it kept me quiet about money. That trend continued intermittently for years.

I couldn't pay my bills, the band couldn't pay theirs. Lawsuits were coming at me from all directions, and again I didn't care whether I worked or not.

"It's pointless," I thought. "No matter how many tickets I sell I don't see any money. I'm always broke and in debt."

My reputation for missing dates got so bad in the mid-1970s that I worked some shows for as little as twenty-five hundred dollars when I should have been getting fifteen thousand. Promoters just weren't willing to take a chance on my showing up. On the occasions I did get my money, by the time I had paid a six-member band, 10 percent to a booking agent, 10 percent to management, bought diesel fuel for the bus, paid for motel rooms, and financed the rest of the overhead, there was little left for me.

There were always plenty of creditors from the lawsuits and money to be paid for child support. I saw no point in working just for my creditors. So instead of paying old debts I often got new ones on impulse.

I again fell into the habit of buying new cars, sometimes once a month. I took a terrible loss each time I traded. I couldn't always qualify for credit, but I was always George Jones. You'd be amazed at the car dealers and other merchants who cater to people in show business. I got to where I expected that.

Waylon Jennings, in 1995, remembered that I was riding in a car with him years ago when I broke out a bottle of cocaine at a traffic light and snorted.

"You can't do that in broad daylight!" he said he told me. "We're going to get arrested!"

"No," he said I said. "There is no way they would arrest you and me."

People who do cocaine regularly think they're above the law. In the words of Hank Williams Jr. they think they're "ten feet tall and bulletproof."

I didn't know that I was on the brink of learning that justice is blind and that I was just as susceptible to harsh law enforcement as anybody.

I had moved to Florence, Alabama, right after the divorce from Tammy and lived there for six years. I bought and sold seven houses during that time, moving on the average of every ten months. I think a lot of that moving had to do with my inner restlessness. I simply couldn't find peace of mind.

I would go on three- and four-day binges during which I took nothing into my body except alcohol and cocaine. I totally refused food. Some folks used to say that I'd gotten so skinny I wouldn't look any worse in my coffin.

I was constantly lonely and confused. Once again I was always by myself, even in a crowd.

I was sitting in the back of my bus one night with my bass player, Ernie Rowell, while traveling to a show. I hoisted a bottle of whiskey, chugged it like water, and threw up, only to blast into another drink. I had become totally self-destructive and fueled largely by self-hatred.

In an interview for this book, Ernie said that during those days I did everything I could to destroy my career and everything I could to destroy my life.

"He hurt both real bad, but neither one would die," Ernie concluded. "The way he lived would have killed

any other career or any other life. None of us thought
he'd pull through."

Ernie kept pleading with me to eat, saying he didn't
understand why I was doing this to myself. I told him I
had no peace and that I never would. I told him not to
worry about me because I was beyond any hope. Ernie
said the sight of me and the sound of those words was
the most pitiable scene he had ever encountered. He
finally went to a brokenhearted sleep that night, and I
went into the next day drinking.

The press kept clobbering me for missing shows, and I
finally got back at them in the mid-1980s when I wrote a
tune with Merle Haggard called "No Show Jones," which
became an album cut and novelty song about seeing me
one minute, then missing me the next.

Merle cut it with me, and the song got a little airplay.
It only reinforced my reputation, but what the hell? If
I've got the reputation, I thought, why not make a dollar
off of it?

My reputation for missing dates got so bad that a few
gamblers made book in various cities as to whether I'd
show up. I wonder now if my management ever placed a
bet on whether I'd make the dates. All they had to do to
ensure I'd miss was get me drunk and full of cocaine.

The Jones Boys and I were booked outside of Washington, D.C., somewhere in Maryland about 1976 and
somebody, unbeknownst to me, organized the gambling.
Those who thought I would show up were asked to sit
on one side of the auditorium, those who thought I
wouldn't on the other.

I walked onstage, the house lights dimmed, and the
spotlight temporarily blinded me. I thought I saw people

stirring. I wondered why they were getting up to leave before I had sung a note. I wasn't drunk and hadn't had time to offend anybody. If they wanted to get angry they needed to give me a minute.

Yet the fans were totally ignoring me, waving money, and hollering and arguing. Was this a concert in a Mid-Atlantic state or a Southern cockfight? I was seeing, before my eyes, the settling of bets about whether I'd show up.

"The son of a bitch made it!" somebody shouted. "This has cost me a hundred dollars."

"I knew he'd make it!" somebody else yelled. "Hell, he missed three other shows here. He was an odds-on favorite to show up this time."

Apparently, everybody was paid in about the time it takes to sing three songs. They sat down, and I could see folks counting their money and putting it in their billfolds. I just kept on singing. Those who won thought I did a pretty good show.

I felt totally lost and without ties for months after the divorce. I had moved to Florence but wanted to be in Nashville, but once there I couldn't wait to get back to Florence. I used to drive from Florence to Tammy's Nashville house, pull through her circle driveway, drive back to Florence, then repeat the cycle. I'd make the two-hundred-fifty-mile trip three or four times a day, stopping only for gasoline. Sometimes I drove alone except for an open bottle of whiskey and a container of cocaine. Sometimes I rode with Peanut Montgomery. We put five thousand miles on his car in one week and never went anywhere except from Florence to Tammy's Nashville driveway and back to Florence.

I was running but not hiding from the demons of loneliness and plain old pain. I had no more money than the cash in my wallet. When I got totally broke, I'd work a show for a few thousand dollars and live off of that until I busted out again. If I was desperate, I'd ask somebody to call a nightclub where I'd packed 'em in during days gone by.

Then they would ask if George Jones could come and play for the door. That meant I'd be paid only from ticket sales. I hadn't worked that way since I'd started in Texas as a teenager. Since I'd take the dates on the spur of the moment, there was no time for advertising. Ticket sales sometimes weren't many, and the money wasn't much.

And I spilled a lot of money.

It's true that I went for days drinking and taking cocaine by myself. But on those times when I went into taverns, I spent money like there was no tomorrow, picking up everybody's tab.

Cocaine was about eight hundred to twelve hundred dollars an ounce, and even with my heavy usage, an ounce should have lasted for weeks. But I'd get wrecked and share it with other people, some of whom I knew and some of whom I'd never met. I've gone through an ounce of cocaine in twenty-four hours.

I went to Peanut and Charlene's house once with forty-seven cents in my pocket. It was all the money I had in the world, despite the fact that I had earned millions of dollars. I had a record on the radio, royalties that were due, and an engagement to sing somewhere. All of that was in the uncertain future. At that moment, all I had was that forty-seven cents. Had I died, I would have left that as my entire estate, along with an obituary that called me the "greatest country singer who ever lived."

That title was suddenly being published as much as "No Show Jones." The same press who were attacking my lifestyle were suddenly beginning to praise my singing like never before.

"The more shows he missed, the more his records sold," said Rick Blackburn, former vice president of Columbia Records' Nashville division. Columbia owned Epic Records, which was the fifth label for which I recorded.

Somebody said I fulfilled the Hank Williams mystique. In the mid-1970s people wanted their country singers to be drunk and rowdy, as Hank Williams had been. In that respect I gave the fans what they wanted and more. Hank lived drunk and rowdy. Trouble is he died the same way. The thought that I would go the way he did began to inhabit my mind. I can remember being too drunk to lie down because the room would spin. I was afraid I'd vomit and strangle in my sleep. Despite that kind of drunkenness, I rarely passed out in those days. I'd instead take a hard, blurred, and long look at the world before I closed my eyes, thinking each look would be my last.

Then, breathing heavily from cocaine, I'd finally yield to a fitful sleep. As soon as the drug began to wear off slightly I was up, sometimes in only two hours, and right back into the bottles.

I told you earlier that Merle Kilgore had worked for Hank Williams when he was a lad. Merle talked recently about a show I did somewhere where I crawled into the backseat of Merle's new car. I had begged to rest.

Hank Williams died while resting in the back of a Cadillac. I guess I looked so bad that some folks actually thought I might be lying down for my last time. They gathered around Merle's car, peeping through the windows to watch me nod off.

"You'd better keep that car," people told Merle. "Jones will surely die this time in the backseat. He'll never wake up this time. That car will be worth a fortune to a collector someplace."

Being called the world's greatest country singer didn't mean a thing then.

About the only thing that kept me semi-sane was the occasional humor from life on the road.

> *It's a measure of people who don't understand*
> *The pleasures of life in a hillbilly band.*

Bob McDill wrote those words many years ago for "Amanda," a hit song for Don Williams and later for Waylon. They're true.

Life on the road is monotonous, tiresome, and sometimes hilarious. Musicians are creative people. When you get six or eight under one roof where there is no entertainment except each other, practical jokes are often the result. Sometimes the jokes are hard. Hard jokes work best in emotionally hard times.

Ralph Land had a date during those days with a girl he met at a Southern nightclub, where she was a singer.

She came onto the bus, and I thought it was high time

I had a date myself. I didn't know she was with Ralph. I was drunk, and wild ideas came easily.

"Who is this girl?" I asked Ralph.

Before he could answer, she sat on my lap.

"I'm the girl singer at this nightclub you're playing tonight," she told me. "I asked Ralph to bring me out to your bus so I could meet you."

The girl was blond and had a big bust. Her neckline was low, but my spirits were lower. I had a bottle in my hand and her on my knee. She had to know what I had in mind.

She flirted and hugged for a long time, so I thought she had made plain what she wanted. I was agreeable, but she was a tease. She said she wanted to be sure she saw me after tonight.

"Now, honey," I told her, "that can be arranged."

The Jones Boys and I had to leave for another show in another town. I didn't get to be with my little bombshell that night.

I lay in the back of the bus thinking about her with every passing mile. Earlier she had sung a song or two inside my bus's bedroom. I liked what I heard and saw. The girl was not only pretty but talented. She was everything a lonely country singer needed.

Despite my hangover, I was up early the next morning. Maybe I could get Tammy off my mind if I could get a new woman into my life, I thought. So I called my manager, whoever it happened to be.

I had several managers before and after Shug Baggott. He and I parted company once, I ran in a few more managers, and then he and I reunited. I can't always remember who was with me when. Records that might indicate that are long gone to too many lawyers. I had as many lawyers as managers to handle all of my legal scrapes. I'll tell you about some of them later.

Billy Sherrill was one of my few constants during those troubled days from the middle 1970s through the early 1980s. He just kept producing those hit records on me, working with my on-again, off-again managers.

"Jones," he told me one day, "don't introduce me to any more of your managers. About the time I get to like one you fire him and hire another. It isn't worth my time to get to know one."

Anyhow, about the girl singer.

"You know the nightclub where I played last night," I told my manager over the long-distance line.

"Yeah," he said, "what about it?"

"They got a girl singer there, and I want to get to know her," I said. "You call that club today and offer her a job opening my shows. Tell her to fly out today because she starts tonight."

I think I agreed to pay her fifteen hundred dollars for each of four shows.

Everything the girl had told me was true. What she didn't tell me, however, was that she was one of *two* girl singers who worked at that club.

My manager called the club and told someone that George Jones wanted to hire the girl singer who had sung there the night before. As it turned out, both had sung.

"Are you sure?" the guy supposedly asked him.

"Yes, I'm sure," my manager said. "He can't afford an-other person on the payroll, but that has never stopped

George. Now send that girl on to our next show tonight. She has a ticket waiting at the airport."

Whoever took that call at the club called the wrong singer at home and told her she was going on the road with me.

I was sitting on the bus in another town before my show.

"George," my road manager said, "that girl you wanted from last night is here. She wants to come on the bus."

I can't tell you how happy I was.

"Just a minute!" I said. "Let me get ready."

I ran into my bedroom and checked my shirt. I put on my suit coat and made sure my hair was in place. Then I hurried back to my seat and tried to act naturally.

"Send her in," I said.

The girl I had admired had blond hair. This one was brunette. The girl I had admired was beautiful, like nature's niece. This one was like Dracula's daughter.

"Who is this?" I asked Ralph. "Is this the girl from the club?"

"Oh yes." He grinned.

I knew I had been drunk, and at that moment I also knew I'd been had.

Then I found out that Ralph had been with the blond before I met her. When I latched on to her, he wasn't pleased. He knew there were two girl singers at the club, and he knew that in the confusion somebody might send the wrong one.

Somebody had. He was so happy.

To make matters worse, the one they sent couldn't sing. At that point I had a woman on my bus who I might get into my bed after she got onto my stage. I didn't want her in any of those places!

I let the girl work one show, paid her for four, and told her I didn't think this was going to work out. I sent her and her money, along with plane fare, home that night after our show.

I would have kept her if she could have sung.

Not long afterward we were somewhere in the Deep South when someone told me that Onie Wheeler wanted to see me.

Onie had been a harmonica player on the Grand Ole Opry and "Hee Haw" for years. Roy Acuff used him on his sets and rarely failed to introduce this veteran country music player to the Opry's national radio audience.

I came out of my bedroom on the bus where I had been well into the whiskey and cocaine. I looked at a guy sitting in my seat who didn't look at me. I stared for a long time, trying to focus my eyes.

"Are you Onie Wheeler?" I asked, and immediately felt dumb. How could I ask the name of someone I'd known for years?

"Yes," he said. "I'm Onie Wheeler."

But he intentionally never looked my way.

I still had the bottle in my hand as, staring and blinking, I began to circle him.

"Are you sure you're Onie Wheeler?" I asked.

"I sure am," he insisted.

I knew my drinking and the rest had gotten out of hand. But if I was beginning to see things, or fail to see things properly, perhaps I was further along than I knew.

"Well," I finally screamed, "you're not the Onie Wheeler I know!"

The stranger turned slowly in his chair, letting light fall gradually across his face. I squinted hard. Then he suddenly stared directly into my eyes.

"Well, I'll be damned!" he shouted. "You're not the George Jones I know!"

He was down the aisle and off the bus before I could say another word.

The band swore they had nothing to do with that.

Chapter 16

My credit was largely shot when I bought a house in the Sherwood Forest subdivision of Florence in the fall of 1975. I put no money down, just assumed the mortgage. The real estate market was soft back then and leaned toward the buyer. A bank held the note on the property. It wasn't making any money off a house it had repossessed, so if it let me take over the payments and I defaulted, it hadn't lost any money. It just got its house back.

Peanut and Charlene helped me decorate, and between times of selecting furniture, wallpaper, and the like we went fishing and camping. Peanut and I wrote songs, as we had for years. I have recorded thirty-eight that he or he and I wrote. Most were album cuts, but there were a few hits, such as "We're Gonna Hold On" and "A Man Can Be a Drunk Sometimes." There were times when it was easy money to get drunk and put thoughts into words and tunes with Peanut, then to record them and have a hit.

But that didn't always happen, and a hit country record didn't pay as much twenty years ago as it does today. I could sell thirty-five thousand copies of a song in 1975 and see the song go number one. A song just about has to be a gold record (sell 500,000 copies) in order to go number one today.

I was constantly in and out of Peanut and Charlene's house and lives in the mid-1970s. One day in 1975 I went to their place and was introduced to Charlene's sister, Linda Welborn. She seemed to be a down-to-earth country gal, and I liked that. I always have. I don't think I've ever been interested in a high-minded woman.

I asked Linda out to dinner, but she turned me down, saying she already had a date. Then she introduced me to the guy. He was kind of a geek, and I couldn't understand why she'd rather go out with him than me. I told her to break her date, but she wouldn't and the guy began to rub it in that she'd rather go out with him.

I reminded him that he was visiting and had to return to his home in another state the next night. I assured him that I'd take Linda out then, and I did.

That was the first date in what became a six-year relationship. Linda lived with me in each of the seven houses I owned during this time. I didn't know that Alabama acknowledged common-law marriages, and when Linda and I broke up, she sued me for divorce.

I had to give her a cash settlement, even though we were never officially married. Once again I didn't argue the divorce case. I didn't even go to court. The whole affair seemed like a joke to me, but the judge who ruled against me wasn't laughing.

I don't think I was ever in love with Linda. I was in love with her ways. Life with her was completely different from life with Tammy. Tammy was a star and wanted everybody to know it. She got upset if people didn't recognize her or want an autograph. Tammy liked fine restaurants, diamonds, furs, and the shine that goes with show business.

But Linda was down-home. She went fishing with me. She didn't have to have a manicure. And if she got one she didn't mind getting dirt under it. We cooked on the grill more than in the oven. We went bowling more than we went to the movies.

Linda had been taken out of the country, but the country hadn't been taken out of her. She made a lot of mistakes with her English, and I liked that. It made me think she was genuine. I had sensed that same kind of reality years earlier in Melba Montgomery. In the country, if you pretend to be something you're not, it's called "putting on the dog." Linda never put on the dog.

My early days with Linda were good for me. I still missed Tammy more than I ever let on to Linda. And if you have to miss somebody, it's sometimes easier to miss them with somebody else. I hadn't handled Tammy's absence too well by myself. I'd see how well I handled it with Linda.

Once again I went on the wagon, and once again it was a ride that lasted for weeks. Looking back, I don't think I ever got sober entirely for myself but always for a woman as well. I just never got sober permanently for one until I sobered up for Nancy and me, although I had been mostly dry for months before that.

I really did try to make my relationships work, and every woman I ever had said that nothing would help things more than my getting sober.

Because I was temporarily sober with Linda, I was able to work more, and I quickly accumulated a few thousand dollars. The Possum Holler club and my business interests remained in Nashville, where my going on extended dry spells was always news in the music community.

"Maybe this time he's quit for good," people would always say.

Whenever that kind of talk began to circulate, I didn't have much trouble borrowing money. Lenders knew I could always work a show somewhere to get cash, and I always had a manager who could convince them that I was once again serious about working.

I borrowed fifty thousand dollars in 1976 and built an A-frame house, my second house in Florence. If Linda and I were going to play house, we might as well do it in as nice a place as I could afford, I figured.

I had started drinking once more and realized once again that a bus is a terrible place after a binge. The sun reflects off of the highway into pained eyes. The constant motion aggravates an upset stomach. But the confinement is the worst of all. After you've done a show, done your drinking, gone to sleep and awakened, you want to get off of that motorized prison. Yet you might have another hundred miles to go before getting home. If you don't want to get drunk to ease the pain of having been drunk, it can be a long and desperate ride.

In December 1975 I had come off a two- or three-day tour, a long trip in my heaviest drinking days, and was ready to bust out upon arrival one morning in Nashville. My fatigue and restlessness were compounded by the fact that I had to drive another two and a half hours to Florence. To this day, after a long trip, I want to do no more than go home. Anything else is a bother.

Billy Wilhite was working as my substitute manager. I think I had fired Shug for a few days. I went into Billy's Nashville apartment to shave and clean up. Despite my hurry to get home, I didn't want to go to Linda and Florence needing a shower.

My layover at Billy's resulted in publicity that clearly shows how unfair the press was to me in those days. A newspaper story claimed I had battered two women, and that was all wrong.

It was only one woman. And I didn't batter her. I didn't even hit her. I tried and missed.

Two women came uninvited into Billy's place. I'd never met them, and Billy barely knew them himself.

Someone played country music on the stereo, and one of the women began to complain. She hated country music.

I asked her why she didn't leave.

"Nobody invited you in here anyhow," I said, "and if you don't like country music, why don't you go somewhere and hear what you want to hear?"

I was too tired to be polite with people whose presence was unwanted.

The woman told me what she thought about country music and me after the other one bolted out the door. As she went through the door herself, she said something obscene, and that set me off.

I had a shaving kit that must have weighed two pounds. I tossed it at her. It hit the wall as she went out. But my throw made her furious.

"I'll get even with you, I promise you!" she said. And she did. She and her buddy sued me for $102,000. The pair claimed I had assaulted them and forced them to drink alcohol.

Why would I have forced somebody to drink when I was staying sober myself for the last leg of my journey home?

But the woman lived up to her promise. She got a default judgment against me, and I got a lot of bad publicity. I didn't see the need to respond to such a ridiculous accusation. I know now that I should have gone to court. After all, I had Billy and his wife as witnesses, and I might have won. But the plaintiffs agreed to a significantly smaller settlement (about ten thousand dollars), and I can't remember if I even paid it. Court judgments against me were becoming pretty plentiful, and many were reduced in a bankruptcy that I'll tell you about later.

But I hated that particular judgment because of the way it made me look in front of fans. Country fans back then would put up with my drinking and missing shows. But they didn't like men who hit women. I didn't like them either, and the point is I wasn't one who did.

I've never gotten to tell my side of that story until now.

*   *   *

Shug was back on my team in 1977, and I have to say that he became very aggressive with CBS in Nashville about promoting my career. He decided that the label should showcase me in front of a national press corps in New York City. His idea eventually worked.

The Village Voice wrote that I should be on a list of America's Top 10 singers in any category. *Penthouse* called me the "Holy Ghost of country music." Several publications, including *The New York Times,* called me the greatest country singer who ever lived, or of all time, and stuff like that. *Rolling Stone* bragged on me real hard, and that was a big deal because a lot of country singers weren't covered by that magazine in those days.

I want you to know here and now that I was mighty flattered. No singer would ever get tired of praise like that. And I don't repeat it to brag but to make a point.

Those things were written about my singing after a showcase I didn't attend. I might have been better off because I missed the show. The fact is I stood up some pretty important people, and the press called me a flake, then went on to say that it was too bad because I had such tremendous talent. Seems to me that I came out all right on the deal, but no one around me agreed. I really made folks furious when I blew off two shows at New York City's Bottom Line club.

The guest list included Walter Cronkite, John Chancellor, Linda Ronstadt, Elton John, James Taylor, Emmylou Harris, the cast from "Saturday Night Live," all three commercial television networks, news wire services, and virtually every print publication in New York.

Rick Blackburn, who was still vice president of Columbia's Nashville division, saw to it that big shots from

Columbia's home office in New York were there. The label bought a bunch of big newspaper advertisements that said, GEORGE JONES AND COUNTRY MUSIC COME TO NEW YORK.

I kept telling people I didn't want to do that show. I was shy because of my old booze and cocaine-laced paranoia. Again, I was no exception. And I had it in my mind that those big-city Yankees would laugh at country music and at me. When I played Madison Square Garden in the 1960s, the big audience was filled with working folks who had gone north to find jobs. I played New York City again sometime in the 1970s, but that audience wasn't comprised of big shots either.

The Bottom Line audience was mostly intellectuals. With the exception of a few singers, I knew that no one there had ever heard of George Jones. I was afraid that once they saw me in person they'd scratch their heads and say, "What's all the fuss about?"

But nothing would do Shug, and he did his job. He persuaded CBS's main office to spend about twenty thousand dollars on rolling out the red carpet and providing a Learjet to fly me to New York.

I was sitting in Blackburn's Nashville office at about one o'clock and told him I'd see him that night in New York. No one in the music business saw me again for three weeks.

Recording artists struggle to get promotional support from their record labels. I had received one of the greatest promotional thrusts in the history of Nashville music and had flatly turned my back on it.

I wanted to do a good job. I really did. But in those days my best work was disappearing.

I was booked a second night at the Bottom Line, and

you already know I missed that date too. (I finally played the Bottom Line months later.)

I guess that my nickname "No Show Jones" was furthered more by the missed New York dates than anything I'd done to that point. Doesn't that prove the power of the press? I'd missed dates throughout the South for years. I missed two at one nightclub and the press circulation about "No Show Jones" branded me more thoroughly than all of my previous misbehavior.

I had told them I didn't want to do those shows.

Shug and I temporarily parted, and I was briefly managed by a guy from Dallas, Caruth Bird. He knew about my reputation for missing dates, and by this time so did anyone who was interested in me anywhere in North America. Caruth decided that guaranteeing my arrival for a show was too much to ask of any road manager whose hands were full trying to get a half-dozen members of my band from show to show. So he got the idea to hire a full-time companion and put him on my payroll.

A string of guys tried to fill that role. The first was my buddy Jimmie Hills. Caruth let me pick whoever I wanted for the job. If I picked Jimmie because I thought he would go easy on me, I made a big mistake. He'd laugh and carry on like he was one of the boys. But when it came time for me to make a show, he turned from a pal into a drill sergeant.

But it did little good. I just had to work harder at running off. If I had worked as hard at putting on shows as I did at running from them, I would have been a terrific performer. That's the obvious logic to a sane man, which I wasn't in 1977.

I didn't cotton to the idea of having a glorified baby-sitter, and that's what Jimmie was, no matter what Caruth called him. Jimmie was paid two hundred and fifty dollars a day plus expenses, not bad wages in 1977, to stand outside men's room stalls to be sure I didn't slip into the adjoining stall. Many times I was in a stall while Jimmie was hollering through the door, "George, you still in there?" He also stood outside my motel bathrooms to be sure I didn't go through the tile ceiling above the commode.

How would you like to live like that? I didn't like it one bit and decided to test Jimmie's skills about midway through my first tour with him. We've laughed about it many times since, but he wasn't too amused at the time.

I played two shows at the Palomino Club in North Hollywood, then decided I wanted to go to Las Vegas on a night off to see Willie Nelson. I was feeling feisty and lonely. My mischief stemmed from determination to give Jimmie the slip. My loneliness stemmed from whatever it always did.

So I paid the Palomino hostess three thousand dollars to go with me to Las Vegas and promised her all I would do was talk. I kept my word. Trouble is I got full of cocaine and wouldn't stop talking, and she went to Jimmie and asked him to pinch-hit as a listener. He reminded her that listening is what she had been hired to do. And while I was figuring out a way to ditch Jimmie, she ditched me—and kept my three thousand dollars!

Meanwhile, my band took the bus and went to San

Jose, California, where I was supposed to meet them the day after my day off.

I sat up all night with Willie in Vegas, driving him crazy, I'm sure, with my constant cocaine babble. Caruth had sent another guy, Bill Starnes, on the road to help Jimmie be sure I wasn't waylaid in Vegas. The next morning the two of them physically walked me from a taxi across a runway to a jet waiting to take me to San Jose. One gripped each of my arms and pushed me toward the plane, as if I were a prisoner.

I hated that. Suddenly, my determination to escape was no longer funny. I lost those guys on the runway. I left them standing with the wind from a jet engine messing up their hair. I wish I could remember how I did that.

Jimmie, years later, couldn't remember how I did it, just that I did. He could only recall that he had only seven dollars in his pocket when I gave him the slip. Having no more than seven bucks in Las Vegas, when you've just had your first failure at your new job, can be pretty scary, I imagine.

Jimmie didn't know at the time that I had watched him go into every bar, restaurant, and men's room at the Las Vegas airport. I didn't really want to abandon him that easily. I didn't want him to get fired. Besides, I feared that Caruth would hire another watchdog I couldn't trick as easily.

Jimmie gave up and started to walk from the airport to downtown, a distance of several miles. And a long walk in the desert is painful. Some folks were charging for ice water in Vegas in those days, and I was afraid he'd get overly thirsty. So I let him find me as I stared at the sky outside the airport's main entrance.

"George, where are you going?" he said.

"I'm going back to see Willie," I said. "Are you going with me?"

"I've got to," Jimmie said. "I don't have no money to go nowhere else."

We took a taxi to the Golden Nugget after I promised Jimmie that I would take a later flight to San Jose. He thought he was really on his toes when he told the hotel doorman and valet to watch me.

"I'm with George Jones," he said. "He's in that there cab. You watch it and be sure he don't go nowhere while I check in."

The doorman and valet would have failed as private detectives. Both stood on the same side of the taxi, and both watched the same door. All I did was lower myself, open the opposite door, and hunker down while I crept alongside a convoy of waiting taxicabs. When I got about three or four cabs away from them, I looked over a taxi's trunk. They were still looking at the same closed door.

I could have robbed one of the cabdrivers, slipped back to my waiting taxi, and the doorman and valet would have sworn I'd been inside all along.

I watched Jimmie open the door to an empty taxi. He looked pretty pitiful as he pulled our luggage out. He sat our bags on the curb and asked the doorman to watch them.

"Oh no," I thought. "Don't let that guy watch them. He can't even watch me inside an idling taxi."

So for a few minutes I watched the guy watch my

bags, all the while watching Jimmie look high and low for me. I was still ducked behind a taxi.

But here's where the story becomes sad.

I've said that the only thing a cocaine user wants is more cocaine. Eventually, more and more gets him less and less high. And out there in the Las Vegas sun, between the taxicabs, I knelt down and packed my nose with white powder. I began to wander aimlessly, and I'm glad now that I did. I became no match for Jimmie, who soon saw and caught me. He said I was about five blocks away.

"George," he said, "where are you going?"

"I'm going to Colbert Park," I told him.

Colbert Park is in Alabama. I had no idea where I was.

Jimmie somehow got me into bed, and I somehow got to sleep. It must have been from sheer exhaustion, as I had been up for about two days drinking and doing cocaine. Jimmie sat by my bedside until I fell asleep, then he took every stitch of clothes I had and put them in another room. He turned out the light and left me in an intoxicated sleep.

I felt refreshed the next morning. I had missed the San Jose show but was still booked in Amarillo. I didn't want to go there either. I showered, shaved, and told Jimmie to order breakfast from room service.

"No," I said, "I've changed my mind. Let's go downstairs and eat. I've got to go to the bathroom. You go downstairs, and I'll be right along."

I guess Jimmie trusted me because I was sober. He went down the hall, and I went out the hotel's back door. I'd proven again that I could give him the slip, so I caught up with Jimmie and went to Amarillo, worked the show, got well into the booze and drugs, and gave him the slip once more.

I chartered a plane and flew alone to Muscle Shoals, a town next to Florence, and told the pilot my money was inside my waiting car. He let me walk to it, and I took off, never paying him a cent.

I never would have done anything like that sober, and my lack of consideration for others when I was wrecked bothers me to this day. I knew the pilot would sue me, and I knew he would win.

I was right on both counts. I didn't even attempt to defend the lawsuit. I simply said, "Pay the man his money and whatever damages he's owed."

There is yet another of the several negative sides of cocaine use, and I experienced that too. Cocaine can sometimes let its user get a thought, no matter how outrageous, and hold it indefinitely. He'll finally do something drastic, or even violent, to get rid of the thought. That happened to me more than once.

One of the worst examples came one night when Linda and I were having a party. A man came up to her to say she had left her purse open. He said he could see inside and advised her to fetch the purse.

"You never know who might be at a party," he said. "Some of these folks have just dropped by. One might get into your purse."

He was right. I didn't know a lot of the people who walked into my house when I was high, and I didn't care. Cocaine limits the user's concentration. He often hears only part of a thought. The only thing I remem-

Merle Haggard and I sing from our *Yesterday's Wine* album, recorded in 1982. *Slick Lawson*

Porter Wagoner, *left*, with me and Little Jimmy Dickens, *right*, backstage at the Grand Ole Opry. *Judy Mock*

Faron Young, *left*, joins Marty Robbins and me in 1982 shortly before Marty's death. *Hope Powell*

Here I am in the studio getting ready to cut a track. *Slick Lawson*

The late
Dottie West and
I were great pals.
Judy Mock

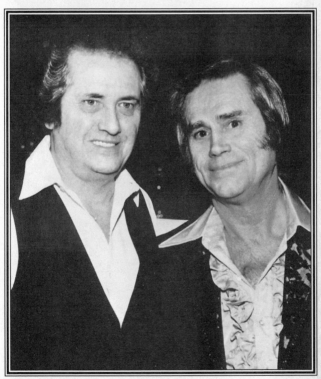

Here I am with my best friend, Pee-Wee Johnson, in 1989.

Hope Powell

Me with my former wife, Tammy Wynette, in concert during the early 1970's. *Private Collection of Tammy Wynette*

Tammy and I in a
1995 publicity shot
for MCA Records.
Harry Langdon

Tammy and I in one of our more recent recording sessions.
This photo was taken in 1994. *Fritz Hoffmann*

My wedding picture, taken seconds after my marriage to Nancy in 1983 inside my sister Helen Scroggins's house.
Adina Estes

Here I am with Nancy in the early 1980's. *Helen Scroggins*

In the mid-1980's, Nancy and I share a laugh
with Ray Charles. *Slick Lawson*

Emmylou Harris is
beautiful in contrast
to Hank Williams Jr.
and me. *Alan Messer*

Chet Atkins, *left,* joins Eddie Rabbit, me, and Mel Tillis for still another "grab-and-grin" shot. *Judy Mock*

In October 1991, President and Mrs. George Bush attended the annual Country Music Association awards show. Here, pictured from the right, are Grand Ole Opry Star Grandpa Jones, me, Barbara Mandrell, Mrs. Barbara Bush, the President, and Barbara Mandrell's daughter, Jamie Dundney. *White House Photograph*

Dolly Parton, *left,* Emmylou Harris, *right,* and I do a last-minute run through lyrics before recording. *Fritz Hoffmann*

Here I am in a practice session with Ricky Skaggs, Trisha Yearwood, and Brian Ahern. *Fritz Hoffmann*

Marty Stuart and I backstage after we cut up inside the Grand Ole Opry House.
Judy Mock

Tracy Lawrence and I toured together in 1993.
Judy Mock

Here are Tanya Tucker and I after a show.
Judy Mock

I congratulate Vince Gill after he won the Country Music Association's award for "Entertainer of the Year."
Judy Mock

Here I am with my favorite female country singer, Connie Smith.
Judy Mock

Travis Tritt and I in 1992.
Rick Diamond

Garth Brooks congratulates me after I win the Academy of Country Music's "Pioneer Award" in 1992. *Judy Mock*

Roy Acuff and I share a moment in his dressing room at the Grand Ole Opry a few minutes before his death. *Judy Mock*

In this shot, Billy Ray Cyrus and I look
like the good, the bad, minus the ugly. *Judy Mock*

Reba McEntire once
asked me to intro-
duce her after I sang
"Who's Gonna Fill
Their Shoes" at the
Grand Ole Opry. I
wish I had done it
because she sings as
pretty as she looks.
Judy Mock

This is my favorite
photo of Nancy,
my reason for living.
Beth Gwinn

My stepdaughter
Adina Estes.
Olan Mills

Nancy and I were photographed in 1993 at a celebrity
softball game held annually for charity in Nashville. *Tammie Arroyo*

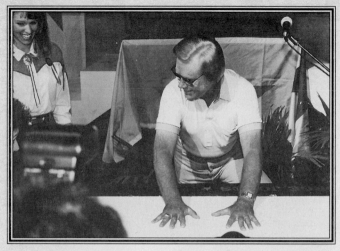

In the summer of 1995 I made an impression in the Walkway of Hands at Opryland. *Opryland, USA*

This historic photograph was taken after overdubbing for the 1992 recording "I Don't Need Your Rockin' Chair," my biggest song of the decade. From left are Alan Jackson, Travis Tritt, me, Mark Chesnutt, Joe Diffie, Patty Loveless, Vince Gill, Clint Black, and Pam Tillis. Garth Brooks is absent. *John Morran*

bered was that a man had been looking inside Linda's open purse. I decided he was trying to steal it.

I was totally wrong, but that didn't stop me from confronting the guy in front of a bunch of other guests and embarrassing someone who had tried to do Linda a favor. She got between us, and the guy angrily left the party.

Not long afterward I was riding somewhere with Jimmie Hills and decided I wanted to get something to eat. He quickly drove to a restaurant because he was pleased that I was actually going to consume food.

I was full of cocaine.

Jimmie and I walked into a café, and I saw the guy who had tried to warn Linda about her open purse. I walked up to him, pulled a pistol from under my coat, cocked it, and placed the barrel against his head. Waitresses dropped their dishes, and people throughout the diner began to scream.

I told the man he was a thief and that he was going to die. He pleaded for his life, and so did Jimmie and others around him. That standoff probably lasted a minute or two before somebody said the police were on the way.

I told the guy I'd kill him the next time I saw him, and Jimmie got me out the door. I don't know why the cops didn't come to my house and arrest me. The Florence police used to regularly look the other way in my behalf.

Linda and I would have a fight, I'd sit in my car behind Jimmie's barbershop, and the cops would call Jimmie.

"Tell George that a new warrant is out for his arrest," they'd tell Jimmie. "We're on the way to get him, so he'd better take off."

Did they think they were doing me a favor? I needed to be arrested. I needed treatment. But it all goes back to the special rules by which show-business people are sadly allowed to live.

I guess the most dramatic incident involving whiskey, cocaine, and me came in 1977 with Peanut Montgomery. My arrest made national news.

I was sitting inside my car watching the river flow outside Florence. Moonlight danced on the churning waters, as black and as troubled as my mind. I had called Peanut to tell him I wanted to talk to him about something and asked him to meet me at the river.

I should say right here that this was after Peanut had gone through a religious experience and become a self-appointed preacher. Here was a guy who had been one of my best friends and drinking buddies. Suddenly, he was telling me, and telling me, that I was going to hell because I drank and used drugs and all.

I didn't want to hear it, especially from someone who had drunk with me for so long. We lived in a dry county, and I can remember when Peanut would stagger with as many as ten empty whiskey bottles in his hands to return to the bootlegger who met him at the door. I always laughed, knowing he couldn't have done that while sober.

I heard his car pull up beside mine that night at the river. I told him something about someone dear to him, and he called me a liar. I knew better.

The drinking, cocaine, financial uncertainty, loneliness, and all-around personal misery were too much to bear. The final straw was Peanut hollering in the dark that I was going to hell because of my sinful ways.

I needed a friend, not judgment.

"You don't know what I go through!" I began to yell, with my car window down.

"You need Jesus," Peanut thundered. "Repent! Repent!"

"Well, let's see if your God can save you now!" I said.

I stared directly through the darkness into his eyes as I picked a pistol from off of the car seat. I intentionally fired over his car roof. I'll believe that until my dying day.

There is no way I could have shot, or shot at, Peanut Montgomery. We were too good of friends who went back too far, no matter how furious he made me with his Bible-thumping.

Peanut's car burned rubber, and gravel flew as it charged off of the riverbank, leaving me in the darkness, alone and ashamed again. But not for long. Peanut went to the police. I was arrested for attempted murder.

In an effort to scare me into straightening up, Peanut decided to file charges against me with the intention of dropping them before I went to trial. That's what he did, and I was told to leave the county, which I didn't. The district attorney said he would keep my file open and refile the charges if he ever caught me inside the county again.

Peanut said I had fired at him and the bullet had struck his car door about an inch below his open driver's window. I never saw a bullet hole. I only saw a photograph of a supposed hole. I believe with all of my heart that someone, possibly someone in law enforcement, doctored that picture to try to help me get my thinking right.

I paced the floor over that one, knowing that the punishment for attempted murder could be several years in prison. My concert dates fell out like never before. No promoter anywhere wanted to take a chance on me not showing up or showing up drunk with a gun.

I have to say that my brush with imprisonment did set me to thinking more than ever about my need to change. But I didn't know how to do it.

I just didn't know how.

Chapter 17

Rick Blackburn and Billy Sherrill were forever supportive of my career when it was under their guidance. I never got any flak from the record label about my legal and criminal woes. Rick maintained his stance about the more trouble I was in, the more records I sold. That actually became the indisputable case beginning in the late 1970s.

I became overly dependent on Rick. I carried his name and telephone number at all times and called him with whatever problem I had. He was the vice president of my record label, not my baby-sitter. But I treated him as such.

I was arrested once and gave the sheriff my name. He thought it was so common that I had made it up.

"Then you call Rick Blackburn at CBS in Nashville, and he'll verify me," I said.

The sheriff did, and asked Rick if CBS had an employee named George Jones.

"No," Rick said. "We have an artist on our label by that name."

"Well, we got a guy in jail that claims to be him," the sheriff said. "And all he's done since he's been in here is sing to the other prisoners. They're having a big time, and he don't act like he cares if he ever gets out. Would you listen to be sure it's him?"

The sheriff held the telephone to the bars, and Rick could hear me singing over the long-distance line.

"That's George!" Rick said. "Where do I send his bail?"

And he sprung me.

Then Rick got the idea for me to record an album of duets. Old and new songs were selected for me to sing with Linda Ronstadt, Emmylou Harris, and some other folks, including James Taylor. I can't remember who else was on the record, which has been out of print for years. I lost my last copy about ten moves ago.

I'd never heard of James Taylor, who I learned is a big soft rock and folk singer.

"Don't you know 'Fire and Rain' or 'Sweet Baby James' or 'You've Got a Friend'?" Rick asked me.

"No," I said. "I never heard of them."

I've never listened to anything but country music. I had heard of the giant rock acts such as the Beatles, but I didn't listen to them. Why should I? I'm sure they did well what they did, but I didn't care for any kind of music that wasn't country. (I listened to the Rolling Stones occasionally just to hear Keith Richards play guitar.)

Ernie Rowell got mad at me once when he brought Neil Young backstage in California.

"Neil Young is here to see you, George," he said.

"Neil who?" I said.

"Neil Young," he said, "of Crosby, Stills, Nash, and Young." He went on to say how much that act was played on the radio.

"But I don't listen to that kind of radio," I told him, "and I ain't never heard of Neil Young."

Neil apparently became angry and left. Ernie later said I was out of touch. I knew that.

I didn't always listen to country radio either. When country stations played songs that were too pop-sounding to me, I changed the dial. I know I wasn't in the fad, but I've never cared about fad.

But I've always cared about country music. Genuine country. That's the simple reason I never listened to anything else. Radio stations that claim to be country today play modern junk with words that don't mean anything. So I don't even listen to what's called country radio anymore, except for WSM-AM in Nashville, where the format is mostly real country music from the 1950s through the 1980s.

Rick played a song for me in 1977 that Taylor had written, "Bartender's Blues." James had made his own demonstration tape, using his own voice.

"That guy is trying to sound like me," I told Rick after hearing the tape.

"He wrote the song with you in mind," Rick said.

"It's a good song," I said. "I'll record it. Now why do I have to sing it with this Jimmy Taylor guy?"

"Because it's going to be on an album of duets," Rick said, "and James wants to do a duet with you."

As I recall, I recorded my part and it was sent to James, who overdubbed harmony. He did an awful good job. I thought then he'd go a long way in the music business.

"Bartender's Blues" was released during the first week of 1978, a terrible time to ask fans who are trying to pay Christmas bills to buy a record. The song was on the *Billboard* country survey for fourteen weeks and peaked at number six. It was my first Top 10 song in two years, following "Her Name Is," which went to number three in 1976. That song was about a guy who was in love with another man's wife. It was a tongue-in-cheek treatment that went, "Her name is . . ." and never told the name of the woman the singer wanted.

The public believed I was singing about Tammy. Several reporters asked if that was true. I purposely hedged on the question. I was ready to let people think whatever they wanted to think if it might sell a few records. I needed the money to pay child support to Tammy.

Once again I wasn't paying a lot of my bills because once again I rarely worked and because when I did, I once again didn't earn enough to satisfy all of the claims against me. I worked many shows and never saw any money from my management. Once again I was usually paid only in cocaine. And once again I was so strung out that I accepted the drug, however reluctantly, as payment in full.

Concert promoters had judgments, some guy in Nashville sued me for breach of contract (claiming that I had agreed to buy his house), and there were various other lawsuits and judgments.

I gave two prices to show promoters. One was the official price listed in a contract. If they paid that, and paid with a check, I couldn't escape tax liability. The other price was less but required the promoter to pay cash. There was no record of that transaction, and I didn't pay income tax on it. I always took cash when I played for the door.

I think every touring country act of the 1960s and 1970s worked that way. I'm owning up to it now because the statute of limitations on my tax liability twenty years ago has expired. And I no longer do business that way.

Today all of my transactions are recorded. If I owe taxes, I pay them. Thank God I have the money to do that at last. And thank Him for a lot of additional organization that Nancy has brought to my life.

Jimmie Hills remembers that I was running late for a show date that I had picked up quickly in 1977 or 1978. I sped to the airport at Huntsville, Alabama, and called Jimmie, who hadn't heard from me in days. He had gone back to full-time work as a barber after deciding he couldn't keep tabs on me for a living.

I don't remember how I got the word about the pickup date. I only remember that I barely had time to drive from Florence and that I feared I was going to miss my plane. The Jones Boys had left Nashville on a borrowed bus and were supposed to meet me at the show.

I had been up for a couple of days, drinking, taking cocaine, and driving aimlessly through the Alabama countryside when I found out about this chance to earn some bucks. I tore into the airport and couldn't find a parking place. I might have had more time than I thought, but when I was taking cocaine, I was usually in a hurry. It has that effect on a lot of people.

It also makes the user highly irritable and impatient. My tension mounted as I drove wildly around the airport, searching for a parking place. By this time I was sure I was going to miss my plane and the few thousand dollars I so desperately needed. So I said to hell with it and parked on the sidewalk—right at the main entrance. I left the engine running for two days.

I ran to the ticket counter, then to the gate. I called Jimmie and told him my car was at the Huntsville airport and that I'd like him to pick it up.

He looked and looked for the car, but he liked to have never found it. That's because he was looking in the parking lots when he should have been looking on the sidewalk at the main entrance. He finally saw the car and couldn't believe his eyes. As he approached the vehicle, he heard the motor running. He saw keys in the ignition. In the back he saw an empty can of Vienna sausages. He knew me well enough to know that was the only food I had eaten for days. And he knew that meant my appetite was suppressed by cocaine.

He contacted the automobile dealership where I had financed the car, and they made keys for him from their service records. They brought the keys to him, and he turned off the ignition forty-eight hours after I had parked.

He couldn't understand why the car hadn't been towed. Then his eyes fell on the dash, where he saw a note. He gave it to me in 1995 when I was writing this book.

"Please," the handwritten note began. "To whom it may concern. I was in quite a hurry, this flight was very important. My name is George Jones with the Grand Ole Opry and I'll be back tomorrow evening."

Numerous security guards and police officers no doubt saw my car. But no one towed it or even tried to turn off the ignition. Jimmie said he couldn't believe the car didn't overheat in the Alabama sun. But that episode shows how I had "friends" who I'd never met who were nonetheless trying to look after me.

I was country music's national drunk and drug addict. There were people whose sympathy for me made them protective and helpful. But again I wish one of them had come forward with legal action to have me admitted to a detoxification ward.

The greatest example of law enforcement's willingness to turn a blind eye in my behalf came on October 23, 1978, two days after the death of Mel Street. Mel was a gifted country singer who had worked shows with me. I loved his style and even wrote the liner notes for one of his albums. He flattered me a whole bunch when he said I had been his greatest influence.

I was drawn to Mel when I heard about his humble raising near Grundy, West Virginia. He grew up poor, then worked construction and climbed towers to help wire the Niagara Power Project at Niagara Falls, New York. He later owned a body shop in Bluefield, West Virginia.

He landed a job on a television show in Bluefield, where he was spotted by Jim Prater, who, years later, became Charley Pride's manager. But in 1963 he knew as little about country music promotion as Mel.

Mel cut a song called "Borrowed Angel" that he had written, and Jim helped promote it. Jim called the same radio stations and asked them to play the song for more than a year. A programmer finally told him to stop calling because his station would not play a record that fans couldn't buy.

Jim was so green in the record business that he didn't know he was supposed to hire a record distributor in order to sell records. He just kept trying to promote a record that wasn't for sale. I was touched by Jim's and Mel's naive innocence.

Mel cut "Borrowed Angel" a second time for another label, wrestled for another year to promote it, only to see it flop again. Nine years later he landed a deal with the Royal American label, hardly a major recording corporation. But Mel's persistence finally paid off, and his little song, first recorded in a little town, entered the national Top 10 in 1972.

Thereafter, he kept hitting commercial paydirt, scoring with "Lovin' on Back Streets," "I Met a Friend of Yours Today," "Smokey Mountain Memories," and others.

The hotter his career got, the more I read that he wanted to sing like me. I felt as though he was a keeper of the country music flame, that he was a country purist during a time when so many other Nashville artists were trying to be "countrypolitan," a term for the blending of country lyrics with symphonic arrangements. Much of the resulting sound was musical mush. It was good music for elevator rides or visits to a foot doctor's office.

Meanwhile, Mel kept singing from his heart, through his nose, by way of his soul. I had tried to do that for years.

I liked Mel so much that I recorded "Borrowed Angel" for Epic, and Mel came to the session. He stood inside the engineer's control booth, and through soundproof glass I saw him weep as I wrung out the words.

When you've been in the public eye as long as me, you hear a lot of people say they admire your work and even that they love you. You develop a sixth sense that tells you who means it.

I sensed sincerity in Mel Street. And I was drawn to him. I'm sure I loved how he loved me. That's one of the reasons I felt protective of the young singer. But I was heartbroken as I saw my influence affect Mel in another way. A sad way. He had heard about my drinking and drug abuse. Perhaps he might have fallen into those traps by himself. So many folks in country music were victimized by those excesses in the 1970s. But I'll never know how much of a negative influence I was on him. People said he wanted to sing, act, and live like George Jones. He lived so much like me it killed him.

On October 21, 1978, I received a call at my Florence home from Shorty Lavender, then my booking agent.

"George," he said, "today is Mel Street's birthday. And today will be his last. He put a bullet through his brain."

I later learned that Mel had eaten breakfast, chatted with his family, casually climbed the stairs to his bedroom, put a gun to his head, and pulled the trigger. He committed suicide on his forty-fifth birthday, as did his father, as did his grandfather, Jim said later.

I was stunned beyond description. We yearn to be

close to people we admire. We can't help but feel close to people who admire us. I was crying, flat hurting out loud when Shorty continued.

"Jim wants you to sing 'Amazing Grace' at Mel's funeral," he said.

"Now how can I do that?" I asked. "I don't think I can get through it, and besides, what about all of the warrants for my arrest in Nashville?"

There was a long silence on the line.

Tammy had sued and won a judgment for forty thousand dollars in back child support. I hadn't paid a dime, and a warrant had been issued for my arrest. The Internal Revenue Service had issued a federal tax lien against my Florence home, and I had been successfully sued by a Nashville hotel that claimed I owed for back room fees. I hadn't paid that judgment either, and another warrant had been issued for my arrest. There were a couple more I can't remember.

These warrants were active in Tennessee, another reason I spent my off time mostly in Alabama. My Possum Holler club was still open, and the Jones Boys still occasionally put my name on a leased bus parked outside to make people think they might see me singing inside. But I didn't go there in the fall of 1978 because I feared being arrested.

In light of the legal threat, how could I sing at Mel's funeral? In light of my love for him, how could I not?

So Shorty called the Nashville police chief and the Davidson County sheriff. He told them that he wanted them to let me come to town, sing at the funeral, and leave without getting arrested. It wasn't for me, he said. It was for Mel Street's family.

And an entire police and sheriff's department took a hands-off attitude toward the arrest of George Jones.

"That's sort of touchy," Jim said in 1995, "but that was back in them days when people would help people out like that."

I was taken, in broad daylight, to a funeral home, where I sang "Amazing Grace" with only my acoustic guitar as accompaniment. I sat on a stool, and Jim remembered that I was skinny and weak-looking. He thought the stress of the moment, coupled with my obvious malnutrition, would topple me from my seat. A lot of folks in the congregation, unaware of my "arrangement" with the law, kept looking over their shoulders toward the back door. That disrupted the funeral, and we paid our final respects to Mel under the threat of my seizure. Folks kept thinking the law was going to stand quietly at the back of the room to put me in handcuffs after I quit singing.

I have to say that Tammy Wynette probably knew I was at that service and could have had me arrested. She was too decent to do that.

Everyone had left the sanctuary when Mel's body was moved into a tiny room surrounded by curtains. His family was brought in and were intended to be the last people to see his body.

But I stayed after everyone else had gone. I was crying and thinking about the Smoky Mountain purity of Mel's baritone, which would ring only in echo on the radio airwaves he had fought to conquer. I thought about the wastefulness of it all. I thought about the scores of times I had thought about taking my own life and wondered why God had given me the strength to live when He hadn't seen clear to give me another dollar for days at a time. Yet I had lasted and Mel had not.

All the while I tried to gather my uncontrollable thoughts, people were whispering through the curtain surrounding Mel.

"George," somebody said, "we've got to get you out of here. You're supposed to be gone. The cops aren't going to look the other way forever. Get out of here."

Folks had my well-being in mind as they tried to rush me from a man I didn't want to leave for the final time. I said something silently to Mel that I've never said out loud. He, God, and an untold number of angels heard it in heaven.

Then I realized that the "Borrowed Angel" Mel had sung about was him. His voice, to me and millions of others, had been angelic. And God had let us borrow it, but only for a while.

"George," someone whispered again, "we got to get out of here. You're going to go to jail!"

And so I left. Someone on each arm whisked me out of the funeral parlor and into an idling car. We sped through town, and a policeman fell into our wake. We were well above the speed limit, but he never pulled us over.

As we approached the county line, he took an exit ramp. I never saw his car again.

I was never more surprised about law enforcement's indifference to me than on October 4, 1978, the day of the internationally publicized abduction of Tammy Wynette. Tammy was at a Nashville shopping center when someone entered her unlocked Cadillac and supposedly forced her to drive about eighty miles, at which point she was beaten and thrown out of the vehicle. A stocking was tied tightly around her neck.

The incident and following investigation were the subject of national television and newspapers for days. Tammy gave a concert a few days after the ordeal and was accompanied by about fifty armed guards, one newspaper reported.

Given my reputation, a lot of people's first thought was that I was behind her kidnapping and beating. There were a lot of whispers on Music Row.

The fact is I was in Florence with Jimmie Hills at the time of the incident. Jimmie would have told that to anyone in law enforcement. But no one in law enforcement ever quizzed Jimmie or me. Can you believe it?

Maybe that was because some officers who investigated the ordeal felt, as I do, that the whole thing was a hoax. Somebody beat the hell out of Tammy, that's for sure. But I don't think it was a kidnapper.

She wasn't sexually assaulted. No money was taken. She wasn't held for ransom. She was just taken on a joyride and beaten by someone who she said wore a mask.

She refused to take a lie detector test.

Later that month a note was found stuck in the iron gates at the house Tammy got from me in the divorce on Nashville's Franklin Road.

"We missed you the first time, we'll get you the second time," it said.

No fingerprints were found on the note, just as none had been found in Tammy's car. The note was left after Tammy had beefed up security at her estate. Cops were roaming the grounds at all hours. Yet no one saw anyone come or go from the property. How did the note get there?

On April 29, 1995, former Nashville police officer Red Smotherman, who had investigated the supposed abduction, discussed the incident with Tom Carter. He said that when he went to Tammy's house to interview her about the supposed crime, she was often an hour late to see him, although she was on the premises. And he felt that her obvious lack of enthusiasm toward the capture of her supposed captor seemed unnatural.

Too many questions remain unanswered. What was her abductor's incentive? And why did she leave her car, filled with birthday gifts for our daughter, unlocked and the keys in the ignition?

I've always thought her assailant was someone she knew. She didn't want to embarrass herself by naming the person, so she concocted a story about a kidnapping, I suspected. After all, the annual Country Music Association Awards were five days later, and Tammy was scheduled to appear on national television. She couldn't go on with a face full of bruises inflicted by someone she knew without being embarrassed.

For the first time ever, Red went on record during a tape-recorded interview to indicate that George Richey, Tammy's fifth husband, had been a suspect.

Red asked Richey to take a lie detector test and said he passed. He asked Richey, among other things, if he abducted Tammy, if he knew who abducted Tammy, and if it was a publicity stunt. Richey was not implicated in any way, Red said.

Lie detector tests are inconclusive and are not allowed as evidence in a court of law.

Then Red told Tom Carter something else he had never told for publication. He suspected that people in my management organization were behind the abduction. I had recently recorded an album, and the proceeds were to go to Tammy to satisfy past-due child support. Some of my managers were anticipating that money. I doubt that I would have seen any of it. I probably would have been paid in cocaine, as usual.

But in the wake of a court order that forced the money to go to Tammy, some of my managers were unhappy, Red theorized. He thinks they might have had Tammy abducted to try to scare her so she wouldn't try to collect money from me again. He thinks they might have been the architects of her kidnapping and beating. They did, after all, want control of my money.

Red wanted to call in Shug Baggott, my head manager, and his brother Sandy, who was sometimes assigned to travel with me. Red wanted to ask them to take lie detector tests but said he was told he could not do that by a superior officer who admits he was then, and is now, a friend of the Baggotts'.

About four years after the incident, Red received a call from another Nashville officer, who said he had found newspaper clippings about Tammy's kidnapping under the sofa of a man who had gone to prison. Red naturally thought the man might be a suspect and wanted to reopen the case but said he was prohibited by his new superior officer.

If the Baggotts had friends in the police department,

could one of them, while on duty patrolling Tammy's estate, have stuck the threatening note in the gate?

I don't know the answers to these questions. But I join Red and his superior officer, former Nashville homicide Detective Sherman Nickens, in thinking that the whole affair was bullshit.

I don't believe Tammy was kidnapped by a street person wanting to act up. It had to be somebody who knew Tammy's car. She didn't have a personalized license plate. And I don't think the cops really wanted to catch whoever did it. Otherwise, they would have questioned me.

I expected, but didn't undergo, police questioning again in August 1979. Shug Baggott and I had gone through an on-again, off-again management relationship since it began. My band hated him and was forever saying that he was taking more money than he deserved while they were behind in their salaries.

It got to the point where band members and members of Shug's management team would get into a footrace to the box office after some of my shows. Each group was trying to collect my money while I was content on my bus with a bottle of whiskey and a bottle of cocaine.

Shug demanded that I work, even when I was too wasted from the cocaine he gave me.

I'll never forget a time when I was supposed to do a week at a club up north, I think in Ohio. I made it to the nightclub but was in no shape to stand, much less sing.

A Memphis doctor, who later was indicted on drug-related charges, was flown to the club to give me chemical nutrition. I was pumped full of shots of I don't know what. But I was still stumbling drunk and couldn't go onstage.

The doctor did what he was reportedly told, and that was to wrap me in medical tape from below my waist to under my shoulders. The tape was tight, preventing me from bending. Unless my knees gave way, there was no way for me to fall down.

I was placed in one spot onstage before the curtain was raised. My bass player was told to extend the neck of his instrument in front of me from my right. My guitar player was told to extend the neck of his instrument from my left. They were told to block me should I lean forward. I was placed near the drums, and Ralph was told to block me should I lean backward. I stood in a man-made, two-foot-square prison containing nothing but a microphone and me.

The tape was so tight I could barely breathe, so you can imagine how badly I must have sung. But taped and bound like a mummy, I was forced onstage. I had officially shown up, so Shug and his cronies got their money.

That went on for a week. Each night the tape was torn from my body, removing hair and skin. I could never get drunk enough to get above the pain, but my managers got their money. I can remember crying and begging them not to tape me up for another show.

I forget who called on that August night to tell me that Shug had been arrested while trying to sell more than two pounds of cocaine to undercover police agents. I braced, waiting for the cops to come and interview me. But again they didn't come.

The press had a field day with the coverage, and Shug was later sentenced to three years in prison. Behind bars, he wrote a five-hundred-page manuscript about what it had been like to manage me and his other perils. I'm sure he had plenty of legitimately negative things to say about me, such as all of the times he booked me on shows I didn't make or all of the opportunities he set up for me that I blew.

He might have even confessed to spending my money, although I doubt it. Shug didn't remain my manager after he went to prison, where he had a born-again experience. He said he accepted Jesus Christ as his personal savior and emerged a new man.

You know what, I'm inclined to believe him. He was good enough to talk to Tom Carter during the preparation of this book. He honestly acknowledged, with tape recorder rolling, that he had supplied cocaine to me and other country singers and named some of them. He pretty much owned up to the wrongs he had done.

God has forgiven him, he's forgiven himself, and I've forgiven him too. There is no percentage in holding hatred, especially at my age.

Shug went to prison, I got out of George Jones's Possum Holler club, and he took it over and was sued for back rent by Kenny Rogers, who owned the building. Kenny sued after learning that Shug was running nude dancers upstairs.

All of these escapades were investigated by the police and covered by the press. And I was never interviewed by either one. And if I had been, I could have honestly said that I didn't know Shug was selling dope or running naked girls.

And in every newspaper and broadcast story, Shug was identified as the manager, or former manager, of George Jones.

Chapter 18

I had my own problems around the time of Shug's bust. They were among the most serious of my entire life. My spending more than I earned finally caught up with me. I filed for bankruptcy.

I could have stayed with Linda in Florence, but during those troubled days I didn't want to be around anyone. So I spent a lot of time in Nashville. There, I could drive down a street and know many of the people inside the music offices. I didn't go inside. I was embarrassed about owing money to so many. It was my own decision to stay away from people. That curiously eased the pain of my solitude.

Loneliness is lessened when you're lonely by choice.

I only knew a handful of people in Florence, and they were sick of me and my drinking, drugging, shooting, cussing, raging, and other outrageousness. They didn't want to be around me. I didn't want to be around them because I was weary of humiliating myself. I couldn't stand daylight around folks who'd seen my dark side.

So I "lived" at the Spence Manor Hotel and Hall of Fame Motor Lodge in Nashville. More than one old-timer in Nashville tells stories about seeing me sitting in my car, or even on a street curb, playing my guitar and singing in 1978 and '79 outside the Spence or Hall of Fame.

I was usually drunk and wasted on cocaine. The Hall of Fame and Spence Manor, then and now, were homes to tourists who came to Nashville for the Grand Ole Opry and other attractions. "Look over there," some were heard to say. "That's George Jones!"

"Naw," their companions often answered. "That ain't him. That man hasn't had a bath or shaved or nothin'. Besides, why would George Jones be sitting out in the sun by himself playing a guitar and singing? That man is a street singer."

To this day Nashville has a few street singers who play and sing for coins along Second Avenue and Demonbreun Street, both tourist areas. Some of the singers make an honest living, and others sing until they get enough to buy a bottle of wine.

I was a street singer only when I was a child. I didn't sing on the streets for money when I was down and out as an adult, no matter who claims differently.

I sang on the street simply to pass the time and because when all else failed, country music was there. When I had no song in my heart, it helped to put one into the air. I sang because I had nothing else to do and nowhere to do it.

I was eventually barred from staying inside the Hall of Fame or Spence Manor because of overdue hotel bills. I had a financed Cadillac, my reputation as the world's greatest country singer, the dirty clothes on my back, and no roof over my head.

I could have worked a show and picked up a few hundred dollars. My fee continued to go down because my reputation for missing shows went up. The missing shows that had once been the exception were now, more than ever, clearly the rule. The few hundred dollars I was getting for some bookings weren't worth it to me. I didn't want to get close to the fraction of sobriety needed for me to travel to a show, work it, and return home. It was easier to hide in a bottle, easier to stay drunk to ease the agony of staying drunk.

In show business people often say that someone is "crazy" when trying to explain his or her irrational behavior. The word is used loosely. But for some time I had seriously thought I was losing my mind, literally going over the edge. That was another hard thing to face, and harder to face while sober. Still another reason to drink.

I had always had a few supporters who said I wasn't uncommonly crazy. They said I was just a common drunk. Those people were gone in the late 1970s.

No one could any longer deny the descent of George Jones because I often refused to be George Jones. I took on two additional and dominant personalities. I even named them. One was "Deedoodle the Duck," and the other was the "Old Man." I quacked like the duck while speaking English, and I moaned like the old man, again in English. I went on for hours, and occasionally for days, unable to speak in my natural voice. I instead spoke only as Deedoodle and the old man. I was a person possessed. The duck sounded like Donald Duck and the old man something like Walter Brennan. They had personalities and passionate convictions of their own. Neither would take shit off of the other.

Sometimes I drove down the road and the duck's voice began to come forward, antagonizing the old man. He'd call him a bad name, and the old man would fire back.

"What the hell do you know?" the old man would say. "You're only a young duck."

"I'd rather be a young duck than a useless old fart," the duck would insist.

Their voices would rise until they were shouting at each other. Their language was hard and aggressive. I'd try to steady the wheel. At times the car would veer under my shaking hand because the two voices were screaming so loudly and violently. They leaped out of me, and I trembled in vain to contain them.

My sanity was regularly taking a leave of absence. On more than one occasion, I struggled to pull the car to the side of the road, crying because I couldn't make the voices stop. The duck and old man made fun of me.

"So you're the great George Jones," one might say. "Wonder what the people would think if they could see you now, dirty and stinking and bawling like a baby? World's greatest country singer, my ass. You ain't nothing but pathetic shit."

I couldn't make them stop.

Maxine Hyder, my friend in Lakeland, Florida, remembers leaving a show in tears because I stood in front of thousands of people talking like a duck. I sang some of my hit songs in the duck's voice, and the audience returned a chorus of angry boos. I could hear myself talking that way, and with every word I tried to stop.

But I couldn't. I honestly couldn't. For years my mind had not been my own. In 1978 and 1979, neither, at times, was my voice.

I knew then that I was going insane. I didn't have far to go. I was totally without emotional or psychological defenses. I had been beaten into submission, but didn't know where to submit. I wanted to rest in someone, but trusted no one.

That's when the financial world fell in on me. And the press jumped on it all.

My only semblance of sanity was my recollection of my roots. When I least expected it, for example, I'd hear the voices of Sister Annie and Brother Burl singing the songs of Christ in a wood-frame Pentecostal church when I was nine. I'd see the arched back of my daddy, ax raised over his head, and hear the crashing of steel against wood that made logs into kindling. I'd hear my mama praying.

And I'd remember how I was always taught, since I was old enough to remember, that a man pays his debts. My daddy was no stranger to credit. But he paid his bills, not always *on* time, but always *in* time.

I put a lot of shame on myself for the legal action I was about to take, listing myself as insolvent before my creditors. I sought full-fledged bankruptcy protection. I just knew my daddy and mama were weeping with the angels about their youngest child's reckless ways, ways that had cost me all of my money. Now they were about to cost the people who had trusted me with credit.

A Nashville bank had sued me for $56,966.70 in overdue loans. I owed $9,000 to Master Charge, $3,500 to Visa, $40,681.14 for a bus loan, $77,901.01 to CBS Records, about $200,000 in lawyer fees, $300,000 in default court judgments, and lots more.

When my lawyer filed the bankruptcy petition, it listed forty-six creditors. I owed $1.5 million.

My net worth was $64,500.

Most of that was equity in a mobile home in Lakeland, and most of the rest was in the plywood furniture inside. And I didn't even live in that house. Nobody did.

I had to go to court time and time again and talk about who I owed what. The proceedings didn't move as fast as I wanted. I didn't like the regular press coverage and wanted to get my name as a deadbeat out of the paper.

I fired my lawyer and hired a new one to speed things along. But the new lawyer's having to familiarize himself with the petition took time, and eventually things were actually slowed down.

Bankruptcy court was much more informal then than it is now, I'm told. I just sat at a table with Tom Binkley, my new lawyer, and listened as he and the judge went over my financial records. No other people, except maybe a court reporter, were inside.

But two things delayed the hearings. First, I couldn't find most of my records. The court would not accept as a legitimate debt something I couldn't document. I'd always done business out of my hip pocket. I had no filing system. I had bought and sold such things as cars, houses, and even a giant boat but had no records to validate the transactions. I could forget about bankruptcy protection, I was told, for money whose spending I couldn't prove.

The second delay came from my drinking and drug use. I was regularly high inside the courtroom.

I'm sure the judge had no idea I was under the influence of alcohol and drugs or I would have been held in contempt of court, but he must have thought I had an awfully weak bladder. I excused myself about every thirty minutes to go to the men's room. Tom said he could see the flask in my pocket, but the judge couldn't.

Neither Tom nor the judge saw my tiny vial of cocaine. I hurriedly guzzled enough booze and took enough cocaine blasts to get a buzz inside a rest-room stall, then floated back to my seat. There, I did nothing but sit quietly and tune out talk about money I didn't have. From that stuffy courtroom, I took mental journeys around the globe.

Old friends who owned music stores, recording studios, and the like listed themselves as creditors. So did members of my band. One Nashville motel wanted $5.64. That must have been for a room service charge.

Johnny Cash and Waylon Jennings helped me. Together, they gave me about sixty-four thousand dollars in cash. I put most of it in a grocery sack, bought an ounce of cocaine, and gave the rest to the court in currency.

The judge got tired of hearing that I could not account for the spending of more than one million dollars. He said I was the most financially irresponsible person he'd ever seen. But I wasn't lying. I just didn't know where it went. How could I have known where my money was when most of the time I didn't know where I was?

Bankruptcy was denied.

I had been in bankruptcy court about fifteen times over six months only to lose my request. I missed a few court dates because I was too drunk to go. I knew the judge wouldn't be amused if I fell out of my chair.

Tom appealed the judge's denial to a Tennessee district court, and I got a judge with a heart, who granted the bankruptcy with an unprecedented payback plan. Tom, who later became president of the Tennessee Trial Lawyers' Association, said he has never seen a district court work so flexibly with a bankruptcy applicant before or since.

Most of my creditors, after the ruling, were paid twenty cents on the dollar. I paid the court five thousand dollars a month until I got permanently sober a few years later, and then I increased the amount of my installments. The court ruled that my royalties from CBS, United Artists, Pappy Daily, and Broadcast Music Incorporated were to be applied to my creditors through the court.

I paid the court's demand in full, and some people who had once trusted me to pay my debts in full took an 80 percent loss.

I didn't even pay Tom right away. In fact, he had to sue me to get his legal fees. He's a kind and forgiving man who is my friend today, and he was extremely cooperative when I asked him to refresh my memory for the writing of this book.

There were many people, such as background singer Jennifer O'Brien, who didn't take a dime. Time and again they were offered the chance to put their names on the list of creditors, but they refused. They said they felt too sorry for me. I'm telling those people here and now how much I appreciate their compassion for the sick sot who was the old George Jones.

I must add a note here about Jennifer and the guys who were in my band from about 1976 until 1980 (except when one or two got mad and quit for a day or two). They were a family who bonded in the way that only traveling show people can. People who live and breathe inside four hundred square feet of motorized steel get closer than biological family and for a very simple reason. They spend more time with each other than they do with blood relatives.

I had missed four shows in a row when the Jones Boys and Jennifer played somewhere in southern Illinois. Jennifer got a call that said her mother, who Jennifer knew had cancer, had only a day or two to live. Jennifer reacted instinctively. She ran to the bus and her family of musicians.

Ernie Rowell took the show to Illinois, fought the fans who were angry about my absence, and worked a deal with the promoter, who agreed to pay the Jones Boys and Jennifer fifteen hundred dollars to perform without me. After the show, Ernie and the other boys told Jennifer they had held a meeting and decided to take her to northern Illinois near the Wisconsin border to be with her mother during her final hours. They drove my bus and arrived at daylight. As a result, Jennifer saw her mother during her last moments on this earth.

"Now here is an envelope," Ernie told Jennifer. "You keep this. Don't open it until we're gone. The Jones Boys and I are going to take the bus and go back to Nashville."

After they had departed, Jennifer opened the envelope to find fourteen hundred dollars. The boys had kept only one hundred dollars to buy diesel fuel and food to get back to Nashville and given Jennifer the rest of their performance fee. She'll never forget that.

I haven't seen Jennifer or most of those folks for years. To tell the truth, I'm a little embarrassed to go around them. Today I'm sober and debt-free. I've got a ways to go before I'm guilt-free.

Linda was living in a rented house in Florence, and I went to see her during the bankruptcy turmoil. I got little solace, as she had me arrested for assault and battery. I think she was just angry because I'd been away. I got out on a three-hundred-dollar bond and went to Texas to see my kinfolk.

Except in my mind, I hadn't been home for years. I visited two of my sisters and went to the graveyard and talked to my mama and daddy's tombstones. My thoughts were melancholy, and my soul was straining to purge itself. I became easily upset, and when I did, the duck and the old man surfaced.

During a blinding thunderstorm, in the blackness of midnight, I wept bitterly over my parents' coffins and wailed as a duck and an old man. The rain splattered mud from their graves onto me. It mixed with the tears streaming uncontrollably down my face.

In that dark and silent cemetery, I wondered where the bottom was. How can I go any lower? When will things ever get better?

All the lawsuits brought against me by creditors were invalid in the wake of my working out a payback agreement with the court. There were still some outstanding Tennessee criminal warrants against me, but I returned to Nashville anyhow. I kept a low profile, and the law didn't catch me. Of course, as I indicated earlier, the law wasn't looking too hard.

Isn't it amazing that all of the people who'd won financial judgments against me, and who could have had me arrested before I was awarded bankruptcy, didn't? Maybe they knew they'd never get their money if I was behind bars, but I don't think so. I stiffed some good friends who somehow knew I didn't want to. And they didn't want to put me in jail. I had better friends than I knew at the time.

So I began to hang around Printers Alley, where all of the Nashville nightlife was still centered in the late 1970s. I often didn't get out of my car. I just watched the tourists or sent someone inside a nightclub to fetch an old friend who I thought might be inside.

I had somehow gotten a used yellow Cadillac when Peanut Montgomery saw me one night. I had a lot of my clothes in the backseat, and he later said he wondered if I was living inside that car. I wasn't. There was no way you could call that living.

By that time I had gone so long without eating much that my stomach had seriously shrunk. It must have been about the size of a baseball. About every three or four days I'd try to eat a sandwich but usually got no more than half of it down before I was full.

I had a case of whiskey, an eight-by-ten glossy photograph of Hank Williams, and some of Hank's cassette tapes in that car. I stared blankly at the picture and listened thoughtfully to the music for hours on end. I didn't speak, unless it was in the voice of the duck or the old man.

Most of my "nutrition" was from the vitamins and minerals inside blended whiskey. My weight had dropped from about 165 in my prime to about 105. My breath stank from the constant lack of food, the way some folks' stinks when they go on a religious fast or rigid diet. I could smell myself.

On the night Peanut saw me, my skin was oily from my not having bathed. My hair was matted by its own natural grease. My clothes, a far cry from the days when I always had a pressed suit no matter how drunk I was, were dirty and wrinkled, as if someone had slept in them. Someone had.

Peanut had been a friend for years, despite my arrest for his attempted murder, and in the space of a moment he'd had enough. Knowing I'd eventually return to Florence, he contacted an Alabama district court judge about having me committed to a psychiatric ward and drug and alcohol rehabilitation center.

But he didn't tell me.

On December 11, 1979, I was in Florence when some men in white coats came to see me. The judge had exercised the legal maneuvers to have me committed.

"Do you love this man?" Peanut said the judge asked him about me.

"Yes, I love him," he said he answered.

I had no relatives in my state of residence. I had none in Texas who were willing to take the necessary legal action. Peanut had to get a court ruling that gave him custody over the life he said I couldn't control. He must have been mighty convincing. If I'd have known what he was up to, I wouldn't have returned to Alabama.

I was taken against my will to the Hill Crest Hospital in Birmingham by the men in white coats.

I think that's the first place I heard that alcoholism is not a moral failure but a progressive disease. The doctors told me I wasn't evil or weak but sick. They told me I had an infirmity that could be treated. They had definite steps toward recovery, which they said was a gradual process.

"It's taken you years to get into this shape," the counselors said. "It will take you years to get well. Don't be in a hurry or impatient with yourself. Recovery is a gradual process that is taken one day at a time. In here and later, when you're out of here, live life one day at a time."

My IQ was measured at seventy-four.

After testing, the doctors said my capacity to rationalize or reason was gone. I didn't know why things worked. I couldn't solve problems put before me. I couldn't perform simple arithmetic. I would have done well to put round pegs in round holes.

The staff tried to teach me practical matters, such as not to let myself get upset, or sleepy, or even hungry. Any of those situations prompted an alcoholic to drink, I was taught. They explained that food intake affected my body chemistry. If certain chemicals got in short supply because of hunger, I would crave a drink and go off the deep end. So I should keep a full stomach, they said.

They told me that alcohol was mostly sugar. They said I had therefore developed an addiction to sugar and that I should try to feed that addiction with lots of sweets, which would help take a part of the place of booze. The hospital was overflowing with cakes and candy that I could eat whenever I wanted.

I couldn't sleep. I had been used to staying up for days on cocaine, never sleeping unless I was drugged with exhaustion or alcohol. During the first few days they gave me sedatives. Mostly the staff gave me love, or at least the appearance of love.

Doctors and counselors tried to determine why I drank and took drugs. They explained the theory of self-hatred to me: Many men who had been beaten by their fathers hated themselves. My young mind felt I was worthless as a human being and therefore deserving of the beatings my dad had given me.

When Dad was no longer around to beat me, I strove to beat myself through various forms of abuse. They said I felt unworthy of anything good, that I had recklessly wasted money, even flushed it down the toilet at times, because I subconsciously felt unworthy to have it. They said I lashed out against women who loved me because I felt unworthy to be loved. Some of their teaching made a lot of sense to me.

I wish it had taken.

Peanut came to see me after two weeks. By then I was dry, but I was far from sober. He entered my room, and I didn't say hello.

"What are you trying to do, kill me?" I yelled.

"No, George," he said. "I'm trying to save your life."

"I'll run my own damn life!" I said. "I don't need you or anybody else to do it!"

Of course I was wrong.

"You put me in this place, and now you get me out," I stormed.

I resented Peanut's involvement because I knew he, at times, had been as big a drunk as me. He had found religion and used to preach to me. That, as I mentioned earlier, made me furious. I'd get drunk and call him "Little Jesus." I threatened to pull out his beard one hair at a time.

I was very hostile, so although Peanut came to see me often, he didn't stay very long. I was too unbearable.

I watched a lot of television and read a lot of cards and letters from fans who weren't supposed to know I was in there. Somehow the reporters got hold of the story. Don't they always? The press had discovered so many of my misfortunes that it didn't matter anymore. It wasn't like the reports were going to damage my reputation.

I had a lot of time to think about God and to read the Bible. I had a lot of time to lie on my back and stare at the ceiling, whose cracks and holes I memorized. I took a lot of mental inventory. I did a lot of soul-searching. I fell asleep a lot of nights on a tear-drenched pillow.

I was financially, psychologically, and emotionally bankrupt. I had no upcoming show dates, no idea if my band had disbanded, and didn't want to see the few people who wanted to see me. And for months I had no longer been able to lie to myself about Tammy and me someday, somehow, getting back together.

"This is it," I remember thinking near the end of my hospitalization. "I have *finally* reached the bottom." In a way, I was actually glad to have gone through so much. The only direction from here had to be up, I was sure.

And on the radio, disc jockeys were playing "These

Days I Barely Get By," my 1975 song about a man who was hitting bottom so hard he was sure he couldn't go on. In part, it went as follows:

> *I woke up this morning aching with pain*
> *Don't think I can work, but I'll try*
> *The car's in the shop, so I thumbed all the way*
> *Oh these days I barely get by.*
>
> *I walked home from work and it rained all the way*
> *My wife left and didn't say why*
> *She laid all our bills on the desk in the hall*
> *Oh these days I barely get by.*
>
> *These days I barely get by*
> *I want to give up, lay down, and die*
> *Worst of all was when she told me good-bye*
> *Oh these days I barely get by*
> *These days one barely gets by.*

The song was cowritten by someone who seemed to know my desperation as well as I did. Her name was Tammy Wynette.

Chapter 19

Nothing would make me prouder than to tell you that my thirty days in drug and alcohol treatment healed me. Nothing makes me more ashamed than telling you they didn't.

I felt so good the day I got out of the hospital that I stopped and got a six-pack. I went to my house, where I had hidden a small amount of cocaine, and used it.

I celebrated my temporary freedom from alcohol and cocaine with alcohol and cocaine.

My treatment had amounted to no more than a monthlong recess from self-destruction. I had rested, but when I went back to the real world, I found my problems hadn't rested at all. They had mounted.

The boys in my band were so unaccustomed to being paid that they still refused to go on shows unless they got their money in advance. I couldn't provide that, as I had no money myself. I had just come out of the hospital. I had no insurance, and I hadn't been working.

I'd finally persuade the Jones Boys to go on the road, promising them their pay after the show, and do my best to deliver. If my managers got the money first, and didn't pay the band, my players understandably got furious.

Drummer Ralph Land was the most vocal of all, and what he said about band members needing their salaries to pay their own bills made sense. My management team thought he was a troublemaker simply because he wanted money that was due him.

Someone anonymously threatened to kill him, and he decided, rightly or wrongly, that the threat had come from Shug or Sandy Baggott. He left my office one evening and called the Tennessee attorney general.

"I'm Ralph Land, and I play drums for George Jones," he said. "I'm leaving Jones's office now and heading for my house." He gave his address, then stated, "If I don't make it there I want you to know who murdered me." He gave the names of the Baggott brothers.

It's hard to maintain morale within an organization whose members aren't getting their paychecks and who suspect each other of trying to kill each other.

And after every show my band and members of management were still physically running to the box office, competing to collect my performance fee to apply to money they said I owed them.

Inside that hospital I had made minimal changes in my mind. Outside my sick world was the same.

So, in the words of Merle Haggard, it was "back to the bar rooms, right back to drinking again." And for me, cocaine went with whiskey as well as water.

Shortly after my hospitalization, I think my alcohol consumption became worse, if that's possible, than at any other time during my approximately thirty years of drinking. In the back of my mind I thought that, with what I had been taught at the rehabilitation center, I could "control" my drinking. All I had to do, I thought, was to enroll in detoxification for thirty days anytime I got exhausted from the booze. I'd dry out, rest, get fed, and even get my thinking right.

I could go into rehabilitation for two thousand dollars in those days. I could afford that merely by getting my share of a weekend's worth of work.

My thinking was really out of whack. I had missed the entire point of detoxification and rehabilitation. Looking back, I think I was discharged too soon.

My mind went right back to playing tricks on me. I went to Florence one day to get Jimmie Hills to cut my hair. I was half drunk and carried perhaps an ounce of cocaine in my front pants pocket. It looked like I had a lump on my leg.

I knew that Jimmie knew I used, and I knew he wouldn't say anything about it. Another customer entered while I was in the chair. He was an IRS agent.

Jimmy introduced the man to me and said he had long wanted to shake the hand of George Jones. This here is so and so, Jimmie said. He's one of your biggest fans, and he works for the IRS.

In my mind, I was sure Jimmie had said FBI. I was certain the man was there to bust me for the cocaine in my pants. I immediately thought of how many Mafia figures had been surrounded by authorities in the barber's chair. I thought of Albert Anastasia, who was murdered by other gangsters while getting a haircut. And so I bolted from the barber's chair.

My hair was dripping wet and I still wore the barber's apron as I sprinted for the back door. There, I was convinced cops were waiting for me outside. Terrified, I yanked a full ounce of cocaine, perhaps fifteen hundred dollars' worth, from my pocket and ripped the plastic bag. I threw it all over the back-room floor. Then I braced for the cops I feared were on the other side of the door.

I charged outside, thinking my momentum might knock one or two down and I could leap into my car for a speedy getaway.

Meanwhile, Jimmie and the IRS agent were scratching their heads inside. The agent wanted a haircut, but Jimmie wouldn't let him take the chair because my time wasn't up.

"George must not be feeling well," Jimmie said. "He's probably back there in the rest room."

Jimmie asked his wife, Ann, who also worked at the shop, to see about me. She walked in the back and saw the floor. It looked like an indoor snowfall. She knew immediately what it was and figured I wouldn't be back. She fired up a vacuum sweeper and began cleaning up the evidence. That much cocaine could have gotten me charged with possession with intent to distribute. Conviction carried a sentence of several years.

Meanwhile, Jimmie and the IRS guy were still waiting for me to return to the barber's chair. Ann had a customer in her own chair. He couldn't understand why she had chosen such an unusual time to vacuum the back room.

If the police had ever learned of that incident and opened that vacuum's bag, we would have all gotten time behind bars.

About this same time, I called a couple of the Adams brothers (who had worked as some of the Jones Boys in the 1960s) to do a few shows with me. I don't remember if they came to Florence or to Lakeland, where I might have called them because a couple of my band members temporarily pulled out again.

It took all of the money the Adamses had to get to wherever I was. They arrived only to find that I was destitute. Not actually. I had a few cents.

"We ain't got any money, George," one said.

"Well, all I got is this change," I said. "That ain't gonna do nobody no good. Hell, we might as well be completely broke."

And so, for the second time in my life and career, I was. I stood at the back door and hurled less than a handful of coins across the lawn. We had a booking, a full tank of diesel fuel in a leased bus, a guarantee of motel rooms to be paid for by the promoter, and nothing else.

Except for a song. And I do mean a song.

I played rhythm guitar and sang "He Stopped Loving Her Today." The Adams brothers flipped, and so did most everyone who ever heard that tune before, or after, it was recorded.

The song had been brought to my attention in 1978 by Billy Sherrill. It had been written by Curly Putnam and Bobby Braddock. Curly had written "Green, Green Grass of Home," which was a big hit for Tom Jones and for Porter Wagoner. Jerry Lee Lewis had put it on an album. Bobby had written hits for Tammy and me. Billy loved "He Stopped Loving Her Today." He said he was unable to sleep the night after first hearing that song. But he thought it was incomplete.

The song is about a man who loved a woman so much it killed him when she left. He had said he would love her until he died, and only on his deathbed did he stop. Hence the idea "He stopped loving her today."

In 1993 I was a guest on a talk show whose host was Burt Reynolds. Alan Jackson, Vince Gill, and Randy Travis were on with me. Alan said he thought "He Stopped Loving Her Today" was the perfect country song.

A lot of folks have agreed with him. In 1992 *Country Music* magazine and *USA Today* published a list of the world's most popular country songs, as voted by their readers. "He Stopped Loving Her Today" was number one in each publication.

To this day, when I sing it in my show, people sometimes applaud from the first note until the last. I've actually had people tell me they didn't hear one word because of the deafening applause.

And I almost missed the song that changed my life and career more than anything, anything, that is, except for my marriage to Nancy.

Putnam and Braddock killed the song's main character too soon in their early versions. Billy kept telling them to kill the guy at a different time and then have the woman come to his funeral. The writers thought that might be too sad, and Billy did too. But he knew the song, on a scale of one to ten, was about an eight. He saw it as a potential eleven.

He gave the song to me, and I carried it for more than a year, also convinced that it needed rewriting. Billy had a notebook about an inch thick that was nothing but rewrites of "He Stopped Loving Her Today."

When we finally got a version that made Billy happy, I went in to record. But I was drunk and couldn't get the melody. For some reason, the melody to "Help Me Make It Through the Night," the Kris Kristofferson classic, stuck in my head. So I sang Curly and Bobby's lyrics with Kristofferson's copyrighted melody. Billy had a fit, and we had a fight.

"You're singing the wrong melody!" he yelled.

"Oh yeah," I said. "Well, the melody I'm singing is prettier than the one you want."

"That may be," he argued. "I'm sure Kristofferson would think so too. But it's the wrong melody."

It took a long time before I sang the correct melody.

That song contains a narration. I hadn't utilized a narration in one of my songs in years and can only think of one I've done since—Tom T. Hall's "I'm Not Ready Yet." Anyhow, the narration pertained to the woman's visit to the funeral. It goes:

> *She came to see him one last time*
> *And we all wondered if she would*
> *And it kept running through my mind*
> *This time he's over her for good.*

Pretty simple, eh?

I couldn't get it. I had been able to sing while drunk

all of my life. I'd fooled millions of people. But I could never speak without slurring when drunk. What we needed to complete that song was the narration. But Billy could never catch me sober enough to record four simple spoken lines.

It took us about eighteen months to record a song that was approximately three minutes long.

On the day we finished, I looked Billy square in the eye and said, "Nobody will buy that morbid son of a bitch." Then I marched out the studio door.

The song was released on April 12, 1980. It became my first number-one song in six years.

I've had my share of career records, such as "She Thinks I Still Care," "White Lightning," "Walk Through This World with Me," "The Grand Tour," and maybe a few others.

"He Stopped Loving Her Today" did more for my career than all of the others combined. I went from a twenty-five-hundred-dollar act who promoters feared wouldn't show up to an act who earned twenty-five thousand dollars plus a percentage of the gate receipts. That was big money for a country artist sixteen years ago.

I was wanted by show promoters everywhere. I was wanted by network television producers. The magazine interview requests were limitless.

To put it simply, I was back on top. Just that quickly. I don't want to belabor this comparison, but a four-decade career had been salvaged by a three-minute song.

There is a God.

* * *

You wouldn't think I could have found a way to blemish such a wonderful hit record and its resulting success. But I did, although only to a tiny degree. I embarrassed myself on national television, but folks just figured I was drunk. Being suspected of being drunk wasn't that damaging to my career by 1981. I mean, what else was new?

The song was nominated for the Country Music Association's "Song of the Year" and I for "Male Vocalist of the Year." Rick Blackburn, still vice president of the CBS Nashville division, wanted to personally see that I made it to the awards show sober. The show has been broadcast during prime time in the fall since 1967. It used to be a ninety-minute broadcast but now runs for three hours.

Rick took me to the Opryland Hotel at 6 P.M. He told me that we had to be in our seats at the Opry House by 7:30 P.M. and that live cameras would roll promptly at 8 P.M.

"I'll be back at seven P.M. with your tuxedo," he said. "You can get dressed, and then the limousine will take us to the Opry House."

I told him I was going to take a nap. I can't remember, maybe I fully intended to do so.

Remember, a lot of my old drinking buddies came around whenever I returned to Nashville in those days. Somebody, maybe Johnny Paycheck, stopped by my room.

Rick returned with Tom Binkley, still my attorney, to find that I had almost single-handedly drunk a fifth of whiskey in the space of an hour. It's a wonder I didn't suffer alcohol poisoning and die. I know now there have been many times when it was a wonder that I didn't die.

I LIVED TO TELL IT ALL   321

Rick expected to find me fresh in my tuxedo when he arrived to pick me up. Instead, I was drunk, unconscious, and naked in the bathtub.

I was supposed to present an award, sing a song, and possibly receive a major music award on an international live television show scheduled to commence in less than sixty minutes.

Tom and Rick turned cold water on me in the shower, and Rick ordered pots of coffee. I cussed and kicked over a lot of furniture, I'm told. I probably wanted to fight but was too drunk to even make a fist.

Rick had spent the last few years trying to convince his superiors in New York City that CBS should keep me in its Epic division. I had disrupted that big deal he had set up at the Bottom Line in New York, but I had redeemed myself with "He Stopped Loving Her Today." He had told the big shots I was a changed man.

I was. I was a worse drunk than ever.

Tom and Rick wrestled me down the Opryland Hotel hall and into the waiting car. We were rushed to the Opry House, where Rick walked me down the aisle to my assigned seat next to him. We'd be seen when the television cameras panned the audience.

Then he made one of the toughest judgment calls of his life. He had invested a lot of money over a lot of years to help rebuild my career. Tonight he was scheduled to get some crowning glory. But he went to the executive producer of the CMA Awards, given on Nashville's biggest night of the year, and told him to scratch me from the show.

"At what point is George scheduled to go on?" Rick asked.

"He's got the third song," he was told.

"He can't go on," Rick said.

"What!" said the executive producer. "What do you mean he can't go on? He's nominated for one of the biggest awards of the night, he has his own song in the show, and you're telling me he can't go on?"

"That's right," said Rick. "He'll embarrass us all."

"This is live television," the executive producer reminded Rick. "It's too late to find a fill-in!"

I guess he wanted me to show my ass live as opposed to having it videotaped.

"Well," said the executive producer, "what about Barbara Mandrell?"

Rick only moaned. He had forgotten that I was also scheduled to do a duet with Barbara, then one of the hottest entertainers in North America due to her prime-time show on NBC. She had recorded a song called "I Was Country When Country Wasn't Cool" that had gone to number one.

I had sung two lines in that song as a featured artist near the end of the recording. The song was a giant hit, an anthem of the airwaves.

I couldn't have sung my two lines any more than I could have sung my middle name. I was that far gone. Rick was even afraid I would pass out in my third-row seat and that much of the free world would see me snoring on Nashville's biggest night.

He was panicked and pissed.

Backstage adjustments were hurriedly made. I didn't get to sing "He Stopped Loving Her Today." Barbara, I was later told, was told to sing her song without me. She was instructed in no uncertain terms not to even acknowledge me in the audience.

So what did she do?

She did her tune to thunderous applause, then brought the final verse to the point where I had come in on the recording. And she spotted me in the audience.

Microphone in hand, she came off the stage and walked down the aisle to my seat. A portable television camera followed her.

When it came time for my lines, she shoved the microphone in my face and hollered, "George Jones!" I was taken totally off guard in front of perhaps twenty million people.

Here's all I was supposed to sing:

I was country, when country wasn't cool
Yeah I was country, from my hat down to my boots.

Not exactly the Gettysburg Address, is it?

I couldn't remember one word. I fumbled and mumbled and said I don't know what. I botched the thing entirely. Barbara headed back to the stage, still singing, and brought the song to a close.

I sat down and wondered where Rick had gone. Embarrassed, he had sunk so low in his seat that for a moment I missed him. Then I decided he might be sick.

"This is great," I thought. "I'm drunk, and Rick has had a heart attack."

I started to ask if there was a doctor in the house but wasn't sure if the live camera was still on me.

"If I ask for a doctor and it goes out over television they're liable to come from everywhere," I thought.

Eventually, Rick sat up and the color returned to his face.

The show went on, and the award was given for "Song of the Year" or "Male Vocalist of the Year," I can't remember which. My name was called.

When Barbara had come to me, I had stood while holding on to the chair in front of me. Now I had to walk down a sloped aisle to waiting stairs that I had to climb on live television while still drunk—very drunk.

I got onstage, was handed my award, and couldn't think of anything to say. So I thanked Johnny Wright and Kitty Wells. Johnny had recorded a number-one song in 1965. Kitty Wells is a true country pioneer who broke a lot of ground for today's female country stars. She was the first woman to record a million-selling record, and it became her biggest hit. That was in 1952. Neither Johnny nor Kitty ever had a thing to do with my career.

"George," Rick later fumed, "of all the people you could have thanked, of all the people who have worked to rebuild your career these past few years, why did you thank Johnny Wright and Kitty Wells?"

"The television lights got in my eyes," I said. "They were the only people I could see."

Rick told that story in a tape-recorded interview fifteen years later and finished with five words: "I'm not making this up."

The continuing success of "He Stopped Loving Her Today" prompted CBS to renew my contract in 1981. The wonderful thing about that song is that anytime anyone wanted to hear it, they had to hear it by me. Another artist had cut it before me, but his version was an album song and did nothing. To my knowledge, I recorded the only single record on that tune.

So Rick set up some high-level negotiations with CBS big shots in Los Angeles, where I was to sign a new contract. The good news is that I was to get a $500,000 advance, a figure that was mighty stout in those days. The bad news is that CBS wanted to be sure the money went to pay my new debts.

After having been awarded bankruptcy, I formed an enormous group of new debts. Tom Binkley said he never noticed a change in my spending habits. Before long, I owed about a half million in back taxes, back salaries, a few default court judgments, and more.

CBS didn't want to go through the legal hassle of having creditors garnishee my royalties. So they agreed to pay me the $500,000 but not let me see a dime of it. All of the money was to go to my creditors.

I agreed to the program, and Rick chartered a jet for Tom, him, and me to fly to Los Angeles for the signing. By this time I had yet another new manager, Wayne Oliver, and he was on hand for the summit too.

Those guys hammered out contract terms for several twelve-hour days. Meanwhile, I sat in a hotel suite, drank champagne, and snorted cocaine. I'm not sure they knew about the cocaine.

At last they sent for me. My new contract was ready for my signing. Rick or somebody ordered new champagne. I was supposed to sign this giant record deal, and then we were all supposed to toast it with raised glasses.

I walked into the room, looked down the length of the

long rectangular table, accepted a polite patter of applause, and then said I had something to say.

"I ain't signing a damn thing."

And then I left. I closed the thick door behind me, but I could still hear men coughing and spluttering.

"What the hell is going on here?" the industry big shots demanded of Tom, Rick, and Wayne. "I thought we had a deal. Why the hell have we been out here for all these days?"

Wayne and Tom came to my room. Their faces were real white. I was drunk and still packing cocaine when I told them they didn't look too good.

"Let's talk," they said together.

"Fine," I said. "We can talk on the way back to Nashville."

"What do you mean?" they pleaded.

"I ain't signing no damn contract that gives money to everybody but me. I want one hundred thousand dollars of that half million for myself, in cash."

They began to pat their chests in half time.

I wasn't bluffing. I was tired of not having any money. Admittedly, I didn't have any because I pissed it away, but I was tired nonetheless.

"You go back and tell those sons of bitches that I'll fly back to Nashville on their Learjet and they can pick up the tab for the high life I've lived while I've waited for them to come up with an agreement that screws me," I said.

I went downstairs and got into a limousine. I told the driver to take me to the airport and the waiting Lear.

I don't think lawyers and executives have ever worked so quickly. I pulled onto a private runway at Los Angeles

International Airport and was preparing to step from the car into the waiting airplane.

Brakes suddenly screeched to a halt beside me. Wayne, Tom, or Rick, or maybe a combination, had a new contract, already written and printed. It gave me $100,000 cash.

I climbed the steps to the airplane with men waving ballpoint pens behind me.

It was the eve of Thanksgiving Day, and the sun was setting in the west. I signed a new contract with CBS Records and got my $100,000. The other $400,000 went to my debts, which were paid with an accounting I never saw.

I didn't care. I figured that I, or rather my creditors, probably got screwed out of about half of it anyhow. I took my $100,000 and bought a new Corvette, a lot of cocaine, and spent the rest on foolishness.

Soon after I recorded "He Stopped Loving Her Today," and before Wayne became my manager, five of the guys in my six-member band quit me forever. They had had it. The guy who stayed, but whom I later fired, Clyde Phillips, had once called Tom Binkley the day before a big Fourth of July festival. He said the band wasn't going until they received their back pay. Tom said he knew who was handling my money, but didn't know where it was going, and miraculously persuaded the band to go to the show, promising them their pay after our performance. The show was one of their last. We were somewhere out west, I think in California, when we had a band meeting. Little was resolved, and we knew it was the beginning of the end.

Those players were among the finest I've ever had. It hurt me to lose them, and it hurt many of them to go. So they got shit-faced twenty-five hundred miles from home. They had done that before, and the bus driver had brought them to Nashville. But there was a problem on this trip. The driver got drunk too.

It was decided that Ralph Land was the least drunk of all after he passed a strenuous test: He remained conscious.

But there was also a problem with Ralph driving. The band, you see, was blind drunk. Ralph was just blind in one eye. And he was only partially sighted in the other. But he squinted through his adequate eye and drove most of the way for most of the length of the nation. When his sighted eye got tired, he covered it after centering the bus between the asphalt and the right lane on the interstate at highway speed. The feel of the asphalt shoulder under the tires as opposed to the smoothness of the concrete told Ralph when he was veering off the road. He knew then it was time to reopen his "good" eye.

Ralph didn't show a lot of sense, but he did show a surplus of courage. And, for the final time, he brought the Jones Boys home.

Chapter 20

In 1980 I went to New York City, where I finally did a show at the Bottom Line. Linda Ronstadt and Bonnie Raitt were there and even sang a couple of tunes with me. I went to Radio City Music Hall not long afterward and got a Grammy Award for "He Stopped Loving Her Today."

Then the New York press blessed me again. "The finest, most riveting singer in country music," said *The New York Times*. That went over the *Times* news wire, and country promoters across the nation were impressed. Country music's popularity, although worldwide and pushed by about two thousand radio stations by then, was still eight years away from the popularity explosion, led by Garth Brooks, that practically registered on the Richter scale.

So anytime *The New York Times* or a major publication

such as *Time* or *Newsweek* acknowledged one of us from Nashville as early as 1980 it was taken seriously by concert promoters everywhere.

Perhaps that's why I was invited to Logan, Ohio, on May 24, 1981. Promoters wanted to throw a gigantic outdoor festival and give me top billing. The show was to be an all-day event. My then manager, Paul Richey, Tammy's brother-in-law, had hired Wayne Oliver to help put together a new band for me that included Tom Killen on steel guitar and bass guitarist Ron Gaddis. Both are still with me.

About the same time, I hired a female background singer whose father, George Morgan, a Grand Ole Opry star, I had known for years. Lorrie Morgan is today, of course, a star in her own right. The recording of "He Stopped Loving Her Today" had a background part sung by a soprano. Lorrie is an alto, but she covered the recorded version perfectly.

People everywhere seemed to regard me differently after that song. I had missed shows due to drunkenness since the beginning of my career. I was still nicknamed "No Show Jones" and probably always will be. People knew if they bought a ticket to see me they were taking a chance that I might not appear. It wasn't an open secret. It was an open fact.

Occasionally, people got vocal or threw things at the stage when I didn't make a date. But after "He Stopped Loving Her Today," their expectations for me were higher, their frustrations more dramatic.

Before the Logan date, the new Jones Boys, Lorrie, and I played Manassas, Virginia, in the spring of 1981. Paul asked Wayne to charter a private jet for Wayne and me, while the rest of the group traveled by bus.

After the Manassas show I told Wayne I didn't want to fly to the Logan date. "I'm tired," I said. "If I can ride the bus, I can get a lot of sleep. And it's been a long time since I've traveled with the band. I think I'll just hang out with them."

Wayne was familiar with my ways. He had promoted some of my shows in the 1970s before Paul hired him to travel with me to try to ensure my arrival at the dates. He'd had a stint as my manager and would eventually have another. Wayne was afraid that if he let me out of his sight, I might not make the Logan show.

"But I'll be on the bus with the band," I insisted. "There is no way I can get away from them. Of course I'll be at the show."

So he trusted me and flew on without me.

Some members of the band had a few drinks after the Manassas show, and I had one or two with them. Then they went to their bunks, and I went to my room in the back of the bus. There, I polished off a fifth of whiskey and got into a hidden bottle of cocaine.

I was not scheduled to perform until 3 P.M. the next day, as the first headline attraction at the grand opening of the Possum Holler Music Park. Possum Holler was obviously a takeoff on the nightclubs I had owned in Nashville. The park's owner, Jim Ryan, owned several other enterprises named Possum this or that or other names that implied an association with me.

I didn't mind. The guy wasn't just trying to capitalize off of my name. I was told that he was the biggest George Jones fan in the world and built the music park only after being assured I would be its opening act. And before my first show was even scheduled, I heard he had booked me for another, on July Fourth of that same year.

Logan, Ohio, is not a bustling community. Its official population was 6,557 after the 1990 census. When I was booked there nine years earlier, more than four thousand people turned out. Rarely had I played a town where two thirds of its residents tried to see me. Three other acts were on the show, but none had ever had a hit record, and to my knowledge none had a recording contract.

I never went to sleep on the overnight trip to Logan. When the band members began to sleepily rise from their bunks the next morning, I was lost in La-La Land, drunk and soaring on cocaine.

Wayne came from a private airport to the bus expecting to find me rested. Instead, he didn't find me at all. I rode all the way to Logan, then decided I didn't want to do the grand opening at an outdoor theater that had essentially been built in commemoration of me. I took off. I had drunk so much whiskey and snorted so much cocaine that I was too sick and exhausted to go onstage.

I staggered quietly off the bus, walked to the back, and inconspicuously lost myself amid the parked cars, traffic, and other activity at the arena's rear entrance. I walked down a sleepy residential street and I came upon two old ladies. I think they were watering their lawns and puttering in their flower gardens.

By now the crowd back at the arena was getting restless. I was ninety minutes late for the show. They would have been even more restless if they had known that Wayne, my band, and anyone else affiliated with the show had no idea of my whereabouts.

Those two elderly ladies had some wine, and we shared it. One had an old guitar. While thousands waited for me to sing inside an arena, I sang for two old women on their front porch. Then I asked one to call me a taxi.

Wayne, meanwhile, had formed a dragnet to find me. I couldn't have gotten very far, he thought, in such a short time. And after all, he wondered, how far could anybody go on foot in Logan, Ohio?

He walked down the same street I had walked a few minutes earlier and ran into the same old women.

"Ladies," he asked, "did a man come by here who was wearing . . ." And he described my clothes.

"Why you mean that nice young man, Mr. Jones," one said.

"That's him!" Wayne said, "That nice young Mr. Jones. Can you tell me where he went?"

"Oh," one of the women said. "He left in a taxi."

Wayne was relieved. "So he took a cab back to the show grounds, eh?" he asked.

"No," said one of the women. "He took it to Nashville."

I was so high on cocaine, which I continued to hit, that I sang to the taxi driver for the entire ride from Logan to Nashville. When we arrived I gave him twelve hundred dollars and that old woman's guitar. I told him to return it to her. He knew her personally and promised he would.

Things weren't going so well back at the Possum Holler Music Park.

Wayne was explaining to the promoter that I had skipped out and was trying to work out some kind of deal. I don't think the promoter was too receptive about dealing with anyone representing me, the person who had ruined his grand opening.

A disc jockey overheard the conversation and took it upon himself to run to the microphone in front of a drunken, impatient, and sunburned crowd. He told them that George Jones was not there, that his whereabouts were unknown, and that no one in the audience would be refunded his ten-dollar price of admission.

All hell broke loose. Furious fans stormed the stage. Wayne later said they "looked like a herd of buffalo in an old Western movie coming over the hill."

JONES FAILS TO SHOW, SPECTATORS STORM STAGE, screamed a headline in the local newspaper. The story and photographs consumed most of the front page.

My band, which had already done a set, ran for the safety of the bus. Deputy sheriffs tried to restore order but to little avail. County sheriff's deputy Ken Berry was thrown to the ground and stomped by six men, according to Sheriff James Jones. Musical instruments and other equipment were bashed on the stage. Lighting fixtures and curtains were torn down.

Then the fans, five of whom were eventually arrested, turned on the bus. They formed a human chain with their hands under the rocker panels and began to rock the bus, perhaps thinking I was on board and too drunk to get off. I had missed two other shows in central Ohio during the previous year. When fans heard I wasn't at the Logan date, they naturally assumed I was wasted somewhere. My band members were careful to stay away from bus windows after someone hurled a rock through one. A fan stood on top of another's shoulders and tried to climb through the broken glass onto the bus.

The bus driver tried to drive out of the parking lot, but people lay down in front of and behind the bus. Had he left the bus in gear, some folks would have been crushed to death.

By then the bus was rocking more violently, as more people joined the attempt to turn it over. Some band members later said they truly feared for their lives.

Members of a motorcycle club happened to be there, and Wayne happened to know them. He yelled through the bus's broken window to one he had met months earlier through Hank Williams Jr. His name was Spook.

"Can you help us?" Wayne yelled. "We're not going to be able to get out of here."

"No problem," Spook yelled, and he and his buddies began knocking a few heads.

Then Spook led the bus away from the riot. About sixty bikers formed a V with their motorcycles in front of the bus, but not before hysterical fans slashed the tires. The bikers accelerated their engines and led the bus through an angry mob. It pulled out of a dirt driveway onto a concrete highway while rolling on steel rims. At that instant, the National Guard pulled into the park.

I know all of this from newspaper accounts and reports Wayne and my band gave me. All the while the riot was going on, I was happily singing ballads to a cabdriver I'd never met before and haven't seen since. He and I had a big old time. Neither of us got mad like those people back in Ohio.

The bikers stayed with the bus at a nearby service station to hold off the angry fans still trying to get on board. The motorcycle gang kept up its protection the entire time the bus was being repaired. Occasionally a pickup filled with hostile fans would pull into the service station lot and the bikers would knock the hell out of a few of them. Then the pickup would speed away with its bloody passengers.

Wayne and the pilot raced to the airplane but not in time. Furious fans had gotten to the runway first and stolen the alternator and other parts of the aircraft. The plane wouldn't crank. Wayne chartered a jet out of Cincinnati to fly parts to the stranded airplane.

Soon afterward, I was a codefendant in a $10.1 million breach-of-contract lawsuit. Also named were Paul Richey and Jim Halsey, my booking agent at the time.

Jim finally told me that he thought I was a tremendous talent and that he enjoyed representing me. But, he said, he spent more money defending lawsuits I brought on than he earned in commissions in booking shows. He let me go.

I was so wasted in those days that I didn't even know. I saw him one night backstage at the Grand Ole Opry House and told him I appreciated all of the work he had been getting me.

"But," I said, "the miles between shows are killing us. Can't you make the jumps a little shorter?"

"George," he explained, "I haven't been booking you for more than a year."

"Then who's been getting my commission checks?" I asked.

Neither he nor I knew.

When Wayne told me about the riot, he said that if the promoter won his lawsuit, it would put me out of business. The promoter, he said, could garnishee my box-office receipts for years to come.

Wayne and Tom Binkley put their heads together and worked out a deal with Jim Ryan in which I would work a free show if Jim would pay the band's and my travel expenses and drop his lawsuit. He would keep all the gate receipts.

I consented.

I worked a noon show on the day of my makeup show for Jim. He sent a jet for Wayne, the band, and me to Florida, then flew Wayne and me in a helicopter to Possum Holler Music Park. As we flew over the arena, I could see that the crowd for the makeup show was far bigger than the crowd for the show I had missed.

I was high in the helicopter but higher on cocaine. And there was no way I was going to do a free show when that many people had bought tickets. Wayne estimated the crowd at between ten and twenty thousand. That meant gate receipts could be as high as $200,000, I thought, plus the promoter was selling food and other concessions.

"I'm not going onstage unless he pays me," I told Wayne.

"We made a deal, George," he thundered. "You can't stand the negative press of another riot, and this time your little ass won't be safe in a taxi, it will be right out there in the middle of the fight."

He had a point. So I lived up to my promise and did a free show for some folks who might have torn my head off if I hadn't. They tell me my performance was one of the best of my career.

* * *

I don't think I've ever pleased an audience more than in a show I once did out of spite. I'd wager that Tammy Wynette and George Richey, her fifth husband and her manager, still fume about it today.

Tammy and I worked shows together long after we were divorced. That wasn't my idea. In fact, I hated to work with her. It brought back too many unpleasant memories, and when some fans saw us together, they got it in their heads that we were going to get back together romantically. But our record company felt that our appearing on the same package would sell a few of our albums.

We were playing an outdoor show somewhere in New York State, and although it was a matinee, the weather was blue cold. Or maybe it just seemed that way to me because I'm from the South.

I told my bus driver to turn up the heater as I waited for my turn to go onstage. He made the bus real hot. That was not a good environment for someone swilling booze straight. I got bombed very quickly.

"I'm too drunk to go on," I told Wayne. "Let's pull off of this job and head for Nashville."

He wouldn't hear of it. He reminded me of riots and near riots in the wake of my hasty departures and ordered the bus driver not to move the coach.

Tammy was supposed to open the show. It was an old custom in country music for "girl singers" to open for men until Reba McEntire became so popular. A few other girl singers had violated that tradition, but Reba permanently broke it. Now there aren't many men in the business who wouldn't give their left arm to open for Reba just for the exposure to the masses who attend her shows. She staged the highest-grossing country music show of 1994.

But back to New York. George Richey said it would be fine with Tammy and him if I went on first. They knew I was drunk and probably preferred to see me open the show rather than miss it.

Wayne helped me out of my dressing room and I staggered down the bus aisle. When I got to the front, I saw two cops. Something about that sight made me feel sober immediately.

"Now, George," Wayne said, "you only have to do forty-five minutes. Tammy has rented an airplane, and it's waiting at the airport. She's paying for it by the hour, and she can't be late. So go on and get off so she can do her show and make her plane."

His orders rubbed me the wrong way. First of all, I wondered, who was he working for, Tammy or me? Second, since I suddenly felt sober, I didn't like the idea of opening for my ex-wife.

"Forty-five minutes, eh?" I thought to myself.

I went onstage and sang every song I could remember that I had recorded. Then I sang every one I could recall by Hank Williams and then Roy Acuff. The people were going crazy.

My band cranked up their amplifiers but could barely be heard above the roar of the outdoor crowd as I started into my next song after two and a half hours. I was freezing out there, but I wouldn't quit singing.

I occasionally looked at the bass and steel guitarists, who frantically dangled their hands, a signal that their fingers were sore.

I kept singing.

I could see George Richey jumping up and down at the side of the stage, yelling at Wayne to get me off. I chuckled as I imagined how mad Tammy must be getting. The clock was ticking on her rented airplane, stuck on the ground while my voice filled the air. Even my sad songs sounded happy to me that day.

"You've got to get him off!" Richey screamed at Wayne.

"Get him off, hell," Wayne said. "I spend all of my time trying to get him on! I sure as hell can't get him off!"

I did forty more minutes, pushing my set to well beyond three hours. And then George Richey pulled the plug on me. He disconnected the sound system! But I wouldn't be outdone. I kept right on singing to thousands of people with no amplification.

By then the band had had it. They walked offstage, and I sang with just an acoustic guitar. The crowd's attention level fell to a hush.

My voice, and my energy, finally gave out. "They ain't gonna let me sing no more," I said as my last shout of the show. The people went crazy.

Tammy had time to do only a few minutes, and she spent a lot of her slot bitching about me running overtime. But each time she complained about George Jones, the place erupted with applause.

I laughed a long time about that one.

A professional is someone who does his job whether he feels like it or not. Friends, by now you must realize that I've occasionally been unprofessional.

I was cold sober, but not too crazy about doing an

outdoor show in the early 1980s at the Washington Monument in the nation's capital, where I was supposed to be part of a Fourth of July program with the Beach Boys and other acts. Approximately seventy-five thousand people were there. I was supposed to be paid fifty thousand dollars for only thirty minutes.

But I should have never been booked on that show. It was a Beach Boys crowd, a rock 'n' roll crowd. My restlessness mounted all day. I was sure that the young people who had come to see the Beach Boys would make fun of me. By the time it was my turn to go on, I was a nervous wreck.

I would have gone on nonetheless if the Beach Boys hadn't run twenty minutes over schedule. By that time the crowd was frantic with excitement, and I didn't think a hillbilly singer could follow one of the greatest rock bands of all time. And twenty minutes is an eternity when you're dreading something.

So I left.

There wasn't much of a stink over my departure. I had been paid twenty-five thousand dollars up front, and I had to give it back. My taking off only got a few paragraphs in the Washington press. I don't think anybody even missed me, which proves my point about my having no business being on that show in the first place. I was a duck out of water.

But I felt differently about a show I agreed to host to celebrate TNN's fourth or fifth anniversary at New York City's Radio City Music Hall. That show was also in the early to middle 1980s, and again I was sober. But I took off from that show too, after riding a bus with my band all the way from Nashville for a program that was broadcast coast-to-coast over TNN.

Here's what happened:

I walked into rehearsal with my band and there was a horn and symphonic string section onstage. I was supposed to sing with them. "I'm a country singer," I said. "I don't have no business singing with these here New York City musicians. I'll be glad to host the show, but I want to sing my songs and sing with my band." I didn't think that was too much to ask.

I rehearsed with my boys, went to my hotel, and returned to Radio City that night to videotape the show. When I walked in, taping had already begun. My friend Ricky Skaggs was acting as host.

"What's he doing out there?" asked Pee-Wee Johnson, my bus driver and companion for many years. "George is supposed to be the host." Pee-Wee asked that question of a lot of folks affiliated with the show. Each time he got the same answer, which was no answer at all.

I figured I knew what the deal was. I had been unwilling to sing with an orchestra, so they ditched me as host and used somebody who would. And then they asked me if I would do a couple of songs anyhow.

"Now why the hell would you want a hillbilly like me doing songs on a big-city show like this?" I asked. "Hell, I might go on barefooted or something."

I thought I was kidding, but then I got the idea to take off my boots. I was going to walk onstage at Radio City Music Hall that way, but instead I said "To hell with it" and left. Without my boots.

I was walking fast and barefooted in my jeans down New York City's Avenue of the Americas with Pee-Wee running behind me waving my boots and dress pants. Pee-Wee is sixty-six years old. He kept hollering for me to stop, and I kept hollering for him to get lost. He was sweating, trying to keep up with me, and his hair was messed up from running. My bare feet were beaming in the bright lights. We must have looked like two old queers who'd had a lovers' spat. But I don't think one person cared or, for that matter, even noticed.

Pee-Wee and I are similar in many ways; we are the same height, have the same color hair and hairstyle, and are approximately the same weight. From a distance, a lot of folks mistake him for me. That cost him dearly one night at another show I didn't want to do, in Augusta, Georgia.

I was drunk and coked up and did a short and terrible show. The people were booing, some were screaming for me to come back, and others were just cussing when I weaved my way off the stage. I didn't get on the bus or into a limousine. Instead, I hopped onto a motorcycle with a sidecar that I had ridden to the show. I went immediately to my motel and parked the motorcycle. I went inside with my booze and cocaine and didn't come out for the rest of the night.

It's a good thing I didn't. I might have been killed. As it was, I was too high to even know a mini-riot was under way.

Pee-Wee walked outside to the Coca-Cola machine. He was supposed to drive the band back to Nashville, or to our next show, the following day. As he rounded a corner, he saw my motorcycle on its side, the sidecar pointed toward the sky. A group of angry fans had found the motorcycle and recognized it as mine. Then they saw

Pee-Wee, who they mistook for me, and began to taunt him.

"Sign some autographs for us, you son of a bitch," one said. "You did a shit show, so the least you can do is sign autographs."

"You don't want my autograph," Pee-Wee said. "I'm not who you think."

"So you're too good to sign autographs," someone else yelled. "You're a rich son of a bitch who's too good for his fans."

"No I'm not," Pee-Wee said. "You're mistaken."

About that time someone hit him, and he went down. Someone else hit him, and two guys jumped on the old man. Those locals beat the shit out of the most trusted and loyal friend I have and broke his jaw in two places.

The police came storming in, and the crowd ran like the cowards they were. I was watching an old cops-and-robbers movie inside my motel and was so high that I thought the movie had a wonderful soundtrack. I had no idea I was hearing the real thing in the parking lot.

Pee-Wee is an old scuffler. He used to own Nashville nightclubs and ran a numbers game and parlay cards. He has plenty of street sense. And so he remembered the faces, among all of the others, of the two men who had hit and kicked him when he was down. He told the cops which way they had gone and without invitation jumped into their squad car.

A high-speed chase resulted, and Pee-Wee was along for the entire ride. The two men were captured. Pee-Wee was hospitalized and underwent surgery that night in Augusta. He returned twice to testify against the men, each of whom was sentenced to eleven months and twenty-nine days.

I have caused a lot of havoc in my life because I didn't go onstage. That Augusta stuff happened because I did.

Chapter 21

In November 1981 I was in New York City, but I don't remember why. I thought I had done an outdoor show, but that's unlikely in November in the North.

The previous day my former manager, Wayne Oliver, and I had been in Shreveport, Louisiana, where I was introduced to his girlfriend. I told him I thought she was cute and asked her if she had a friend. She did and said she would bring her to New York as a blind date for me. By this time it was over for Linda and me, but I hadn't been home long enough to move out.

Wayne's girlfriend's friend was the former Nancy Sepulvado—the current Mrs. George Jones.

To say it was love at first sight is unoriginal. It's also true. We began talking seconds after we were introduced, and we continued all night. I felt closer to her in hours than I had to many folks I'd known for years.

We saw the sun rise over Manhattan, and then Nancy went to her own room. Soon she went home.

I went back on the road, but her memory was calling me home. Home to me, already, was anywhere she was. So I sneaked out one night on Wayne Oliver and showed up in Shreveport, where Nancy lived and worked. For a few romantic days and nights we went to dinner and movies and spent time together just walking. She had no idea I was missing shows simply to be with her.

Wayne found me. He always could. It was as if he had a network of George Jones spies. I never had an associate who could track me down anywhere in the world more effectively than Wayne Oliver. He wasn't too happy about my absence, and neither were the promoters and fans who had been expecting me. I was booking for fifteen to twenty-five thousand dollars a night, and I often got a percentage of the gate. I probably missed about fifty thousand dollars in income just to be with Nancy. But I didn't care. My career was hot, and I had once again reached that comfort zone where I could call my booking agent and tell him to find a concert promoter for a show the next day. Because I gave the promoter so little notice, I often agreed to play for the door. Even if I only played thousand-seat honky-tonks and set ticket prices at ten dollars, I could pick up twenty thousand dollars in a weekend. But I was usually broke by the next weekend after sharing it with everyone entitled to a cut.

Money has just never been that important to me. I always suspected that love was. That lifelong suspicion was confirmed in the person of Nancy Sepulvado.

I was immediately intrigued by her energy. She worked harder than most men, and I had no idea in

1981 that someday she would work that hard to rebuild my tattered career and shattered life.

Nancy was a divorced mother of two daughters and supported her household by building telephones on an assembly line. She was paid by the hour and received time and a half for overtime. She usually worked a forty-hour week, then fifteen additional hours. She had worked for her employer for twenty years, having gone to work when her first daughter, Adina, was three weeks old. Nancy wore work gloves and a shop apron and could assemble a telephone with all of its components in about one minute. Something about all of that impressed me, what with my family's background in manual labor and all.

Wayne forced me to do the responsible thing and go back on the road to work my shows. I'd look at the crowds and, as always, see a sea of faces. But this time each was Nancy's. No teenage boy ever fell harder for a girl than I fell for Nancy.

So I called her and asked her to quit her job. It was snowing in Shreveport when my long-distance voice suggested she become my constant companion. She never forgot that, and hearing her tell the story pleases me to this day.

Her boss tried to warn her. He told her that musicians were no good and I was the worst of the bunch. He said he had read about me and repeatedly told her I would leave her stranded. He said he couldn't believe she would give up a job where she was a utility operator with seniority to run off with a country singer as if she were a silly, starstruck girl.

She told him she didn't want to hear it. She told him she knew what she was doing. She told him good-bye.

Nancy took fourteen-year-old Adina and hit the road with me. (Her other daughter, Sherry, lived with her father.) The Jones Boys traveled in the bus, and Nancy, Adina, and I traveled in a recreational vehicle.

Nancy was looking forward to spending the rest of her life with me. Then she discovered my addictions. She hadn't heard that much about my behavior. She is not a nosy person and didn't care for the tabloids or gossip magazines. I had made plenty of police and court news, but none in Shreveport. She hadn't followed my life and career with the closeness of a devoted fan. She had heard that I drank heavily, but by 1981 that was common knowledge in this country and abroad. I mean, there are people who have no interest in Santa Claus, but they know he wears red. She certainly had no idea that I had been in drug and alcohol rehabilitation.

After spending some time with me, she decided I drank too much. She developed a plan to help me because Nancy always wants to help the people she loves, and she never has to be asked. But before she could pursue the drinking problem I pulled out the cocaine. She had never seen that drug.

I've already told you how cocaine altered my mind, often making me mean. Real mean. Nancy was exhibiting nothing more than a naive country girl's curiosity when she asked me what cocaine was. Remember, this was 1981 in Shreveport, Louisiana, and Nancy was an untraveled person who worked in a closed and controlled environment. I had spent my life in the fast lane, and she had spent hers working, paying her bills, and going to bed at a regular time. I took none of that into consideration.

I was high and thought she was making fun of me when she asked about the cocaine. As I've explained, the cocaine user is paranoid and insecure. I stupidly thought she thought she was better than me because I felt I needed the drug and she didn't.

So I hit her.

I would have never done that sober, and my heart was broken when I sobered up. I had physically hurt a woman who, in a matter of months, had made more sacrifices for me than many women I'd known had made for their men in years. I begged her forgiveness.

She gave it and then decided there was a "devil" living inside of me. I don't know if she meant that literally, but "devil" is the word she used. She even used the word years later when she talked to Tom Carter about that time of my life.

She said she was bound and determined to get the devil out. Little did she know that the project would take years. Little did I know that once Nancy finally got me straight, it would last indefinitely.

Some folks think she saved my career. She did. She also saved my life.

Although I was "officially" living with Linda in Alabama, I hardly went there again except to leave forever.

Linda supposedly has told folks that one night someone called and warned her that people were on the way to kill her or me. I don't know if that's true. I sure don't know who called, if anyone. But I do know she left. I guess she thought she was running for her life. When she took off, I wasn't far behind her. I never saw her again.

I gave Linda a lot of grief. She got a lot of cash, cars, furniture, jewelry, and other things out of me. I don't have anything bad, or anything else at all, to say about her. I understand she eventually married.

I can't remember if I was doing cocaine, but I was slobbering drunk once when I went to Waylon Jennings's house. He was really high himself; at the peak of his cocaine addiction, he was consuming fifteen hundred dollars' worth each day.

I was raising hell inside his place and finally began to doze off. Some folks think people can't sleep if they're using cocaine, but they can if they've used it for three days and nights because they finally reach a point of exhaustion that even the stimulating drug can't dent.

Waylon never drank and doesn't know much about alcohol. He decided that since I was almost asleep, I would pass out if he gave me an enormous straight shot of booze. He sat me upright, and I drank a tall glassful. The sugar in that much alcohol quickly energized me. But then Waylon and a friend of his did the wrong thing by leaving me alone, thinking I would nod off. They heard me raising hell seconds later.

Waylon came into the room to see about me, and I hurled a picture with a solid metal frame from off of his wall directly at him. He said later that the frame, because it was so heavy, could have killed him.

I proceeded to demolish much of his furniture and art. I did all of this in the home of a man who'd been a longtime and proven friend, to a man who had been there for me when no one else, except Johnny Cash, had been.

Waylon jumped on me and called for the help of his friends. One was his guitar player. I kicked that guy in the hand and broke his thumb. That put him out of work.

Meanwhile, I continued to tear hell out of Waylon's house. Waylon sat on me, but even though he outweighed me, he began to tire. He later said he was probably exhausted from his own drug consumption. So he called for a rope, and someone brought him something, perhaps an extension cord.

He tied me up and threw me on his couch. I was helpless but cussing him all the while. He left me there alone and called my manager, who probably took his time getting to Waylon's house to get me. Not a lot of folks wanted to be around me when I went into one of my drug-induced rages.

By the time my manager arrived, I had settled down or maybe had even partially slept it off. Waylon said they untied me and walked me out and I acted as if nothing had happened.

My point is I wasn't acting. I didn't immediately remember the ordeal. Later, when reminded, my longterm memory gave it all back to me.

The same was true during that first of a few times I hit Nancy. The next day I never remembered. Blackouts, by then, had long been a part of my booze- and cocaine-soaked life.

Nancy, Adina, and I eventually moved to Muscle Shoals, Alabama, a neighboring city to Florence. Adina saw me drunk and wasted on cocaine and was certainly old enough to know what was going on. She couldn't handle it and sometimes left to move in with her daddy in Shreveport. But each time she returned to Nancy, and each time I was glad.

I fell in love with that girl as quickly as I did her mother. On a few occasions I got on a rampage and no one except Adina could settle me down. I felt strangely compelled to obey her and not abuse her youth and innocence.

Nancy began to look after me around my friends who she thought took advantage of me. She recalled that one Saturday night I was passed out from a binge and Peanut and Charlene Montgomery came to my house wanting a few thousand dollars to air-condition the church where he was pastor. I gave him the money, and Nancy and I went to the church the next morning for a service. The place was so cold Nancy said she nearly froze. She wondered out loud how Peanut had gotten the place air-conditioned overnight, and I think she asked him about it. Maybe Nancy and I misunderstood and Peanut had had the church air-conditioned earlier and needed me to pay for the work after it had been done. But that isn't the way Nancy remembers it. She thought Peanut was trying to hustle me financially, and she and the Montgomerys didn't hit it off.

I hadn't been to church in years, and when Nancy and I went Peanut preached against people who aren't married but live together nonetheless. He knew that Nancy and I were shacking up, and she felt like he was intentionally preaching directly at us. That made her and me angry. I was in a foul mood and raised hell for the rest of the day, she recalled years later. "That wasn't a very good Sunday," she simply said, and never complained.

I continued to mistreat the woman who loved me. I bought drugs in the Florence–Muscle Shoals area from a man who ran a recreation hall. Nancy occasionally went with me to visit his place of business. At first she had no idea I was going there to score cocaine. She said she wondered why so many people who never participated in recreation visited this recreation facility. They just went into a room in the back. She began to suspect that it was a drug outlet, but she became confused when she saw Peanut and Charlene come and go. She didn't think a preacher would be around any illegal behavior, so she couldn't figure out what was going on. Many times I left her sitting on a bench in the recreation hall while I went into that back room. When I kept coming out with a very changed personality, her suspicions were finally confirmed.

As I've said, Nancy was naive. But I also think she just always wanted to believe the best about me, so it was easy for her to kid herself about what I was really up to at times.

She finally came face-to-face with the proprietor, my drug connection. Nancy has the courage of a sky diver when she's convinced about something. And she was convinced this guy was trying to earn money at my physical and emotional expense. She told him what she thought about drugs and about him. It wasn't a mild sermon.

Nancy was never one to speak her piece and quit. She wanted to get me off of drugs, and she decided to cut off the flow at the source. She made friends with a guy whose nickname was "Big Daddy," who knew my dealer.

The dealer and his cronies, I decided, were watching our house. The instant Nancy would go to the grocery store or some such place, the dealer or one of his runners would come to my door. She'd come back, and I'd be gone. Then she'd begin a fruitless search all over Florence and Muscle Shoals to find me.

Big Daddy, for reasons neither of us know, intensified his friendship with Nancy. He would call her and whisper my whereabouts over the telephone. He told her never to tell anyone that he was her informant. She would go to where he had said. She often walked in as the dealers were shoveling cocaine up my nostrils, while I sat there in a helpless haze. I was often a zombie, sometimes barely breathing.

It wasn't long until Nancy heard that the dealers had taken out a life insurance policy on me. She suspected they were trying to kill me through an overdose. Given my reputation, any coroner would simply think that I had ingested the overdose by myself. He'd never suspect murder.

There was another reason why those hoods were determined to keep me on cocaine. While they weren't my managers, they were their business associates. Once again it was that tired old story of men owing me money and paying me with cocaine.

And I'm positive they felt it would be easier to cheat me out of the money they owed me if they could keep me high. They could more easily manipulate me when I was wrecked. That's why, when I couldn't buy it or they didn't owe me anything, they would give me free cocaine. They wanted to keep me wasted so they could get their way with me.

Nancy got wise to their methods and quickly got to the place where she wouldn't leave me by myself. She sent Adina for groceries or to run errands, even though Adina wasn't old enough to legally drive. Adina, like most teenagers, was eager to drive a car, but it didn't matter. Nancy insisted that Adina learn to drive so she could stay with me to protect me from the thugs.

They quickly grew to hate her. At last they decided they were never going to catch me alone so they could pump me full of cocaine, so they boldly walked into my house when Nancy was there. That made her furious, and the cussing and screaming were on. She called them everything she could think of—right to their tough and lined faces. I can't believe one of them didn't put a bullet through her head.

Sometimes they brought me things, such as a guitar, with cocaine hidden in its case. They'd leave, I'd open the case to see the instrument, and come face-to-face with the white powder. I was too weak to resist, especially when I had been drinking. They knew that because they knew I was an addict. They had helped sustain that.

Other times when they marched unannounced into our house, one would sneak me into a bedroom while the others distracted Nancy, who was kicking and screaming. It's easy to distract someone who's hysterical.

Then the men would quickly leave, and Nancy would start looking for me. Her search ended when she found me babbling, cursing, and screaming in the voices of the duck and the old man. Today I can only vaguely remember her falls into tearful pieces. To this day I can't believe she stayed. A hundred reporters have asked her why she did.

"Because," she always said, "when he was sober he was the best man I ever knew. All I had to do was find a way to get him permanently sober."

I've only told you the beginning of her travails. Nancy thought she was hopelessly outnumbered, and she was. By now she was aware of the power held by the criminals who hated her and wanted to possess me. They had strong ties to local law enforcement and owned several "legitimate" businesses that they used to launder drug money. The cocaine addict feels totally helpless. People have asked me why I didn't go to state or federal authorities. My altered mind was convinced that those people would be of no help either.

Nancy's only ally was Big Daddy, who continued to call her secretly. One night he told her these men wanted her out of my life permanently. He stressed the permanent part, and she knew what he meant. Nancy feared for her life.

I think I was out on the road when Nancy drove across a bridge over a river that runs through Florence and Muscle Shoals. Adina was in the car.

Suddenly, the car was rammed from the rear. Then it was hit again, and again. Nancy lost control, the car began to veer toward the railing, and Nancy and Adina thought they were going to plunge into the water to their deaths. Adina became hysterical.

Nancy struggled with the wheel, and to compensate for the thrusts pushing her to the right she turned sharply to the left, into the face of oncoming traffic. The traffic had nowhere to go, as there was no shoulder on the bridge. So each time Nancy was about to have a head-on collision, she turned instantly to the right. She got the car straight, only to have the car behind her try to force her again into the water below.

The drive across that bridge should take about sixty seconds. Nancy said she felt it took her a year. As she drove her battered car off of the bridge onto land, the mysterious car behind her turned abruptly and vanished.

Nancy could not kid herself. She knew she had just undergone a serious attempt to kill her and her daughter.

I had failed miserably at quitting booze and drugs by myself and had responded to professional treatment mostly while I was under a doctor's supervision, not when I was on my own. I had never had a companion, a friend, whose sole mission in life was to save mine. Nancy was relentless. She was going to see that I whipped my addictions if it killed her.

My bouts with paranoia returned. I was often positive that I saw and heard things. I was terrified of those sights and sounds. I wondered if they were real or just my cocaine-prompted delusions.

I sometimes became convinced that my enemies were walking around my house. I thought I heard footsteps in the grass. I would bolt the doors and windows and sit with a loaded pistol, waiting for them to burst through the doors and try to kill Nancy and me.

I just "knew" that platoons of criminals were stalking me by circling my house. The fact is they might have been, but not every night, as I imagined when I went on my week- or two-week binges.

I wouldn't let Nancy and Adina go outside, which made for a real problem at sunrise, when Nancy had to take Adina to school. She couldn't let Adina, an illegal driver, drive to a public school. So she asked Adina to sleep outside our house, in the car. That way Adina didn't have to dress in the house and Nancy wouldn't hear me rant and rave the whole time, insisting that I wasn't going to let her leave.

I'd go to sleep at sunrise. I felt safer then. And Nancy would quickly ease through the door to drive Adina to school. It was a taxing and trying routine for both of them.

And still Nancy stayed with me.

She was preparing to leave the house to pick up Adina from school one day when the telephone rang. By this time I loved Adina even more than I would have had she been my very own.

"Nancy," said a voice on the line, "we want to come over and see George."

Nancy recognized the voice of one of the drug pushers and told him to go to hell. She told him not to bother coming because there was no way she would let him inside.

"But what about Adina?" the man asked.

"What do you mean?" Nancy said.

"We have her," he said.

The line went dead.

Nancy's daughter, the girl who would become my stepdaughter, had been kidnapped by drug dealers wanting to get to me. Nancy lost it. She began to cry and scream uncontrollably. She tried to call back the man who she thought had called her. There was no answer. Thank God that on that particular occasion I was straight. I was able to try to comfort Nancy for a change. But nothing I said or did worked. Calling the police, in bed with the criminals, was of no use, we agreed. Nancy was obsessed as she feared for the life of her first child.

Within minutes the telephone rang again. This time it was Big Daddy. He had intercepted Adina. He told Nancy not to ask how. He said that she was safe with him inside a nightclub he owned. Nancy was instantly relieved and started to race out the door to get her daughter when I told her not to act so fast.

"This is a setup," I said. "They know that nothing could get you away from me except Adina's safety, right?"

"That's true," she said.

"All right," I continued. "They probably know that Big Daddy has told you where Adina is. You'll go there, and while you're inside, they'll plant drugs in your car. Then when you start home, the police will stop you, search your car, and you'll be arrested."

Nancy understood my theory. She understood that the police were not only no help but also a big part of the threat. But more than that, she understood that her daughter was in trouble. Nancy would march into live gunfire for a loved one, and she bolted into Big Daddy's dive yelling, "Where is my girl?" I think she had a pistol in her purse.

Nancy parked her car so she could see it while she was inside the club. Big Daddy gave her the sign, and she walked immediately to him. There, tucked under the bar, quietly sat Adina. I think Big Daddy had given her popcorn and Coca-Cola, and the hoodlums in the joint might not have known she was there. If they did, they didn't bother Adina under the protection of that giant man.

Nancy and her daughter came safely home. She put her key in the lock, but the door eased open by itself. The thugs had come in her absence and given me a little cocaine until I had a buzz, then mercilessly crammed it up my nose repeatedly until I was out of my mind.

It had been another day and night in the early courtship of George and Nancy Jones.

Chapter 22

In 1981 I had a hit record entitled "If Drinkin' Don't Kill Me (Her Memory Will)." Much of the public thought the tune was about Tammy Wynette, although we had been divorced for six years. Most people hadn't yet heard about Nancy and never really knew that much about Linda since my profile with her was always low.

Knowing what people thought about Tammy and me, I often changed the words of "If Drinkin' Don't Kill Me" when I sang it publicly, particularly on national television:

> If drinkin' don't kill me
> Tammy's memory will. I sang.

The song rode the *Billboard* country survey for fifteen weeks. I followed that with my one hundred and second single record in twenty-five years. It was called "Still Doin' Time" and was about a man who lived in a cage of taverns from which he could not escape. He was "still doin' time." The song became my second number-one record in less than two years.

Some folks might be disappointed because I haven't put more information in this book about my recording sessions and song selections. I usually let whatever producer I was working for select the songs, then I selected from his selections. I'd usually pick ten from about twenty-five prospective songs. Why not? I wasn't writing myself anymore, and my producer, whoever he happened to be at the time, always brought me songs from the best writers in Nashville. I've never understood singers who listened to hundreds and hundreds of songs before deciding which ten or eleven to record. Do they really think their own judgment is that much better than the accomplished producer and songwriters working with them?

I can't tell you a lot about my recording sessions either. First of all, I've worked so many of them too drunk to walk but not too drunk to sing. I can't remember much about them. Secondly, there have been so many at this point in my career that they seem interchangeable. Thirdly, I've always believed that once you sing a song your best, you go on to the next song. The only time I rerecorded and rerecorded a tune was when I was too drunk, high, or both to get my part right. I've already told you about some of those songs.

Billy Sherrill had nervous obsessions about retakes. He'd call me at home and say my version of a song had some flat notes or improper phrasing or something.

I'd tell him to listen again.

He would, but then he'd call again, insisting that I come in to rerecord. I complained a lot, but I always went back to grant the producer's wishes. Then, if the record flopped, no one could say it was my fault.

I could not help but be astonished about the reverse parallel of my life and career. The more anguish I underwent in my personal life, the more my career flourished. Somebody suggested that was because my songs were autobiographical. Each time I came up with a new single it was as if I were giving a confession set to music.

Those songs, in many ways, did reflect the circumstances of my personal life. I didn't care. The press had made my personal life so public so frequently for so long I didn't care what people knew, didn't know, or thought they knew about me.

If folks bought my records because they thought I was breaking down, which I happened to be, then so be it. When all else failed, I could always get as many shows as I wanted because I was hot on the radio.

My bouts with paranoia, in fact, became worse, although that seems hard to believe. I suppose, at this point, much of my entire life story seems hard to believe. I'm fortunate that there were always a few musicians, managers, road managers, old friends, girlfriends, record executives, hoodlums, songwriters, ex-wives, ex-cons, and others who can verify my story.

I've often thought that the biggest criticism I'll get of this book is that people will swear no sane man ever lived as I did. Well, you must have realized by now that there were times when I was totally insane. But I lived through all I've told, and I lived to tell it all.

I was more "sure" than ever in 1981–82 that I was being followed, and I had some days when I simply had to get out of town to run from my pursuers, real or imagined. I would demand that Nancy take Adina out of school so we could drive. We had no destination, I just wanted to be in motion. That's when I felt safest.

If we became hungry, we would check into a motel and eat what little food we had taken along, such as canned sardines or fast-food hamburgers. I was too frightened to go out for food. I just knew the bad guys were on my tail.

My cocaine-induced paranoia had reached hysterical proportions, and the only thing I did to lessen that was to take more cocaine. I've already explained that the cocaine user wants nothing but more cocaine. Once he gets really high, he thinks the only thing he *needs* is more cocaine.

God, I was sick.

Whenever I disappeared from the Muscle Shoals–Florence area, the gangsters who had invaded my life became worried. I had additional reasons to suspect by then that they had formed an alliance with my management. I wanted to interview some of those people who were on my former management team for this book. Many apparently did not want to be interviewed. One did not return calls on three occasions.

I told Nancy that there was no point in our slipping out of northwestern Alabama to find peace when I was convinced I was being followed wherever I went. What kind of peace would we find?

So, I decided, we would leave by dark of night. I told

Nancy to pack everything she could. We left a lot of things behind, intending to fetch them later.

Adina, still too young to legally drive, followed in another car. There was no room in Nancy's and mine. It was jammed to the roof with belongings.

We eased through the late-night, quiet streets of Florence–Muscle Shoals. We stopped at a red light, went forward, and I did what I did about every fifteen seconds, which was check over my shoulder for Adina. I didn't see her car. The young and inexperienced driver had somehow gotten lost.

Adina, then and now, is bright. That child had the sense not to drive aimlessly through the night trying to find Nancy and me. She instead did what Nancy predicted she would do and drove back to the house we had left. But we weren't sure of that at the moment.

When Adina arrived at our home, so had the drug-dealing thugs. They didn't make their presence known to her. They knew that Nancy and I wouldn't be far behind.

Nancy drove silently into the Florence city limits and came to a full stop at the first stop sign. She gently accelerated through the intersection. No one was in sight. We were not that far from the house we had fled—the house where we prayed Adina would be safely waiting.

Then the red lights and sirens came on. Police cars sped around Nancy and forced our car to the curb. Before she could turn off her engine, two cops stood at her window. I was sitting in the passenger's seat going out of my mind. I knew she hadn't committed any moving violation. I was sure, therefore, that the cops had stopped us on the hoodlums' behalf. I continued looking over my shoulder out my window, thinking someone was going to walk up to our car and shoot me for trying to run from Alabama.

"Out of the car!" a cop yelled at Nancy.

"What for?" she said.

"You ran that last red light," he said.

Nancy called him a liar and asked him how much he had been paid to stop her. With that, he spun her around and slammed her against the car. She was kicking and screaming when he locked her handcuffs into place.

Nancy and I were loaded into a police car and taken to jail. She was thrown into a cell by herself while I was left standing free. Nancy was sure she knew what was about to happen.

Adina, meanwhile, was still waiting in the car all by herself in our driveway, hoping we would return to the house she had no keys to enter.

Nancy continued yelling and cussing inside the police station, telling the entire force that it was accepting payoffs from the Florence and Muscle Shoals goons. She hadn't run that light and everyone in that place knew it, she kept insisting.

"How much are they paying you crooked cops to arrest me?" she demanded.

An officer walked to her cell and told her that if she would simply calm down everything would be all right. She spat through the bars on him, and then she spat again. I'm glad the bars were between them. Otherwise, he might have hit her.

Then I joined in with the authorities. "Nancy, just calm down," I said. "If you'll calm down we can work this out. Everything will be fine."

Boy, was I wrong.

"George," she said, in front of the cops. "Don't you realize what they're going to do? They're going to leave me in this cell and take you somewhere and fill you full of cocaine."

She meant they would incapacitate me with the drug so I would lose the courage to try to leave town and their clutches again.

One of the officials said I'd have to step out of the cell area while Nancy's arrest was being "processed." I did, and in no time I was put into a squad car and whisked to the recreation hall. I was taken by uniformed officers to the back room.

Consciously, I'm sure I knew what was about to happen. But I couldn't believe it, not with the cops wearing uniforms and all. In the shadows I saw familiar faces. On a table I saw a familiar sight—a pile of cocaine. I was put into a chair, and someone stood on each side of me, shoveling tiny spoonfuls of the powder up my nose and yelling at me to inhale harder.

I was back at the police station in about thirty minutes, Nancy figured. I was, she said, "higher than a kite." I'm sure I was delirious.

Nancy, without explanation, was suddenly released from custody and told to take me home. A jailer opened her cell, and she kicked him hard in the leg. She continued to kick him, until another official grabbed her, then she kicked hell out of him too.

Why wasn't she arrested for assault and battery on a police officer? They had done nothing to her except let her out of jail, yet no arrest was made and no charges were filed when she attacked them. Obviously, there was never any intention of arresting Nancy for anything. The cops had wanted to put her in a cell so they could take me to their bosses, men who controlled me through the strings of cocaine.

I think Nancy called Big Daddy to ask if he knew Adina's whereabouts. He told her he had reason to believe she was safe, at home, untouched in our driveway. And she was. She never unlocked her car doors, and she never thought about leaving.

Then Big Daddy told Nancy what he had said earlier about certain people in Alabama holding a fat life insurance policy on me. He wondered aloud how much cocaine I could take without overdosing. There was more talk about what an autopsy would show, and Big Daddy asked, "How do you know there would be an honest autopsy?"

They could keep me wrecked and control my finances. They could kill me and collect from an insurance policy. Whether I was dead or alive, they couldn't lose.

Nancy pulled into the driveway we had tried to run from and there, sobbing inside her car, sat Adina. Mother and daughter ran into each other's arms. I did my best to struggle out of the car and to my feet. We went into the house that now, more than ever, seemed like our prison. My drug-soaked mind was even more altered by the stress of having tried to flee, only to get caught, only to be returned against my will.

Nancy called Big Daddy the next day, and he talked to her about the wisdom of my trying to run. He told her I should get out of town at any cost. If I stayed I would die because I had figured out too much about my associates' ties to the drug world. He urged us to try to leave again, explaining what I already knew: I would have to quit show business. After all, how could I go underground if I was making public appearances in front of thousands of people?

I was willing to quit. I had told Nancy that the three of us would go away and that I could walk away from the music business forever if that's what it took to save our lives.

Eventually, we did follow Big Daddy's advice and leave Florence–Muscle Shoals, but of course I didn't permanently quit show business. I didn't have to do that.

Somehow, somebody apparently found out that Big Daddy had been supplying information to Nancy and me. We were living in Louisiana when we got the call from someone who said Big Daddy's head was in a parking lot—detached from its body. His murder, to this day, remains unsolved except to the person or persons who committed it and the law enforcement officials who conspired to let them.

And still Nancy stayed with me.

Nancy and I tried again to leave Florence–Muscle Shoals. Leaving in the middle of the night hadn't worked, so I decided we would rent a truck, load the furniture onto it, and drive to a place we had rented in Lafayette, Louisiana.

I think the bad guys must have been watching us load and were intent on not creating any problems until the instant we pulled away from the house. That approach, they might have figured, would be even more intimidating.

And that's what happened.

We had loaded everything into a moving van, including Adina's car, and the truck had departed for Lafayette. Nancy, Adina, and I were about to leave in Nancy's car when some of my associates pulled up.

Nancy later recalled coming into a room once before, after they'd had me for two days. She found me crying and sitting on the floor as they forced me to ingest cocaine. They kidnapped me on our second moving day and gave me similar treatment.

Nancy had about twenty dollars when I was taken this time. She was crying and begging the men not to take me, and I couldn't stand to see her that upset, although I knew it was justified. So I tried to comfort her. "I'm going to go with these guys for a few minutes. I'll be right back," I said.

She stopped crying, and I shouted, "Don't leave me, Nancy." She didn't know what to do.

To make a long story short, Nancy was contacted by Pee-Wee, who found me and took me to my new residence.

Nancy had an insight into me that no other woman has ever had. She realized that, with my shattered nerves, I simply couldn't take pressure. So she began to assume more and more of my business responsibilities. That wasn't hard for her. She didn't have to take them from me because I just let them go.

She learned about booking shows and how much money goes to a booking agent. She learned about recording contracts and when they come up for renewal. She learned how to get the biggest advance possible out of a record label and how to commit that label to promoting its product.

The greatest mystery of the entire recording industry, to me, is that a record label will spend hundreds of thousands of dollars producing an album, then let it lie on the shelf without investing any money in its promotion.

The recording industry can be very underhanded. That's hardly a secret. In the old days, I saw acts that sounded like current successful acts come to Nashville and record labels tie them up in contract so they couldn't record elsewhere. The label might not record them at all or might not release their records if they did. But the new act, because of the manipulation, wasn't a threat to the label's established act.

Nancy learned the ins and outs of the business in both its legitimate and dark sides.

I worked a show shortly after the attempted move to Lafayette, and the drug dealers showed up. I was already high, and when they came with their stash I was ready to accept. Nancy tried to reason with me.

Let me say here and now that Nancy never really nagged me. She realized early in our relationship that when I was high, I didn't like preaching and I didn't like nagging. They served no purpose except to worsen things.

I've seen her get up and begin to repair a house that I had forgotten I'd totally destroyed the previous night. She never mentioned what happened, and I was too ashamed to ask. To this day, when women ask Nancy for her advice as to how they can help alcoholic husbands, she urges them to do many things, but the one thing she insists they don't do is nag.

Yet on this particular day, she didn't want me to be with the men who had forced us out of Alabama. I wouldn't have wanted to be had I been sober.

Nothing would do me, and I put Nancy out of our hotel and locked myself in with the dealers. I got too wrecked to do that night's show, disappeared, and Nancy didn't hear from me for two weeks.

She had no idea if I was dead or alive, except she figured my death would have made the television news. She watched the news many times, fearful of what she didn't want to see. She read newspapers, looking for what she didn't want to find.

I called our new home in Lafayette one day and told her I was coming home and told her to tell Adina. I said I wanted to get professional help. Nancy later said Adina was elated, thinking we were at last going to have a home and a drug- and alcohol-free life.

I was wrecked when I arrived, and Nancy later remembered that I looked like "death eating a cracker." I don't think she wanted Adina to see me with my weight loss, babbling and out of my mind. The duck and the old man were ranting uncontrollably.

Adina had been too optimistic. For some reason she had really believed this time my pledge to make a life for the three of us was sincere.

I don't remember why I wanted us to stay at a motel that night. Perhaps I had no reason at all, or perhaps Nancy thought Adina wouldn't see me on what she prayed would be my final binge.

I had come home as a filthy and mentally destroyed man. But, after fourteen days, I had come home.

Adina went into her motel room, and then Nancy took me to ours. I don't remember anything else about the next several hours.

Nancy said I suddenly turned on her and called her by the names of the men who sold and forced drugs on me. She knew their names well. She said she told me she was not those men but that I insisted she was. I was mad at those men for providing me with drugs, and I was furious at her for pretending not to be them.

When I awoke the next day, Nancy's face was an enormous bruise. Someone had torn her clothes and undergarments off of her and beaten the hell out of her.

That someone, she tearfully said, had been me.

I insisted it couldn't have been. I begged her to tell me who had done this to her so I could get even. God, I was sick.

Throughout the attack, she said, I kept calling her by the men's names and telling them they could take this and take that for wrecking the lives of my family and me.

And then, Nancy said, I snapped to my partial senses and saw her bleeding and battered before me. She said I begged her forgiveness, and that of Adina, who had been pounding on the door that separated our rooms. Nancy said I got on my knees and pled.

I remembered nothing.

And still Nancy stayed with me.

There was other mistreatment. I've thrown Nancy off a bus during a cocaine-laden high, leaving her stranded at a truck stop without money. Bobby Birkhead, my road manager, threw a hundred-dollar bill out of the bus window on a couple of occasions as the bus pulled away

from Nancy. Had I known he was helping her, I probably would have fired him. I was that insane.

Once an eighteen-wheeler rolled over the money. Its
wake took the bill away, and Adina was left searching in
the dark for the money that would have gotten her
mother and her home.

I've stopped for refuelings at airports and, while
Nancy was using the ladies' room, ordered the pilot to fly
away and leave her, with no money or luggage.

Why did I do it? I'm not making excuses when I say I
didn't. The whiskey-and-cocaine-drenched demon that
lived inside of me did it. I was a different man inside the
same body you see today.

I was a different man.

Nancy grew to believe that drugs are the enemy of the
world. Good people do bad things while under the influence of drugs, she insisted. She refused to blame me and
always blamed the drugs.

Nancy hates drugs. She'd fire anyone in our organization who used them, on or off duty.

And I would too—now.

Nancy left me once. It was when we were still in Muscle Shoals. She said she didn't want to, but she had to
leave to preserve her sanity. She honestly felt she was
having a nervous breakdown. The fact is she probably
suffered an untreated nervous breakdown.

She always kept Adina's and her own clothes packed
and two credit cards in her brassiere. Armed with these,
she got into her car and got as far as the end of the street.

"But if I go it won't serve any purpose," she later remembered thinking, "except that the drug dealers will
kill him."

She stopped the car and cried uncontrollably. Then she turned around and came home.

And so, for the duration of 1982, Nancy pressed on—locked into the seemingly unending and impossible task of rehabilitating George Jones.

Chapter 23

I feel inner restlessness today less than ever. Far less.

Yet, when I least expect it, restlessness occasionally bursts through, although I'm sixty-four. It obviously isn't as strong as it was during my crazy days. That's a good thing for several reasons, including the fact that I'm too tired to roar the way I once did.

My life was once running ninety miles per hour down a dead-end street. Cats, not humans, have nine lives, yet I must have used up nine times ninety.

There is a saying in Alcoholics Anonymous. An alcoholic will either sober up or he'll wind up locked up or covered up. One of the two would have been my destiny if I hadn't finally, finally quit drinking and using drugs.

TV's "60 Minutes" did a documentary about the Rolling Stones in 1994 in which Mick Jagger said that using drugs was a waste of life. The interviewer asked how long it took before he realized that.

"About twenty-five years," Jagger laughed. "I was a quick study."

So was I.

I don't think I'd been drinking or using drugs when Nancy asked me to go to the store one day in 1982. The sun was high and I wasn't, so I didn't have my usual paranoia toward my enemies, real or imagined. I had no reservations about going to the market.

I had worked two or three shows and had bought a new pickup. I told Nancy I'd be right back with a loaf of bread.

I returned a week and two thousand miles later. What can I say? In those days I still had to sometimes get away on impulse. I still had the restlessness.

Nancy alerted law enforcement authorities, and I understand an all-points bulletin was issued regarding my whereabouts. Nancy feared the evil ones had found me and that I was dead. But I didn't consider her or her worry when I took off. A heavy drinker and drug user is selfish and often doesn't think about anything except his own elusive peace of mind.

I pulled off the highway, got a bottle, and soon had that golden glow that all binge drinkers know. I had the steering wheel in one hand, whiskey in the other, and the sun in my rearview mirror. I headed east toward Florida, where I still knew a few folks. I didn't bother to see any of them. In fact, I only talked to one other person on the entire trip, and that was by accident.

I pulled over to take a drink and pee beside the road. I was too drunk to notice that I had stopped near a hitchhiker. The passenger door swung open and an old black man climbed into the seat.

When I first heard the noise of the door I jumped, thinking the drug dealers had followed me.

But this guy was too dirty and too scrawny to hurt anyone. He wasn't carrying a gun. He didn't look as if he had the strength to lift one.

"Now where do you think you're going?" I asked.

I didn't realize that the man expected me to ask that, believing I had stopped to give him a ride. He was drunk too.

"Where are you going!" I asked again, meaning, "What are you doing in my truck?"

The man was going to Fort Myers, Florida. But he had a thick, drunken accent, and I had a thick, drunken ear.

So when he said "Fort Myers" he pronounced it "Fouh Meyuus," or so it sounded to me. I thought he said "Four miles."

"You're going four miles?" I asked.

"Fouh Meyuus," he said.

"Well, I don't know what the hell is so important four miles down the road, but I'll give this old boy a lift," I thought to myself.

I had never thought that a lot of black folks cared for country music. My pickup radio was set to a country station, and the old man told me that his favorite singer was George Jones. A couple of my records were played, and he sang along, telling me all about myself.

I'd never previously seen this guy in my life.

"Have you ever met George Jones?" I asked.

"Oh yeah," he said. "I's bin all over the world with him. Him and me is like that."

He held two fingers together. Because I knew he was lying, I could think of one I wanted to hold up for him.

I passed the bottle to him each time I took a swig, and he seemed to be having a wonderful time. By that time I was sure I had driven seventy-five or eighty miles.

"Now where did you say you were going?" I asked.

"Fouh Meyuus! Meyuus!" he insisted.

"Well, goddamn," I thought to myself, "this is the longest four miles I've ever driven. I think this old boy just wants my free whiskey."

A person usually can't smell too well when he's soused, but I could sure smell this guy. I used the power switch to roll down each of our windows.

"Tell me where you're going!" I yelled, above the noise of incoming wind.

"Fouh Meyuus, goddamnit," he screamed. "Fouh Meyuus."

"This son of a bitch must think it's four miles to the end of the earth," I thought. "Four miles my ass. I've been driving him for two hours!"

I had to do something to get rid of this guy, or at least his smell.

"All right," I said. "Maybe you can see your destination better from the bed of the truck. I'll stop, and you climb back there."

"Fouh Meyuus," he muttered as he moved from the cab to the bed.

I drove through Fort Myers, and the old drunk was waving and pounding on the roof of my cab. I didn't know we had reached his destination. He was trying to get me to stop, but I thought he just wanted another drink.

"I don't guess he's used to whiskey that good," I thought, and zoomed right past the place where he wanted to get out. By then he had stood up in the pickup's bed and begun to stomp. He was doing all he could to get me to stop, but I didn't get it. So I just hollered out the window at him while he staggered inside the bed. "I know, 'Four miles, four miles,'" I yelled, and kept on driving.

"Boy, that guy is making so much commotion, that booze is doing him better than it is me," I thought. I took another swig.

I had to pee and pulled to the side of the road. He jumped out of the truck bed. I think the wind had sobered him up a little because when he said where he wanted to go, I understood Fort Myers.

"We just came through there," I said. "Why didn't you say something?"

He began to scream and jump up and down. Once again I couldn't understand him. Then he peed and was still doing so when I sneaked to the truck. I burned rubber getting away from him. Blinking, he was holding himself and looking at me as I sped down the highway.

Stories like that are funny to me now, but only because they're a past-tense part of my life. I walked into Nancy's and my house after my absence and Nancy remembers that I made no explanation about where I'd been for a week. I simply told her about the passenger whose speech I couldn't understand and then sat down as if nothing had happened.

I think I ate the bread.

* * *

They say folks can go home again but that they can never return. I had not lived in Texas since I had divorced Shirley. I wanted no part of Florida, Alabama, or Tennessee. My records were doing so well that I felt I could live wherever I wanted and still work. Maybe if I slipped away, the cocaine pushers and crooked managers would finally give up on me.

And that, in essence, is what happened in time, although I continued to use cocaine and underwent additional abuse for a while after the move.

I told Nancy we were going to move to East Texas to be near my sister Helen. I wanted to eat with my brother and other sisters too. I wanted to walk the dirt where I had walked as a child, when drinking and failure were something I saw the grown-ups do and wondered why they did. I wanted the soothing safety that went with the tall arms of the East Texas Big Thicket once again.

I knew my life could end any day from circumstances induced by my lack of food and excessive drinking and drug use. I knew that others, such as Elvis Presley, had officially died of heart failure but that the heart failure was drug-induced.

I frequently expected each binge to be my last. But I didn't care. I was unhappy to the point of misery and didn't know why. I was head over heels for Nancy, but on the other hand I was furious at her for being nice to someone I hated so much—me. So sometimes I sought to punish her by getting drunk and drug-soaked. What a pathetic existence. I would have preferred peace in death over misery in life. So when people told me I was drinking myself to death, my first thought often was "Pour another drink."

My feelings for Nancy then were nothing like they are today. An alcoholic and drug addict doesn't love himself. Someone who doesn't love himself can't really love someone else, not to the full degree.

Returning to Texas helped me stop drinking for a while. I went on a sobriety binge. And then I got the idea to stay in Texas and once again make my home part of my livelihood. I had owned the Old Plantation Music Park when I was married to Tammy in Florida. I had "owned" the two Possum Holler clubs when I had lived in Nashville.

I told Nancy we would open a recreational vehicle park, featuring live country music and other attractions, and call it Jones Country. Working on the place, I knew, would keep me busy. The busier I was, the less I would drink. I think my dry period lasted several months, with only an occasional slip.

I started working clubs again and often played for the door because I didn't want to commit to an advance booking. Nancy and I (Adina was living with her father at the time) moved into a used mobile home, so our overhead was next to nothing. I'd perform on Friday, Saturday, and Sunday nights, then work all week at clearing land with rented equipment. Nancy cooked at home, and all we did was work, eat, and sleep. Helen's kids worked with us, and they were mighty inexpensive laborers. Tom Binkley, my attorney back in Nashville, handled my delinquent credit cards, and I got my credit rating built back up once again.

And each time I saved a few more thousand dollars from working weekend shows, I bought a few more acres. Finally, I had all the acreage I needed. We put in bleacher seats that went up a natural slope. We built an economical stage and put a sheet-metal roof over it. We had electric hookups for recreational vehicles and another area where folks could camp in tents. There was a concession stand and a restaurant too, and Nancy and I pretty much lived on the property after building the facility.

I don't think there has ever been a time when I saved more money faster than when I built Jones Country. We barely had a grocery bill because we grew a lot of our own food.

Nancy was working in the garden one morning when I approached her. "If you're going to be the next Mrs. Jones," I said, "you'd better get up from there and let's go get a blood test."

Not straight out of Shakespeare, is it?

We didn't even change out of our work clothes. We washed our hands and drove to Woodville, where we took the blood tests and bought the marriage license. We came back to our trailer, and I called Helen. I asked her to have a preacher and some witnesses at her house the next morning.

We got up the next day, took showers, put on our work clothes, and went to Helen's. She, Uncle Dub, the preacher, and a cake were there to receive us. The preacher, Nancy, and I stood before the fireplace in Helen's den. The preacher said his part, we each said "I do," and that was it. Helen took some Instamatic pictures.

That was enough ceremony for me.

Helen also cut the cake, and I told her that Nancy and I didn't have time to eat. We had a park to build.

That was on March 4, 1983.

We drove twenty miles to Jasper, Texas, and ate at the Burger King. I paid for our hamburgers with a twenty-dollar bill. When the change was returned, it was all the money we had in this world. At home we had one sack of beans. That was the extent of our pantry. That's how we started our married life.

But the month's installment on the mobile home was paid. Our food, because of the garden, and the sparse amount of cash would last us until I could get to a weekend show and pick up a few hundred dollars if I played for the door or a few thousand if I played somewhere where the promoter had adequate time to advertise.

I was interested in building Jones Country more than in performing. So I sometimes went back to deciding on Thursday morning whether I would work on Friday night. I resorted to calling a few honky-tonk owners personally, usually in Texas, and told them I'd come and play for the door. I'd ask for the telephone number of their local country music station, then call the program director and ask to have my telephone voice put on the air.

"Howdy, folks, this is George Jones," I'd say. "I'm going to be at such and such ballroom tomorrow night from nine until one for three big shows. I want you all to come and hear me 'cause we're going to have a mighty big time."

Nancy and I would drive to the dance hall, and there was almost always a crowd waiting. That's what you call show business by the seat of your pants.

I don't know what else to say about Jones Country except that once again the biggest names in country music played my outdoor park, and I owned it for six years. Country stars put on concerts during summer holiday weekends, and we had a dance hall that was open on weekends year-round. The dance hall featured name entertainers, including Johnny Cash, George Strait, Janie Fricke, Little Jimmie Dickens, Waylon Jennings, and others.

There was also a country store at Jones Country.

I might still be living in the East Texas woods next to Jones Country except that my recording and touring careers got so hot I couldn't handle the responsibility of the road and run Jones Country as well. Rather, Nancy couldn't.

In 1983 I had "I Always Get Lucky with You" and "Tennessee Whiskey," songs that were number one and number two in that order. I went to number three and to number two in 1984 with "You've Still Got a Place in My Heart" and "She's My Rock." In 1985 I topped at number three with "Who's Gonna Fill Their Shoes," a song that is a part of my live show today. And the hits, thank God, and the fans, continued.

As I mentioned, Nancy had pretty much become my manager, and there was no way she could approve the road bookings while trying to run Jones Country from our touring bus. I didn't want anyone to cook at Jones Country except Nancy because no one else's cooking could suit me. She'd be cooking one minute and working with a maid to clean the bathrooms the next. She was totally overloaded.

One day a customer complained that he couldn't get his camper where he wanted because of a tree. Nancy got tired of hearing him bitch and fired up a chain saw. He's lucky she took the saw to the tree and not to him.

She was about to drop dead from too many irons in the fire, and then, just when she thought she might actually be seeing the end of my drinking, I started again.

That was the final straw. I was going to have to sell the place or lose a wife and manager. So in 1989 Nancy and I returned to Nashville to be near my record label, as well as the recording studios, music offices, and all the rest that went with the life of a traveling recording artist.

But before we were married and before we returned to Nashville, there were additional wrinkles in our life.

In 1982 I had decided to visit Helen and let her have me committed for drug and alcohol abuse for the second time in my life. I was once again determined to get off the booze and cocaine. Of course, the treatment didn't take.

Nancy, Adina, Nancy's dog, and I started out for Helen's house in Texas. Nancy was driving while I sat in the back, drunk and snorting cocaine. I had gotten to where I would do that in front of Adina, who couldn't stand the sight or sound of it. She covered her ears each time I sniffed the stuff.

She was sixteen.

Nancy wasn't sure of the route but couldn't manage to look at a road map, drive, and watch me in the backseat. I guess she was afraid I'd take off on foot if she stopped the car to study a map.

She suddenly began to plead with me for the thousandth time to stop using cocaine. "George," she said, "it's a good thing your mama's not alive to see you doing that. It would break her heart."

Nancy had touched my weak spot.

"You can whip that stuff. Just throw it out the window. Go ahead, throw it out."

"Please throw it out, Daddy," Adina begged. "Please."

The two of them worked on me for miles. I took a big snort, then, during the few seconds of resulting courage, I threw a big and expensive bag of cocaine out the window. Nancy and Adina clapped and cheered.

None of us knew that a mere trace of the stuff had blown back into the car. Or perhaps it fell while I was snorting.

In a short while I was missing my cocaine. I wanted it back pronto, and there was no way to get it. So I pulled harder on the whiskey, while Nancy struggled to find her way to Helen's and the hospitalization I had promised to undergo.

The accelerated drinking and my frustration at wanting the missing cocaine made me mean. I climbed over the front seat and sat next to Nancy.

"You don't even know how to drive," I told her. I put my foot on top of hers and pushed the accelerator to the floor. In no time we were going ninety-one miles per hour. At least that's what the newspaper reported was on the radar belonging to the cop who stopped us. He arrested Nancy for speeding, reckless driving, and driving without a license. (She had no license from that time she was stopped in Florence for supposedly running a red light.)

And then the cop saw me.

"Isn't this George Jones's car?" he asked Nancy.

It must have killed her to admit that it was.

The cop immediately called agents for the Bureau of Narcotics. They brought a drug dog.

"Why are you calling the drug dog?" Nancy, in handcuffs, asked.

"'Cause that's George Jones's car," he said. "He's a dope dealer."

Let me say that in all I've ever done I've never once sold narcotics or illegal drugs. I've given away plenty but never sold any.

The cop was joined by a posse of other cops and agents. They turned the drug dog loose, and wouldn't you know it, he smelled a trace of cocaine on the floor of the car or in the cracks of the upholstery. I was arrested for possession of cocaine and public drunkenness.

We had a convoy of stopped cars, red lights, Nancy's barking dog, a barking drug dog, a crying teenager, and two adults in handcuffs about twenty miles south of Jackson, Mississippi, on Interstate 55.

GEORGE JONES CHARGED WITH COCAINE POSSESSION, screamed the headline in the next day's Jackson newspaper.

If I hadn't thrown away the cocaine bag, they would have caught me with enough to charge me with distribution. I might still be in prison.

Nancy, Adina, and I were taken to the Hinds County jail. I was put into one cell and the women into another. Nancy, naturally, began raising hell. That woman can be as loud as she is tender, and she is the most tender woman I've ever known.

"Who the hell put this woman and kid and dog in this cell?" said the sheriff, who had walked in and wasn't amused. "Let them out right now."

At first he didn't say a thing about me. I wondered if I'd been too quiet. Maybe Nancy knew what she was doing with all of her yelling and screaming.

But then we were all released on our own recognizance, and Nancy again took the wheel of my 1991 Lincoln. They had popped me for public drunkenness and then turned me out while I was still drunk.

Nancy and I have scratched our heads many times over that. I just think the sheriff, deputies, and jailer got tired of hearing her cuss and scream. I'll bet the cop who arrested us wished he had stopped public enemy number one instead. It would have been more peaceful.

Tom Binkley eventually made some kind of deal with the district attorney and judge. I was sentenced to return to that part of the country and give a show whose proceeds went to a charity or police fund. Meanwhile, a newspaper reporter wrote a story in connection with the incident that said, in part, that I was "a loser beyond help, Godless and friendless, a moral pauper who is perpetually ashamed of himself and you wouldn't take him home to meet Ma either."

How dare they say that about me? It was all true, but how dare they say it? I sued for libel, claiming my character had been defamed and my good name smeared. I forgot whatever came of that lawsuit. I know I didn't win any money. The defendants might have used truth as a defense and had an open-and-shut victory. Or maybe it was just thrown out of court after the judge stopped gasping in disbelief.

Nancy, Adina, and I stopped at a motel after we were released from jail. I started drinking Bloody Marys and breaking the glass as I finished each one. Mother and daughter were crying, and I eventually passed out. I don't know if I was that drunk or if I just wanted to get away from their noise.

I awoke with a terrible hangover and decided I didn't want to go to Texas and drug and alcohol rehabilitation after all. So I took over the driving and headed back to Muscle Shoals. My system was filled with that day's booze and yesterday's cocaine. And I got crazy. I accused Nancy of setting up the arrests and suddenly stopped the car. I pushed her, Adina, and the dog out and took off. They started walking and came to a farmhouse. A woman answered the door, and Nancy told her she had been riding in a car with George Jones.

"Well," said the woman, "I got a police scanner and he's just had a wreck about two miles from here."

And I had.

I was put into an ambulance, and someone brought Nancy and Adina to it. They rode with me to the emergency room and the detoxification center at Hill Crest Hospital in Birmingham. That's how I arrived for my second thirty-day span of rehabilitation.

I met someone in the hospital who was a George Jones fan. That fan knew someone who Nancy thinks was a relative. That relative "befriended" me and brought me cocaine while I was undergoing treatment for cocaine. The drug showed up in my urine.

The hospital had no authorization to keep me after thirty days. The doctors realized that I was scoring the drug inside the hospital and released me.

You might more accurately say I was expelled.

Chapter 24

This may be my favorite chapter.

It has to do with the beginning of the end, the actual end, of my alcohol and drug abuse.

I went home after the 1982 hospitalization and immediately got some cocaine from a vial I'd hidden in the refrigerator. Moisture ruins cocaine, and it's a wonder that frost or thawing hadn't ruined mine. I held the powder under my nose and snorted as I'd done thousands of times.

And something inside me clicked. I hated the drug. I had hated it for a long time but craved what I hated. Only persons who've undergone an addiction will understand that. But after that single blast by the refrigerator, the craving was gone. The stuff suddenly sickened me.

Maybe all of the treatment that had saturated my subconscious mind suddenly burst into my conscious mind. Maybe it was nothing less than an old-fashioned miracle. After all, most miracles unfold gradually, and I had been gradually struggling against cocaine since the first night I had tried it in the back room at the Possum Holler club.

I didn't finish that vial that day. I put the powder down the sink and haven't used the drug since. The master monkey was off my back.

Unfortunately, the struggle with the booze went on awhile longer.

My last hospitalization, in Birmingham, where I had stayed coked up, had served to create a desire in me to *want* to quit drinking more than ever. Even though I got staggering drunk for several days after the hospitalization, I asked Nancy to take me to Florida, where I had briefly been treated for alcoholism years earlier.

Nancy had watched a lot of films about alcoholism in Birmingham, had attended a lot of classes, and had generally learned a lot about living with an alcoholic. Maybe she sensed in me a different kind of desire to quit drinking. I don't know.

I said earlier that maybe I just got too old to drink. By that I mean I might have finally gotten wise, or my body got tired, or both. Who knows why I suddenly wanted sobriety so badly. I was consumed with getting sober. With getting well.

Nancy called the Florida facility, but the head doctor didn't want me.

"Won't you please do something to help him?" Nancy pleaded. "I know this is saying a lot, but he is worse than he's ever been. Please help him."

"There is no help for George Jones," the doctor told

her. He didn't want her to bring me. Nancy took me anyhow.

She and I entered the hospital and immediately got into a loud argument. I was drunk, of course, but even so was astonished at the filth. There were cigarette holes in the bedding, lint on the floor, and other signs of neglect. Nancy said the place looked like a drunk tank in a small-town jail. I was so drunk, and so outraged, that I didn't hear her stressing that she wouldn't let me stay there.

She took me out almost as quickly as she had taken me in. I was dry for a few days afterward. But then I'd start to drink on and off and get so drunk that my system couldn't process any more booze. I would throw it up as fast as I swallowed it.

After a day or two of that, I might pass out, then wake up sober enough to tough out a two- or three-day hangover. After that I wouldn't touch the stuff for a few days. Then I'd resume drinking, and each resumption would be for a longer period of time than the previous binge.

I didn't know it, but I was wobbling on my last drunken leg, going down for the final time, truly preparing to drown in a sea of alcohol.

I got drunk in a motel and lost my spirit more than ever. I lost my will to drink more, I lost my will to get sober. I would have just as soon been dead but was afraid to die. For a few days I drank to the point of unconsciousness, awakened, groped for a bottle, and drank more. Nancy thought I was going to die of an alcohol overdose. She could do nothing with me. She couldn't even call the police. I wasn't drinking publicly, so I was violating no law.

I strongly resisted her suggestions that we go back to the hospital in Birmingham. She reached out to me over and over, and each time I returned her compassion with hostility.

And still she stayed with me.

She wanted to call Pee-Wee, but I wouldn't let her. So she tricked me by saying she had to check on her mother.

Pee-Wee answered the telephone.

"Hi, Mom," Nancy said, not sure how much of her conversation I was understanding.

"Nancy?" Pee-Wee said.

"Yes, Mom," she said. "It's me. How have you been? How are you feeling?"

"What's the matter with you, Nancy?" Pee-Wee asked. "You're talking to Pee-Wee, not your mother." He might have thought she had grown tired of fighting my drinking and decided to join me by getting drunk herself.

Debbie Doebler, our financial manager, was there, and she figured out what was going on.

Debbie took the telephone, and Nancy began to speak to her in code. She mentioned the names of the motel and city where I had holed up. She talked about Birmingham, and Debbie knew Nancy meant the alcohol rehabilitation center.

Help was on the way.

Debbie translated for Pee-Wee, who, like the trusted and loyal friend he is, drove with Ron Gaddis, my bass player, for hundreds of miles to the motel. He said he walked in to see me sprawled on the bed, unable to rise. He picked me up as if I were a child, put me in the front seat, and, with Nancy and Ron in the back, started the drive from Biloxi, Mississippi, to Birmingham.

I continued to abuse Nancy, so she got on the floor, where I couldn't see her. She rode over the hump for several hours. She wanted me to forget she was around, thinking that if I saw her, I might insist on turning back.

I had lapses into and out of consciousness. When I was awake I was profane and aggressive.

Then Pee-Wee stopped and bought a Hank Williams tape. Years later he remembered that whenever he played it, I settled down and sometimes even went peacefully to sleep. The instant he took it off, however, I awakened and became hard to deal with all over again.

With Pee-Wee manning the tape deck, Nancy on the floor, Ron in the backseat, and me out of my mind, we rolled into Birmingham. The doctors and nurses were waiting.

Understand that I wouldn't let anyone take my bottle from me. So whenever I awakened in the car, I drank straight from the bottle. I didn't know at the time that these were my final drinks on the last lap in the race against death by drunkenness.

I was lifted from the car and placed into a wheelchair, the bottle still in my hand. No one tried to take it. My heart rate, blood pressure, and all the rest were measured with the booze in my clutches.

Of course I argued with the staff and showed them the rude and shameful behavior they'd seen countless times in drunks. A doctor eventually gave me a shot and told Nancy she could rest—I would be asleep for about two days.

And I was.

My blood alcohol level, upon admission to the hospital, was a blink from being over the fatal line. When the doctor did his calculations, he told Nancy and Pee-Wee that officially I would have died from a mere two more ounces of liquor. I'm sure I consumed an ounce or two with every swig.

My departure from alcohol had been decades late. But it had come in time to save my life, my tired and shattered life. That life, from that day to this, has been drastically different.

While I can swear there has been no cocaine, I won't tell you I have been totally sober from that day in 1983 until now. There were slips early in my sobriety, when I thought I could still play with the drug of alcohol. I was wrong.

A lot of nosy people are obsessed to know the day and the hour that I pitched my last drunk. I can't answer that and probably wouldn't if I could. I didn't record the date because I don't want to remember. Just let me say that I'm so thrilled with sobriety that it hasn't been long enough since I last was drunk and never will be. But I will say that I've been sober for several years now.

There are still some things I haven't learned about this disease called alcoholism. I was taught that a true alcoholic can't ever have any alcohol in his system without craving more. If that's true perhaps I'm not an alcoholic in the modern sense of the word. Perhaps I was always just an old-fashioned drunk.

I still drink today.

I'll have a beer on a hot day, and during the summer I might consume as much as a six-pack in a month or two.

Nancy and I rarely go out to fine restaurants, as I prefer the down-home, meat-and-potatoes places. But when we do, I occasionally have a glass of wine before dinner and drink no more. I don't squirm in my seat, fighting the urge for another drink. I don't have any urge.

I don't drink whiskey at all. I don't like the taste. I'm not sure I ever did. I used to drink whiskey because I wanted to work up a good drunk. Whiskey is less work than beer or wine.

People write me letters and ask how to help a friend or loved one stop drinking. I've never understood why they would ask someone who took so long to achieve sobriety himself.

They should be asking Nancy. I had been drunk for thirty-five years before meeting Nancy. I was mostly sober within two years afterward.

I think the most solid advice I could give anyone is to try to find ways to like yourself. The chronic drug or alcohol abuser hates himself. I'd also encourage trying anything, anything that might work. Don't be shy about seeing a minister or professional counselor or undergoing rehabilitation.

Alcoholics Anonymous, which I never attended regularly, has worked wonderfully for millions of people around the world. When you participate in those meetings, you leave your ego at the door. The first thing they teach you is to admit your problem, which is easy for a lot of folks. After all, they wouldn't be there if they didn't think they had a problem.

Most of all I'd remind anyone who wants to get away from drug or alcohol addiction that they can, no matter how many times they've failed in the past. If George Jones can get sober, anyone can.

Remember that a stumble is not a fall. If you've had the problem and think you're permanently sober, only to get drunk again as I did, the next day is a new day. It's the first day of the rest of your life. Sobriety has nothing to do with your past and little to do with your future. It has everything to do with the moment at hand. Seize it.

There are many proven routes to sobriety. Each is a journey of different steps. No step on any of the paths is harder than the first one.

Take it.

Then take another. Take the steps one at a time. Be concerned about nothing other than the current step. Only after completing the step should you take another, then gradually another, and gradually another on the only road to true personal fulfillment, a life that is free of substance excess.

Chapter 25

It was a sweltering August night in Nashville, where I was doing one of two evening shows. I did the first at Opryland, where I had played five nights a week since April. I was scheduled to rush to the Nashville Network studios later for a guest shot with Lorianne Crook and Charlie Chase on "Music City Tonight."

The first show was important to me. Its audience was filled with talent buyers from across the nation for fairs, concerts, and the like. I wanted to do a great show so they would be inclined to buy my services for 1995.

But the sound was terrible. I had done a sound check and was using a soundman who worked for me regularly. Yet my monitors weren't right, and the air was filled with feedback and distortion. There was simply no excuse. A singer can't give his best through a sloppy sound system. I politely apologized from the stage, urged the soundman to get it right, and went into another song. The sound was still terrible, and I was becoming increasingly embarrassed and frustrated. But I was determined to make a good impression in front of the standing-room-only crowd of very important people.

Instead, I got into a fistfight.

I lost my temper and bolted over to where my soundman sat in the wings. I clobbered him, and folks in the first two rows saw me. The band kept playing to try to cover up my actions, but not for long. One or two of them quickly left their instruments to hold me back. The next day, each of Nashville's daily newspapers carried stories that implied I had started a free-for-all. It was nothing like that, and it was over in a matter of seconds. I do wish, however, that I hadn't done that in front of the audience.

I didn't realize that night that my nerves were frayed due to a heart condition that would soon result in a triple bypass. I had been drug- and alcohol-free for about several years, so I certainly wasn't impaired when I jumped on my soundman. A month later my doctor would tell me that my nerves were irritated by an acute heart condition that I didn't know I had. He said that's why I had such a short fuse the night of the Opryland fracas.

I was physically hurting, but still didn't know why, when I returned to Opryland the next day. I asked my band to lower the keys on each of my songs. I wanted to make things as easy as possible for myself.

But nothing helped.

I finished the show with "I Don't Need Your Rockin' Chair" and afterward did not have the energy to talk.

Nancy remembers that I didn't say one word during the thirty-five-minute drive to our house.

The following day I didn't ride my tractor to mow our yard, as I had planned. I was simply too exhausted.

I continued to feel rough through September 7, 1994, when I celebrated my sixty-third birthday five days early. Nancy and I received over three hundred guests. A half-mile-long driveway leads to our front door, and Nancy had lined the road with balloons and other adornments. The place really looked festive, and guests dined from tables filled with prime rib, chicken, and all the trimmings. Everyone seemed to be having a wonderful time—except me. So I left some of my guests and went to bed.

I felt badly about leaving my own party, but I would have felt worse had I not lay down. The last guests to go were Waylon Jennings, Connie Smith, Jimmy Dickens, Carl Smith and his wife, Goldie Hill, and WSM radio personality Keith Bilbrey, who walked up the terrace to the house to sing "Happy Birthday." I appreciated that.

But not as much as I appreciated the feel of my sheets.

I experienced chest pains all night and blamed them on indigestion. I canceled all of my appointments the next day.

Nancy began to insist that I see a doctor, but I didn't want to do that. I was afraid he would order me to miss a show at Opryland, and I wanted to work the entire summer without missing a single date. I was determined to show all the Nashville music industry that the days of "No Show Jones" were ancient history.

So Nancy called my daughter, Susan, to come give me a visual examination. Susan's only medical credentials were that she liked to play nurse when she was a little girl, when she may have put a Band-Aid on a puppy. But I didn't want any professional people in the house.

Susan stared at me long and hard.

"He's got a weird color," she finally said. That was the extent of her diagnosis, but it was enough for Nancy, who called Opryland and canceled my Friday-night show without my permission.

I still refused to see a doctor, so this time Nancy called Roy Dean Johnson, son of my longtime friend Pee-Wee. Roy worked for the fire department.

"Roy," said Nancy, "since you work for the fire department, could you bring out one of your EKG machines and check George?"

"Let me ask the chief," Roy said.

"No, I can't do it because George lives in the wrong county," Roy said. "My chief said I can't bring this county's equipment to George's house."

During all of these efforts to get half-baked medical attention there was something I didn't know: I was dying by the day.

The fire chief who wouldn't let me use his equipment called to say that Roy had a cousin who lived in my county who was a paramedic.

So here came Nancy once again. Directly and indirectly, there is no telling how many times that woman's caring persistence has saved my life. This proved to be one more example. "Roy's going to come out with his cousin, who is a paramedic, and they're going to give you an EKG," she said.

I was still pretty indifferent, so I asked if I had to be there. "My God," I told her. "I'm fine."

I was checked with the portable equipment from the fire station and told that my heartbeat was irregular. I was also told that more equipment, the kind found in a doctor's office, was needed for an accurate diagnosis. I thanked the men for coming and told them I'd be okay.

"That's just fine," said Nancy. "But I'm not going to sleep tonight if you don't go to the doctor. I'm not going to do anything."

After more arguing, I agreed to go to a county medical center, where I felt I would attract no attention. Nancy talked to the staff and was assured that the press would not find out I was being examined.

A doctor determined that I was dehydrated, probably from days of diarrhea. I had no viral infection, so he was curious as to why I had the diarrhea. Nancy later decided that diarrhea without a virus was God's way of telling me something serious was wrong.

Someone gave me a shot of glucose and explained that I needed to replenish my bodily fluids. After an hour of people poking me, taking blood, and putting thermometers into my mouth, I was ready to leave. After all, I was still sure there was nothing wrong with me. I had simply agreed to go through all of this to satisfy Nancy.

"I'm going to let you go home because your heart rate checks out," said the doctor.

As they were undoing the medical machinery, I burped. And the needle on the device jumped dramatically.

"If George Jones isn't having a heart problem, then what did that mean?" Nancy said, pointing to the graph. No one else had noticed.

"Oh my God!" said the doctor, and put nitroglycerin under my tongue. "You can't go home, George!"

If I hadn't burped, and if Nancy hadn't noticed the effect, I might have walked out of that place never to walk back.

They took me from the medical center to Nashville's Baptist Hospital, and I was angry with Nancy during the entire ride. She had earlier made some banana pudding, and all I wanted to do was go home and eat it. I had granted her request and seen a local doctor, and now I was lying down in the back of an ambulance with tubes coming out of me en route to a hospital!

That's mighty frustrating when you're convinced that nothing's wrong.

When the ambulance arrived at the hospital, the hospital staff made good a promise to keep me anonymous. As I lay on the ambulance cot, they covered me from head to foot with a sheet—the way they do a dead person—so I wouldn't be recognized. I must have looked like a mummy.

I was taken into a room for more tests, still insisting that my problem was no more than indigestion.

At one point I was wheeled from one room to another, and in the hall I spotted Nancy.

"You and your damn PKG," I said.

"You ain't even saying it right," she fired. "It's EKG."

I didn't care if it was IUD.

A doctor soon approached Nancy and said he was going to show her my problem. He drew a picture of the heart and the arteries that surround it. One was 100 percent blocked, another 95 percent, and a third 50 percent. The doctor then showed Nancy, on paper, how he would surgically bypass the blocked arteries to ensure the flow of blood through my body. He even showed her where he would take substitute arteries from my leg and chest.

He was talking about open-heart surgery.

I refused to talk about it, but not for long. The doctor told me I could live without the surgery—for about two days to a week.

Nancy said I didn't say anything else.

During the next two hours I thought a lot about the rest of my life. I didn't ponder how I would spend it, but *if* I would spend it. Nancy showed me the drawing, and later the doctor explained it to me personally.

He also said that once he opened my chest, he might find a fourth artery that was blocked and have to bypass it as well. I told him I didn't care if he found a hundred. I told him to do whatever he had to.

Waylon Jennings had gone through a similar operation in the same hospital a few years earlier. Nancy tracked him down somewhere on the road, and I talked to him.

"Is this thing really going to work?" I asked.

"Yeah," he said. "And you don't have a choice."

"Well," I said, "if it saved you I guess it will save me."

On September 11, 1994, I agreed to go under the knife at daylight the next day, my sixty-third birthday.

Connie Smith joined Nancy by my side at 5 A.M. Jimmy Dickens, Waylon, and Keith Bilbrey were close behind. Connie, Jimmy, and Pee-Wee had come by the previous night. Merle Haggard called every few minutes. Alan Jackson and Doug Stone called often. Garth Brooks and Reba McEntire sent enough flowers to start a nursery.

Many of those who came to the hospital sang gospel songs and held hands in united prayer. When the chips are down, there's no denying that country stars are there for each other.

And that's also true of the fans.

The press somehow got hold of the fact that I had been hospitalized after complaining of chest pains. The hospital public relations department kicked into gear and began issuing official information. The day I went under the knife, when it was still as black as midnight outside, so many fans came to the hospital that they were given their own waiting room. The hospital staff was wonderfully considerate. Someone went to the fans' room regularly to give them an update on my progress. Something like that is so meaningful when you're looking at a life-threatening situation.

And then the mail started. Nancy stopped counting the cards at ten thousand. We kept every one.

I don't remember much about the surgery. In fact, I don't remember anything. I was pumped full of shots and can't even recall being taken from my room to the operating room.

My daughter by Tammy, Tamala Georgette Jones, is a registered nurse, and she was waiting with Nancy and my sister Helen when I came out of surgery. Of course I had tubes running in and out of my body, and Nancy said my skin was about the color of flour. I choked a lot, and Nancy thought I was going to strangle. Georgette assured her that my behavior was a normal reaction to what I had been through, and after a while Nancy settled down.

I was listed in critical condition, as are all open-heart patients, and doctors at first let only Nancy see me for fifteen-minute intervals. With each visit, she noticed a return of my color, she said. Not long after I became conscious, I grew bored with that room where I lay alone. I asked to be moved to where I could watch television and where Nancy and Helen could join me. Nancy had a bed of her own and rarely left my side until I came home five days later. I arrived two days sooner than most open-heart patients, I was told.

I went through the depression that is normal for open-heart patients. Nancy spent a lot of time on the telephone getting advice from Jessi Colter, Waylon's wife, and from Charlene, wife of Billy Sherrill, who also went through the ordeal. I had my worst times in the mornings. I was grouchy and didn't like the fact that I couldn't eat the same foods I used to eat.

Naturally, I had to give up cigarettes after about fifty years of smoking. I didn't like the fact that my tastes were different and that I was a different man entirely who I hadn't yet come to know. I had developed a new sense of mortality. I knew then, more than ever before, that someday I was going to die.

In those days after surgery, I didn't want to see anyone except Nancy, and I wore her out. I wanted her to do everything for me that I would have normally done for myself. She grew physically and mentally tired and sometimes went into the backyard to cry. Then she returned to the house as if nothing were wrong. I never knew until later how much stress she was under.

Doctors blamed my irritability on the strong, painkilling drugs I was taking. Drugs can really affect the thinking of someone who's otherwise been drug-free as long as I had.

I started physical rehabilitation soon afterward. I rode a stationary bicycle for an hour a day, three days a week. A few days later I tried to drive my car. But even with its power steering and brakes, the twenty miles to Nashville and back was an exhausting experience. It showed me how totally weak I was from a procedure in which I had been cut from the bottom of my rib cage to the bottom of my throat. Then utensils were used to separate my chest and lay it wide open. My doctor said my body had been extremely traumatized, and he was right. He said it would be months before I felt fully recovered, and he was right about that too.

I returned to work ten weeks after the operation with a show on November 18, 1994, in Davenport, Iowa.

RECOVERING JONES GAVE ALL HE HAD, read the headline on the review in *The Dispatch,* the Moline, Illinois, newspaper that covered the concert. The review began: "The legendary country singer who has influenced so many, with the voice so often emulated by others, has long been the standard by which other country balladeers are measured. His visit to Davenport was no exception . . ."

I deeply appreciated these remarks of reviewer Ellis Kell, who went on to report that I had apologized to the crowd for my lack of wind and that the audience had been extremely supportive. They were.

I left the stage to a standing ovation, and believe me, I was moved beyond words.

That show was supposed to be a part of a three-day tour, but I had to return to Nashville. I didn't have the stamina to make the other dates. As of this writing, almost ninety days after the procedure, I'm walking, talking, and generally living at a slower pace.

Undergoing life-saving surgery is like few other things in this life. It happens to millions, but when it happens to you, it's as if it never happened to anyone else. People were wonderful to support me, but there is only so much anyone can do. Eventually, it's only you and the doctor. You're asleep on your back, and you pray he's not asleep on his feet.

You tell yourself he's done this many times before, and you hope that doesn't mean he's done it so many times he won't pay attention.

And then you finally realize that it's beyond your control. The doctors and nurses may hold the surgical instruments, but your life is in God's hands. Once again, God gently tightened his loving grip on the life of George Jones.

And that life goes on.

Chapter 26

I don't care much for many of today's young country singers. They're not country—they're clones. Many got their recording contracts because they sound like someone else.

I told you earlier how, when I was coming up, the record companies looked for artists who sounded different, who had their own style. But today's country music industry is a lot like the television industry. It's in love with reproducing itself.

Country music has been mass-marketed for a long time. More recently it's been mass-produced.

I've heard a lot of fine young acts who can't get a record deal because label big shots think they don't sound like anybody else. The powers that be are looking for another Garth, Reba, or Alan. If Randy Travis had come to town last month, he probably wouldn't have gotten a record deal. He's too good and too original. His tone is traditional and his phrasing shows Lefty Frizzell's influence, yet his vocals are distinctive. And he doesn't wear a cowboy hat or pimple cream. Today's labels are looking for pretty boys and girls. The way today's artists look is more important than how they sound.

On September 8, 1990, a duet between Randy and me called "A Few Ole Country Boys" was released. The song rose to number eight on the *Billboard* country survey.

The day it did my telephone rang.

"George," somebody said, "do you realize you made history today?"

I thought about that for a while. There was a time when I would have said, "Talk to my lawyer."

"No," I said instead. "I don't know nothing about me and no history."

"You became the only country artist in history to have a Top Ten song in each of the past five decades," he said.

I was still thinking about that when he said, "You've been in the Top Ten now for half a century."

Three years later the telephone rang again with more unusual news.

"George," said the caller, "you need to be sure to go to this year's Country Music Association Awards show. You're nominated for induction into the Hall of Fame."

To my way of thinking that's the highest honor in all of country music. And that's what I told the crowd when I was inducted. I even said the award meant more to me than all of my others put together. In my acceptance speech, I politely scolded radio program directors for refusing to play veteran artists. I'm sure my remarks, broadcast coast-to-coast and overseas, annoyed a few programmers and hurt my own airplay.

It went down shortly afterward.

I accepted a standing ovation from members of the Country Music Association and realized that praise from my peers is the greatest praise of all. I took my bow, walked calmly offstage, and fell apart. I stood in the wings and cried. My tears, needless to say, were tears of joy. The award had been given to George Glenn Jones from Kountze, Texas. That's all I've ever thought I was.

I pondered all I had done to slaughter my career and how, even in the face of reduced airplay, my concerts were drawing more fans than ever. I wondered why, but not for too long.

My curiosity gave way to gratitude. The CMA had given the coveted award to someone who, just thirteen years earlier, had come to its awards show so drunk he could barely stand upright. This was the same CMA that had given me those awards in the 1980s that were later found in a garage sale. I've never felt so simultaneously happy and undeserving as I did during my Hall of Fame induction.

I almost had as much gratitude a year earlier.

Something happened then regarding the handful of some truly talented young country singers on the scene today. My record producer, Norro Wilson, brought a song to me called "I Don't Need Your Rockin' Chair," about an aging man who is a little slower at, but not finished with, his craft.

The song was my attitude set to music, and Vince Gill, Mark Chesnutt, Garth Brooks, Travis Tritt, Joe Diffie, Alan Jackson, Pam Tillis, T. Graham Brown, Patty Loveless, and Clint Black joined me on the biggest-selling song I've had so far in the 1990s.

Yet despite that all-star lineup, airplay was limited and the tune only rose to number thirty-four. Nancy got on the telephone and, in typical devotion to my career and me, personally asked program directors around the nation to play my song. Her loving efforts shouldn't have been necessary. They were hardly effective.

I have a theory as to why. It's because George Jones, the lead singer, was a senior citizen. The country music industry today is an industry where youth will be served. So we have artists making records about life who haven't yet lived much life.

I look at the shape of contemporary country music, and I'm saddened. There has never been a time when country radio was so disrespectful of its elders. I suppose the same can be said of the country music industry as a whole, including the record companies.

With the exception of MCA and, more specifically, Bruce Hinton, chairman of MCA's Nashville division. What a limb he went out on when he signed me to the label a few years ago. I can't think of another record company executive who would have signed a senior artist, particularly one with a reputation for misbehavior. And Bruce has stuck by me. He's a man who is more interested in his artists' art than in their age.

Bruce still has a recording deal with Bill Monroe, who is in his eighties, because Bill is the father of bluegrass music. No other major label honcho in Nashville would give Bill or me a deal.

I asked Tom Carter to make Bruce the last person to whom he spoke in connection with the writing of this book. Bruce told Tom that he signed me, and continued to record me, because he thought I was the world's best country singer and because he would never have been able to forgive himself for not documenting my work when he had the power to do so.

I'm forever indebted. With the exception of Nancy, Bruce has done more to prolong my career than anybody. If someone ever makes a movie about my life, I won't approve the script unless someone is cast as Bruce Hinton.

I won a major music award from the Country Music Association two or three years ago. I had gone to pee at exactly the same time the award was bestowed. So when I was announced as winner, Nancy leaped from her seat and accepted it on national television, telling the audience I was in the john. I was delighted that all of America got to hear about my urinary habits. But from the platform she thanked Bruce Hinton. I was so pleased about that that I wasn't even angry that I missed my acceptance.

I'll say one more thing about Bruce. He's a genius of the art of selling records. He knows how to move records. Here I am a radio artist without radio airplay who is selling albums into the hundreds of thousands of copies. That's because Bruce knows how to promote through media other than radio, such as print press, television, and significant concert exposure.

Think about this. As of this writing, Bruce has sold more than one million albums by a group called the Mavericks. He has done so without the group's ever having had a Top 10 record.

The man knows how to promote.

* * *

Rock 'n' roll music, historically, has been fickle. Its star singers made millions of dollars, then were forgotten by rock radio in about five years. Country radio, on the other hand, used to play its seasoned singers right in with the new for years. When I was starting out, radio played my songs among those by Ernest Tubb, Roy Acuff, Bob Wills, Gene Autry, Hank Snow, and many others.

But look how country and rock have changed roles.

Rock radio today plays Tina Turner, Rod Stewart, the Rolling Stones, Eric Clapton, Elton John, Paul McCartney, Bob Seger, The Eagles, and others in full rotation. Those people are in their late forties or early to mid-fifties.

Merle Haggard, Johnny Cash, and Charley Pride, meanwhile, can't get country airplay. Yet if it weren't for those guys and artists like them, today's young singers would have had no role models. Those veterans paved the young artists' road to success. Many stations that won't play veteran acts wouldn't even be on the air if it weren't for interest generated by the older artists in their stations a few years ago.

But country radio doesn't seem to care. I worry about the future of a country music industry that has no respect for its history.

In February 1994, Nancy and I drove thirty miles through Nashville's worst ice storm in recent history to the Bradley Barn Recording Studio, owned by Owen Bradley, the legendary producer of hits by Patsy Cline,

Loretta Lynn, and many others during the 1960s and 1970s.

Bruce had come up with the idea for me to record a duet album with many of today's hottest stars and some of the industry's most established, including Vince Gill, Ricky Skaggs, Alan Jackson, Marty Stuart, Emmylou Harris, Tammy Wynette, Mark Chesnutt, Mark Knopfler, Trisha Yearwood, Dolly Parton, and the world's best rock 'n' roll guitarist, the Rolling Stones' Keith Richards.

Electricity went out at our house the night before the first day of the recording session. With no heat while temperatures fell below freezing, I feared I would get sick and be unable to do the session. A lot of artists who had changed their touring schedules would have done so in vain if I failed to appear. So Nancy got up during the night to pile blankets on me to be sure I stayed warm. She got up repeatedly thereafter to be sure they hadn't come off. I was reminded of the songwriter who, years ago, wrote "Little Things Mean a Lot."

After the duets album was released, radio didn't know what to do with it. I mentioned earlier that it was reluctant to play the first single from the album, "A Good Year for the Roses," by Alan Jackson and me. Alan was white-hot on radio, and programmers wanted his voice. But some didn't want his if they had to take mine. The vast majority of Alan's other single records have gone to number one. His duet with me became his first single not to crack the Top 50.

Yet on June 5, 1995, at the annual Music City News Country Awards, the song was named "Vocal Collaboration of the Year." That award, given on prime-time national television, is a people's choice award. The fans do the voting and have to pay for each vote by dialing a 900 number that shows up on their phone bills. It's doubtful that any radio programmer, or entertainment industry big shot, casts a vote. They wouldn't spend their money.

I was happy. The fans liked what I had done despite the absence of airplay. I care a lot more about my loyal fans than I do the come-lately radio programmers who are boycotting veteran artists.

Alan accepted the award and called me to the stage. I had no idea he and I would win, so I had already left the show after having presented an award to somebody else. Marty Stuart came on after Alan and told coast-to-coast viewers that George Jones had gone home early to watch a rerun of "Matlock." Actually, it was "The Andy Griffith Show." And although I'd seen Andy many times before, his show was far more interesting than most of the stuff I hear on modern country radio.

Keith Richards and the Rolling Stones were in the middle of a standing-room-only concert tour when the Bradley Barn album was released. It was the Stones' first tour in ten years. They were drawing upward of fifty thousand people each night. Someone suggested that MCA release the duet between Keith and me as the next single and forget about pairing me with one of the popular young stars.

"We don't want to do that," said an MCA executive. "No one in radio wants to hear two old men on the radio. Isn't that a shame?"

Despite the confusion, the album's sales will likely have topped half a million by the time this book is published. I wonder what it would have done with hearty promotion and radio airplay. I wonder how little it would have done had it not been for Nancy's and Bruce's tireless efforts and the national press they generated. Thank God the newspapers and magazines still have an interest in artists with gray in their temples.

I want to stress here and now that I'm thankful, above all else, to still be working, with or without radio support. A whole lot of recording artists don't have the privilege of still working without broadcast of their recordings. I've told the fans I'll tour as long as they come to see me, and I mean that.

But that doesn't eliminate my sense of injustice for my buddies in the business. I just don't think it's right that some gorgeous young girls who sing flat can get airplay today while Loretta Lynn and Connie Smith can't even get record deals. Country music, the music of the common man, has become uncommonly ruthless in the way it treats the proven greats.

I hope I can be around in a few years when today's record company and radio decision makers are getting older themselves. I'd be curious to see if they'll be tossed aside and, if so, how they'll handle it.

In 1995 I went into the studio with Tammy Wynette for the first time in seventeen years (with the exception of the one song we did at the Bradley Barn session). The 1995 effort was an album called *One*. I had said years ago that I'd never record with Tammy again, so this experience taught me to never say never.

Recording with Tammy, in many ways, was like old times. Our ability to harmonize was still there, and we went on a thirty-city tour, including some stops overseas, that began on June 6, 1995, at Nashville's annual Fan Fair.

Twenty thousand fans sat in a driving rain to watch Tammy's and my return to the concert stage. Many could have gone home, but I didn't see one leave. I was touched.

Tammy and I put a song on the album called "Look What We've Started Again." Some record promotion folks hoped the title might suggest that Tammy and I were getting back together romantically. They thought such rumors might sell albums. As I've said before, I don't care what people think if it will help sell albums.

I may never again say never about recording together. But regarding our romantic reunion I will forever say never.

The album's coproducer was Nashville's hottest and certainly one of its most talented, Tony Brown, who produces Reba McEntire, George Strait, Vince Gill, Wynonna, and more. Its other producer was Norro Wilson.

We went into the studio for six days to do ten songs, then returned to rerecord some of the vocal tracks. The sessions were fun and filled with goodwill. Yet they had an air of sad uneasiness.

"We might as well have as much fun with this project as we can," said Norro, "because we already know that radio isn't going to play anything we record." That statement was repeated openly several times during the next few days inside the control room. "Damn, this is going to be a good record," observers repeatedly said. "What a shame it won't get on the air."

Someone kiddingly suggested that we alter the photographs for the cassette and compact disc jackets. It was thought that we might put Tammy's and my bodies under the heads of young fashion models. "Then the people at radio will think you all are a new act and play the record," said one studio musician. "Hell, they'll put it on their playlists without even listening if they think you're young."

One music magazine said that the reunion of George Jones and Tammy Wynette was to country what the reunion of the Beatles would be to rock 'n' roll.

I don't agree, but a lot of smart folks felt that way about an album featuring Nashville's best studio musicians behind singers whose separate careers have sold more than 60 million records. There's something wrong when even the album's producers thought the project was commercially dead in the water before it even got to retail shelves.

Time will tell.

Nancy, bless her heart, immediately started calling radio people to ask them to play the record. She wanted me to do a bunch of radio interviews. I refused.

"Why should I kiss radio's ass?" I asked.

I feel badly for Tammy and a lot of talented people who worked very hard making that record. We're all mighty proud.

Instead of making a new album, I'd have been more content to be at home—cutting the grass at the only place I've ever owned mortgage-free in my life. (If you think I'm not in high cotton, let me tell you that I am. I have my own brand of pet food—George Jones' Country Gold Pet Foods. And the stuff is a runaway hit. Who needs radio when there are pet stores?)

Riding a lawn mower over my acreage is the most

relaxing thing I do, along with feeding my cattle. Mowing and feeding are unlike the entertainment business with its crooked road of lies and deception. When you mow you don't wonder which direction you're going in, you can follow the path. When you feed, you don't wonder about bullshit, you can see it.

These days Nancy and I spend a lot of time doing nothing with our time. We walk hand in hand over our grassy slopes and return to watch the sun set in our pastures and over our bonded souls.

We are two people whose lives are as one.

At sixty-four I've turned twenty-one. I have found peace, and peace has found me.

Mine has been a stormy, but more recently, wonderful life. I hope to see a lot more of that life—now that I love it at last.

Chapter 27

I have to be one of the most fortunate people in show business. Many entertainers my age see their careers coming to an end, yet I'm on the brink of one that's brand new.

It appears I'm about to get my own prime-time talk/variety show on The Nashville Network.

We'll shoot pilot versions in 1998. If the network and I are pleased, the shows will go into full production, and we'll do thirteen original, one-hour programs. The shows will be rerun, giving us a total of twenty-six air dates for 1998. The programs are tentatively scheduled to run each week immediately after the Statler Brothers Show, the sixty-minute variety program that runs on Saturday nights and is the highest-rated offering on TNN.

That's a great "lead-in" for my show.

I'd love to see the George Jones Show catch on so I

can work television more and the road less in upcoming years. I did 120 one-night engagements in 1996, and am scheduled to do ninety-six in 1997. That, plus the television show, is enough. I'm too old, and the miles are too long, for many more of the one-nighters. I've been a sailor on the cement sea for almost a half century.

The concerts I do in 1997 will be inside smaller halls. I don't like to play the 20,000-seat rooms because I can't always draw enough people to fill them. To do so, I have to be billed with a younger, hot act. Such acts charge a lot of money to concert promoters, and many promoters who sell 15,000 to 18,000 tickets lose money because of inflated performance fees. I think the young acts have gotten their performance prices so high that they're putting promoters out of business.

I don't want any part of that.

I'm going to use local bands to open my shows in 1997. I can still draw enough fans to earn my fee, and the promoter will make a tidy profit. Then, if I'm lucky, he'll ask me to come back and play again.

I've learned to look at the long-term in my career.

My television show, if it becomes a reality, will be country with a capital "C." Maybe my earlier remarks were too hard on some of the young acts. I think a lot of them record some of the junk they do because that's what their producers order.

But I'm going to tell the viewing audience that they've tuned into a country show and if they don't want real country music, they should change the channel right now.

Reckon that will make the sponsors happy?

Any young act with a record deal will be invited to

appear on my show. And the veteran acts, of course, will always be welcome. My only requirement is that the acts keep their music, and its performance, country. I don't want people coming on with elaborate choreography or giant choirs. I don't want smoke and mirrors. I want artists to sing the kind of music they'd sing if they could sing whatever they wanted—as long as what they want is country.

I'm going to try my hand at interviewing, too. I'll have a writer who'll research the artists' histories so I can talk to them intelligently. I want the performers to be relaxed, and the viewers entertained.

I'm going to give it my all, and I hope the fans know that what they see, good or bad, is sincere. I really think I can do talk television, but I don't think Jay Leno or David Letterman have to worry about their jobs.

One of the things I appreciated most about 1996 was the fact that I acquired a second home. It's a comfortable condominium in Coco Beach, Florida, where Nancy and I go to get away from everybody.

We lived there for three weeks before I let her hook up the telephone, and three more before I let her give out our number. She had a fax machine, her only link to the outside world.

The place is on the water, and we can sit on the balcony and watch the waves.

Nineteen ninety-six brought disappointment for me in that my estrangement from my two sons was solidified. The two sued me for record royalties they felt were owed to them. Their mother, my late wife Shirley, took half of the songwriting royalties I earned through the time of our divorce. After she died, my two sons thought they were beneficiaries. They thought the songs had earned millions of dollars.

I had to give depositions, and we reached a settlement. I could say it was painful to fight my own offspring in a lawsuit, but that would be a gross understatement. I had been an absentee father, but I can't undo what I did in my reckless years. And I would never add fuel to the flame of my deficient fatherhood by purposefully trying to swindle my children.

I sat for what seemed like hours giving sworn testimony that resurrected a lot of painful memories. I'm not very high on the boys' favorite persons list, and I deeply regret that. Perhaps things will be better among us in our next lives.

I sold my quarter horses and got into the miniature horse business in 1996. Don't ask me why. There is no money to be earned from the tiny horses. In fact, they cost me money. They're about the size of a really large dog. But I have a trainer who prepares them for show competition, and somehow Nancy and I find that relaxing.

My greatest hits album went platinum in 1996. That means a million people bought recordings of songs that I have sung for decades. The sales of this album sent me a message. I realized that people want to hear my traditional sound more than anything else I've tried. I recorded "I Lived to Tell It All," an album whose title was taken from this book. The record sounded like the

George Jones of old, and I'm already scheduled to record another album for MCA in 1997. Any songwriters reading this might as well realize that I don't intend to cut anything trendy. Bring me some hard-core country music and we'll talk.

I think the fans need some time to realize that I'm back to recording in my old and original style. I had a giant hit with "Rocking Chair" and a strong hit with "High Tech Redneck." Those were uptempo, novelty songs. The fans have been accepting through the years of my less serious work, such as "White Lightning" and "The Race Is On."

But I think singing the emotional, sensitive songs is what I do best. And so I'm going to do it some more. My future work will be mostly ballads, sad songs, and waltzes.

Nancy and I hope to become executive producers of a puppet show in 1997. That's right—puppets. Our friend Jeff Greer has designed puppets that resemble country music legends. There's Porter Wagoner, Johnny Cash, Conway Twitty—you get the idea. We're shopping the proposal to various television networks for a program that is country music's answer to the Muppets.

Friends, there is just no end to the diversity that I'm developing at this stage in my career. I'll be sixty-six going on adolescence, and I'm ready for brand-new opportunities. I won't mess up this time around.

People have asked me about my favorite development inside the country music industry in 1996. That's a hard one. But I'm going to have to say that I've been swept off

of my feet by LeAnn Rimes, the fourteen-year-old singing sensation whose first album, "Blue," opened at number one and stayed there for months.

People make a big deal about her young age. I think
they should make a bigger deal about her singing. That
child is brilliant for ANY age.

I saw Patsy Cline live. I worked with her. Not since
Patsy have I heard such a no-bluff voice. And I loved the
fact that LeAnn's first single record, written by Bill Mack,
was penned for Patsy in 1958. I have no doubt that
Patsy, had she lived, would have had a big hit with that
song.

Right out of the box, LeAnn faced resistance from
American radio. Her first single incorporated a yodel,
and country stations thought it was too country. Imagine, LeAnn had the number-one country record in the
nation, but some country stations wouldn't play it. The
word on the street was that one station said it didn't fit
their "young country" format. A fourteen-year-old who
didn't fit a "young country" format? What a crock of shit!
I hope LeAnn becomes a billionaire, buys all of those
stations, and fires their program directors.

Is anything more ridiculous than American country
radio?

LeAnn Rimes will have a giant career in the music
industry. And her music, still new to many folks, will
live forever. A voice like that comes along about once in
a century. In her, God has given us His 100-year wakeup
call.

I cut a duet with Hank Thompson in the fall of 1996.
Hank and I go back, and I was pleased that he asked me

to record with him. I was thrilled that some of the hot young singers, such as Vince Gill, cut with him too.

I think it's wonderful when the youngsters help out the older artists who paved the way for them. Some of the young hotshots take themselves too seriously for that. There will come a day when their careers cool, and then they'll have to live with young singers who treat them like yesterday's news.

Finally, the most significant thing I did in 1996, and in my entire life, was write my life story. It was published on May 6, and by July had climbed to number six on the *New York Times* bestseller list. The paperback you're holding is a reprint of the hardcover, plus this chapter.

It has been decades since anything I've done has prompted so much public interest. Nancy, Pee-Wee, Adina, and I went to autograph sessions from coast to coast. On several occasions, I signed more than one thousand copies of my book at one sitting.

And the press was wonderful. I don't think I read a negative review, and we were given full pages with pictures in *Newsweek, The Washington Post, Los Angeles Times, USA Today,* and more—much more. I was asked to be on any number of network talk shows.

I was truly touched by the forgiveness of the country fans who bought my book. Years ago somebody said that country fans will forgive you for anything if you're honest with them. I did my best to be honest in my book, and I think the fans have given me amnesty.

One book signing stands out in particular. It came in the heat of the summer during Nashville's Fan Fair. A radio station announced that I would be at the George

Jones Gift Shop and Museum at 2 P.M. on a Wednesday to sign my book.

A two-block line had formed by 8 A.M.

I stayed until I had autographed every book in the store, then sent out for more. We even signed books that people were running to buy at other stores.

I'm glad I wrote my book, I'm glad it set the record straight, and I'm glad the fans took it in the spirit in which it was intended.

I'm glad I told my story. I'm glad I lived to tell it all.